# The Liberalism Trap

# The Liberalism Trap

*John Stuart Mill and Customs of Interpretation*

MENAKA PHILIPS

# OXFORD
## UNIVERSITY PRESS

Oxford University Press is a department of the University of Oxford. It furthers
the University's objective of excellence in research, scholarship, and education
by publishing worldwide. Oxford is a registered trade mark of Oxford University
Press in the UK and certain other countries.

Published in the United States of America by Oxford University Press
198 Madison Avenue, New York, NY 10016, United States of America.

© Oxford University Press 2023

All rights reserved. No part of this publication may be reproduced, stored in
a retrieval system, or transmitted, in any form or by any means, without the
prior permission in writing of Oxford University Press, or as expressly permitted
by law, by license, or under terms agreed with the appropriate reproduction
rights organization. Inquiries concerning reproduction outside the scope of the
above should be sent to the Rights Department, Oxford University Press, at the
address above.

You must not circulate this work in any other form
and you must impose this same condition on any acquirer.

Library of Congress Cataloging-in-Publication Data
Names: Philips, Menaka, author.
Title: The liberalism trap : John Stuart Mill and customs of interpretation / Menaka Philips.
Description: 1st edition. | New York : Oxford University Press, [2023] |
Includes bibliographical references and index.
Identifiers: LCCN 2023006188 (print) | LCCN 2023006189 (ebook) |
ISBN 9780197658550 (hardback) | ISBN 9780197658574 (epub) |
ISBN 9780197658581
Subjects: LCSH: Liberalism—Philosophy. | Democracy. | Mill, John Stuart, 1806–1873.
Classification: LCC JC585 .P443 2023 (print) | LCC JC585 (ebook) |
DDC 320.5101—dc23/eng/20230228
LC record available at https://lccn.loc.gov/2023006188
LC ebook record available at https://lccn.loc.gov/2023006189

DOI: 10.1093/oso/9780197658550.001.0001

Printed by Integrated Books International, United States of America

*For Nora*

# Contents

*Preface* — ix
*Acknowledgments* — xv

1. Is Liberalism Inescapable? — 1
2. Disciplined by Liberalism: Contestations, Pedagogies, and the Exemplary Mr. Mill — 15
3. Mill Reconsidered: From a Crisis of Certainty to a Politics of Uncertainty — 37
4. The School of Virtues: Emancipating Women, Wives, and Mothers — 59
5. Earning Democracy: Class Politics and the Public Trust — 88
6. Governing Dependencies: Between Authority and Self-Determination — 116
7. Politics, Possibility, and Risk: Beyond the Liberalism Trap — 145

*Notes* — 155
*Bibliography* — 191
*Index* — 207

# Preface

The problem this book explores can be illustrated by an affair featuring the Russian president. In the summer of 2019, Vladimir Putin announced that liberalism was dead. Interviewed by the *Financial Times* ahead of the G20 summit in Japan, Putin punted on Russia's interference with US elections and turned instead to the failures of liberalism, an idea that had become, in his words, "obsolete." Using fundamental disagreements over LGBTQ rights, multicultural politics, and migrant protections as examples of liberalism's decline, Putin argued that its defenders were tone deaf to the demands of the "overwhelming majority." The liberal idea, he concluded, had "outlived its purpose."[1]

Putin's pronouncement quickly captured the news cycle. Asked about the interview, then-President Donald Trump seemed ready to agree with the Russian autocrat, though he also mistook the latter's use of the term "liberal" to refer to California Democrats.[2] Most others correctly understood Putin to be attacking a tradition of western political thought originating in the nineteenth century.[3] A few noted that Putin's critical assessment had become fashionable "among reactionaries" in several countries, bolstering the rise of far-right figures like Jair Bolsonaro, Matteo Salvini, and Marie Le Pen. In that reactionary fashion, for instance, Hungary's Viktor Orbán claimed that alternative visions of the world are taking hold, visions that "are not Western, not liberal, not liberal democracies, maybe not even democracies, and yet are making nations successful."[4] Those who were loath to side with Putin but reluctant to praise liberalism argued that while the liberal idea is not *yet* obsolete, it is "on the ropes" and its systems clearly "under pressure."[5]

European Council President Donald Tusk was more forthright in his criticism of Putin's assertions. At the G20, Tusk told his audience: "We are here as Europeans also to firmly and univocally defend and promote liberal democracy. What I find really obsolete are—authoritarianism, personality cults, the rule of oligarchs."[6] *The Financial Times* itself published not one but two separate rebukes of Putin's comments, suggesting he was posturing on the world stage to downplay liberalism's successes, particularly in terms of economic development.[7]

By no means were reactions limited to politicians and reporters. Putin's claims about the fate of the liberal idea became part of a series of scholarly responses to Raymond Geuss's critique of the liberal tradition in his curious commemorative of Jurgen Habermas's ninetieth birthday. For Seyla Benhabib, Putin's and Geuss's overlapping pronouncements against liberalism warned of "strange bedfellows," while for Martin Jay it suggested a "guilt by association" which "may not be a fair tactic—although in this case, it is hard to resist."[8] The exchange made clear the extent to which public and scholarly debates can merge around the question of liberalism and its value. As a "vexed object of attachment," the idea has as firm a footing in academic circles as it has in public debate.[9]

Putin's interview clearly sparked a broad conversation about the vitality and utility of the liberal idea. But one must wonder why it worked so well as to capture the attention of news media, pundits, scholars, and political officials alike. After all, Putin's comments were in many ways quite *mundane*. This is not the first time that liberalism has been declared dead by its critics or revived by its defenders. A little over a century after its birth, Herbert Hoover announced that "liberalism was under attack "even in the great countries of its origins."[10] And though Francis Fukuyama declared its universal triumph in 1989, thirty years later he made headlines again for observing that the "liberal world order" had begun to falter and, perhaps, to reverse.[11] Because challenges to liberalism have emerged sharply in places like the United States and Europe—exemplars of the liberal tradition—they are especially damaging to "the reputation of that system as a whole."[12] In the intervening years, Fukuyama argues, the uneven distribution of globalization's gains and particularly the rise of identity politics have ruptured any liberal consensus, deepened social resentments, and made feasible the popularity of politicians like Putin, who have capitalized on these challenges in their appeals to the people liberalism forgot.[13] For detractors, Fukuyama's concerns about liberalism's future reinforce their criticisms of the celebratory bell he rang in 1989. After all, we are reminded, "what counts as victory in the field of ideas, theory or ideology will always be contested."[14]

Still, many have tried to "keep the ship afloat," with book after book released "trying to breathe new life into liberalism" in the face of these challenges.[15] The *Economist* even chose to mark its 175th anniversary by devoting a series of issues to liberalism's rise, decline, and prospects for resurrection in the twenty-first century. Presidents, legacy media, news blogs, pundits, and scholars all carry on debates over whether the "comfy Western consensus" over liberalism is under threat.[16] At the very least, all this talk of its relative health indicates that the liberal idea is well and widely attended to.

For precisely that reason, liberalism remains a reliable and convenient flashpoint for political conversation. In fact, Putin's *Financial Times* interview later makes clear that the real object of his ire was a specific set of rights-based claims and democratic practices, which have been undercut by his regime and for which Russia has received sustained criticism. However, by couching policy questions on LGBTQ rights or minority protections in the language of liberalism, Putin effectively reframed the ensuing debate away from issues of democratic legitimacy and his regime's own conduct and toward an assessment of the liberal idea itself. His critics fell in line. Taking various defensive positions, they outlined either what liberalism *has* achieved or more cautiously, what liberalism *can* achieve but has not yet. Others accepted its demise.

Thus, following his interview, coverage of the G20 summit as well as related conversations between scholars narrowed in on the fate of the liberal idea as much, if not more, than on Russian policies.[17] By directing his interview toward a discussion of liberalism, Putin worked a sleight of hand—centering our focus on the life of an idea while quietly shifting his regime's policies into the background.

And therein lies the liberalism trap.

My primary claim in this book is as follows: we are, in both public discourse and in studies of political thought, too preoccupied with the idea of liberalism. Focus on liberalism has become habitual and in so becoming, burdens interpretive practices among scholars as well as political debates in society at large. As the Putin affair illustrates, liberalism can become a discursive ploy, redirecting political conversations about specific practices and policies toward debates about the life and times of the liberal idea. Attentiveness to the idea is narrowing our range of inquiry. My claim, importantly, is not a statement about bad readings or biases. The problem of the liberalism trap runs much deeper. Liberalism is used to outline a set of theoretical and evaluative practices that organize how we think. We tend to approach political questions, histories, and texts in terms of their presumed relation to liberalism, and we understand the significance or utility of these things in terms of what they might tell us (or not) about liberalism.

This is an issue of *interpretive method*. Liberalism has become a discursive anchor that weighs down how we approach politics. Our attachment to this idea does not simply bias critical inquiry and deliberation. That attachment restricts the conditions under which such work is possible. The book offers an argument about how a familiar idea can transform into a methodological trap for political thinking.

The book makes three critical interventions. The first concerns interpretive habits: how can reliance on liberalism, as a methodological frame for inquiry, bind contemporary politics, from the media coverage surrounding a G20 summit to the erudite discussions that have marked political scholarship for nearly a century? I concentrate my study in the following chapters on the field of political theory. In its attentiveness to ideas and their implications, the field is poised to query how, and with what effects, conceptual attachments can shape our political perspectives. Yet, as I argue, approaches and debates within the field have become subject to the conceptual dominance of liberalism as an interpretive frame. This tension, between critical practice and interpretive habits, affords striking insight into the challenges posed by the liberalism trap.

Second, it outlines how the interpretive habits involving liberalism impact scholarly work through a study of the liberal tradition's now preeminent figurehead: John Stuart Mill. Popularly seen as liberalism's "founding father," Mill offers critical resources for identifying the effects of the liberalism trap and, as the book advises, for escaping it. Reading Mill through his status as a liberal icon has displaced the fundamental appreciation for *uncertainty* that informs his politics. Instead of a liberal ideologue, I identify Mill as a cautionary radical, a progressive thinker caught up in the challenges and the opportunities of doing politics without the conceit of certainties. The uncertain attitude Mill embraces is at once a condition of possibility and of risk. Recovering that condition not only reinvigorates our understanding of Mill but also informs how we approach our own political contexts and challenges.

The book's third critical intervention involves the politics of canon construction and "canonization" itself. Over the past few years, increased attention has rightly been paid to the exclusionary effects of canon construction—particularly as concerns representations of gender, race, and non-western contributions to political thought. I add to this work by drawing attention to the politics of inclusion into the canon. We ought to concern ourselves with the ways in which canonical *recruitment* can contain a thinker or a text's receptions and in turn limit how they are read into contemporary political thought. In Mill's case, for instance, I suggest that contemporary discussions around gender equity and postcoloniality might engage a Millian interest in uncertainty. That interest disrupts reliance on ideological anchors like liberalism, enabling a wider, even if more complex, range of possibilities for political analysis and collaboration.

These interventions attend to the varied effects of reading through liberalism in studies of politics—from the way we approach questions of political import, to the way we take up texts and authors to address those questions. In all, the book initiates a discussion about the dangers of the liberalism trap, and in so doing, invites consideration of what we might discover beyond it.

# Acknowledgments

This book is a product of the teachers I've been blessed to know, and who have come through my life in many forms. By the light of their minds, as J.S. Mill would say, I have learned so much and am learning still.

I wouldn't have had the opportunities I've had without the sacrifices my parents have made. They left everything they knew and loved in Sri Lanka when the war broke out and pursued a much different life than they had likely imagined. My mother, Amali, is a cultural anthropologist. She brought me along on her early field work in India, embarking on an academic career with a stubborn six-year-old and later managing a multigenerational household mostly on her own—I now look back with amazement at her strength and stamina. She remains my foremost mentor in feminist theory and practice. My father, Rajan, masks his real vocation as a political commentator with a daytime career in urban planning. Peppering story time with his own distillations of Marx and Engels, and biographies of US civil rights leaders, he set the tone of my interests and became my first editor and critic. I still write with my parents in mind. Needless to say, my early plans to become a virologist by day and a singer by night stood no chance against the examples they offered, of a life spent with ideas. I am obliged to them for that.

It seems unfair that I could have exceptional role models at home only to encounter more out in the world, but I did. In Canada, John Shaw, Brent Pavey, and John Barnes made lessons on religion, politics, and English a delight and encouraged my first experiments with writing. I am fortunate too to have had Barbara Arneil, Bruce Baum, and Mark Warren as professors during my time at the University of British Columbia. At Northwestern, Daniel Galvin, James Druckman, and Sara Monoson led wonderful seminars that invited fun and creative applications of political theory. Lars Tønder, and Elizabeth Beaumont (then at the University of Minnesota) were especially generous with their time; early discussions with Lars and Liz were essential to developing what would (eventually) become this book. But it was Laura Janara's contagious love of political theory that first sparked my own. Her invitation to discuss a future in the field changed everything. It was also Laura who suggested I work with the exceptional Mary Dietz—and that remains the best advice I have ever followed.

Mary brings political theory to life. Her phenomenal lectures, precise and insightful readings, and ability to guide without leading are the gold standard of academic research and teaching. From Mary, we learned to follow the text—and the questions, challenges, and confusions it generates—into the analysis. My fascination with J.S. Mill, and the idea for this book, first germinated in her classes. Serendipitously, my introduction to Mill in Mary's class coincided with James Farr's fantastic seminar in American Political Thought. Jim stumped me with an incisive comment on a paper concerning the US political tradition. "I get the contestation part of the argument," he responded, but suggested that I interrogate my own assumptions about "the 'liberalism' within which it all allegedly unleashes itself." Clearly, that comment had legs. It is a great privilege to have worked with Mary and Jim and to now call them friends.

These formative teachers are joined by the amazing colleagues I learned from in graduate school. In Laura Montanaro, Andrew Clarke, and Clark Banack, I found brilliant, lifelong friends—and delightful people to travel with. Bai Linh Hoang, Giovanni Mantilla, and Michael Julius kept classes lively and life fun in Minneapolis, and I am thankful to know Libby Sharrow—an inspiring scholar, and fellow X-Filer. The truth is still out there.

At Northwestern, Nick Dorzweiler, Alison Rane, Samara Klar, Kharunnisa Mohamedali, Emily Alvarez, Joshua Robison, Rachel Moskowitz, Christoph Nguyen, Ari Shaw, and Thomas Leeper became family. They made five years in Chicago wonderfully rich and all too short. I also benefitted from Ross Carroll's and Doug Thompson's excellent leadership of the Political Theory Workshop, where I first put some of the ideas in this book up for consideration. There was no better place to do so, as Ross and Doug created a space in which intellectual exchange, collegiality, and lasting friendships rounded out our training in political theory. Nick and Alison, Désirée Weber, Chris Sardo, Lexi Neame, Anna Terweil, Boris Litvin, Lucy Cane, and Arda Gucler helped nurture that space, and I am thankful for having been part of their community.

And then of course there's Jennifer Forestal. My compatriot, my co-author, my WhatsApp sister—who has read and commented on too many drafts of this project. One never knows what life after graduate school will entail, especially after being immersed in a program where political theory was well and widely respected. What started as a lifeline in those early days of being freshly minted theorists in unfamiliar departments across the country has transformed into one of the most supportive and productive friendships of my life. Working with Jeni is a collaborative dream—from simultaneously co-editing paragraphs online (it works!) to dividing and conquering the appetizer and drink lines at conferences. Reader, if you can find your own Jeni, you'll be better for it.

The arguments about Mill and about liberalism I make in this book were given at various conferences over the years. I am appreciative of the perceptive comments and questions that came from audiences, panelists, and discussants at APSA, WPSA, CPSA, and especially APT and BIAPT—which include those from Daniel O'Neill, David Williams, Jeanne Morefield, Eric MacGilvray, Michael Goodhart, Alasia Nuti, and Terrell Carver, as well as Inder Marwah, whose wonderful work has enriched how I read and understand Mill. Thanks also to Anne Manuel for facilitating visits to the John Stuart Mill Library housed at Somerville College, Oxford, and for invitations to participate in the events she has organized for the archive.

I could not have asked for a better editor than Angela Chnapko who, along with Alexcee Bechthold steered the project smoothly through the various stages of academic publishing. Sincere thanks also to Brid Nowlan for copyediting and to Derek Gottlieb for indexing. And it was a special delight to work with my talented friend Kara McGuire (Also Known As), and her colleague Katie Frederick, who conceptualized and designed the book's cover.

I found my first professional home at Tulane University thanks in large part to Tom Langston and Nancy Maveety who brought me on board. I learned much from colleagues at Tulane, who read draft chapters and advised me through my first years in the profession. This is especially true of the PoliChix (Chris Fettweis's moniker, which we hate to love, but do)—Mirya Holman, Christina Kiel, Celeste Lay, Casey Love, Anna Mahoney, Virginia Oliveros, and Izabela Steflja. What a wonderful group of scholars to learn from—and a better happy hour crowd cannot be found.

I also found a true a family of friends in Mary Grace, Patrick, Meredith, Kelly, Brandon, William, Madeleine, Kara, Seamus, Trey, Nikki, Paul, and Krysia. Even in the thick of writing, pandemics, parenting, and hurricanes, they make life a joy with Friendsgivings, pizza challenges, beach getaways, and so many costumed escapades. It doesn't matter where we are, Core Group is forever. And because (as Jeni would say) space matters, I must acknowledge the place where I discovered this family: New Orleans. A city of haunting contrasts, great revelry, and deep magic. In the immortal words of Anne Rice, "as soon as I smelled the air, I knew I was home."

My move to the United States for graduate school began with a brief year in Minneapolis. As a fresh-faced student in a new country, I had plenty of reason to be anxious, and I would have been had it not been for Nance and Brian Longley. They made me welcome, offered great conversation, delicious meals, and time with their family. But I owe them a special debt of gratitude for their daughter Nora—an incomparably beautiful soul. Nora and I were chance roommates in Vancouver, and years later, fortune would bring me to her home city for graduate school. I am grateful for that extra time with her. Before she left, Nora told me she was proud of me, and that is an honor I hope one day to earn. This book is dedicated to her.

My own (very) large family of accomplished aunts, uncles, and cousins spread around the world has been a steady anchor in the sometimes-nomadic life academia can involve. There are few things I look forward to more than our chaotic reunions, the 1,000 daily group messages, and Zoom chats between 10 generations, across 5 time zones. And by far the most loved Auntie there is, my sister Mira is one of the best and brightest people I know. Along with my mother, she was there for me at a particularly difficult time; the project would not have crossed the finish line without her. To my dragons Jai and Rami—whom I carried in one form or another while writing this book—my thanks for the daily reminders to laugh, dance, and play.

Now to Geoff Dancy. He managed breakfasts and bedtimes whenever Mill demanded my attention and lent his considerable editing skills to this manuscript (more than once). I met Geoff on an elevator in Minneapolis, where he hatched a five-year plan. As with most things he sets out to achieve, he executed that plan with aplomb. Far past the five-year mark, through four cities, with two great kids, dearest Bellatrix, silly Elvira, and so much more to come—the Philips Dancy Krewe can parade with the best of them. In Geoff, I have found a sharp mind that can spar and inspire, a friend always ready to support and to encourage, and a partner with whom I have built a life that feels like an adventure. There is no greater gift than that.

# 1
# Is Liberalism Inescapable?

*As soon as you label a concept, you change how people perceive it.*
Adam Alter, *The New Yorker*

To be trapped by an idea is to be beholden to it, to become so deeply entangled that our perceptions are bound to it. Understanding that entanglement and its effects in the context of liberalism constitutes the central aim of this book. What I call the liberalism trap is not a problem of the idea itself, but of our collective infatuation with it.

Preoccupations with liberalism—a fixation on working out its meaning(s), origin(s), and future(s)—are becoming methodologically customary, and with troublesome consequences for the study and practice of politics. In the scholarly context, liberal preoccupations generate interpretive habits which detail not only why, but *how* scholars of politics must center analyses and debates around questions and presumptions about liberalism.[1] And in the broader public sphere, concerns about the death and/or resurrection of liberalism have been the lifeblood of political discourse for over a century.[2] From academia to political punditry, no idea in modern history has enjoyed as much study and use, and from all angles, as has the liberal idea.

Notably, when the term "liberal" appeared around the fourteenth century, it referred to noble and generous spirits, characteristics befitting free men and gentlemen. Research using Google Ngram data suggests that the word gained a more political meaning in the late 1700s, as use of terms like "liberal policy" or "liberal principles" began to gain traction.[3] The *Liberales* group of Spain was among the first to adopt the term as a political identifier in 1812, during its fight for universal male suffrage, a constitutional monarchy, and land reform.[4] By 1815 "liberalism" had made its first appearances in the context of Western European party politics, associated with themes of free inquiry, self-government, and a market economy, though "it remained an obscure and marginal category."[5]

Over the past two centuries, those simple beginnings have given way to a conceptual powerhouse, imbued with an almost human-like agency through pronouncements about liberalism's birth, its health, its responsibilities, and its failures. And that agency is widely felt. Thomas Nagel observes that virtually every political argument in the western world is a variation on the theme of liberalism.[6] But ongoing interrogations of liberalism's imperial past and its transnational grip today indicate that this is by no means a strictly "western" phenomenon.[7]

The breadth of arguments about it also reveals liberalism's conceptual elasticity. The term's evolution, Harold Laski noted, has incorporated "winds of doctrine so diverse in their origin as to make clarity difficult, and precision perhaps unattainable."[8] For John Dewey "liberalism has meant in practice things so different as to be opposed to one another," something Judith Shklar warned might result in the term becoming too "amorphous" to be of much use.[9]

Evidence of this elasticity can be found in everyday political conversations. On matters of public policy, for instance, liberalism has been used to both justify and challenge regulations concerning what women wear, while proposals for universal healthcare in the United States have been viewed as a battle for and against liberalism's survival.[10] For some pundits on the right it is a political ideology devoted to big government and interventionist social agendas. Meanwhile, critics on the left see it is a platform for free market and elite interests that impedes the efficacy of democracy and the achievement of social justice. And despite disputes over who, or what, is or is not a "liberal,"[11] the subject of liberalism's life and prospects throws together "socialists, conservatives, social democrats, republicans, greens, feminists, and anarchists" in sometimes unexpected ways.[12] Debates about liberalism have made for uneasy bedfellows over the years—a point some have toyed with for narrative effect.[13]

Liberalism's conceptual elasticity offers a clue to understanding its popularity as an object of constant praise and censure; there is always room for renegotiating its meaning and value. The life of this idea has been nourished by continuous discussion of its past effects, its present significance, or its future possibilities. Though both its critics and defenders tend to evaluate the success of liberalism as a measure of the political consensus it achieves, in reality, victory in the realm of ideas should also be judged by sheer *persistence*. The endurance of this idea relies less on collective agreement over its value and more on a collective need to attend to it in political analysis. Even for some of its most ardent critics, liberalism maintains a hold they cannot seem to shake. As Wendy Brown says of left politics, an attachment to the liberal idea reflects "an organization of desire we wish were otherwise."[14]

But the wishing otherwise Brown desires maintains an active connection to the idea, and keeps it, in a word, alive. Brown's lament thus captures something of the nature of liberalism's victory in political discourse—it is not one of consensus but of inescapability. Whether we love it, hate it, or remain endlessly ambivalent about it, the liberal idea is defended, critiqued, and assessed across the political spectrum. The question of liberalism's power, then, is not about universal appeal (or emerging decline) but about its *discursive resilience*. On that score, liberalism's dominance in the realm of ideas is unparalleled. And this is precisely why declarations of its death, along with attendant efforts to keep it alive, might be almost comical if not for the very real effects our deep attachments to liberalism are producing: from conflicts over policy to conversations between academics, those attachments are directing the way we think about and do politics.

## A Tumultuous Affair: Political Theory and Liberalism

The effects of preoccupations with liberalism are best on view in the so called "ivory tower" of academic political theory. If even a field oriented around the interrogation of ideas and practices can become caught in the liberalism trap, it would offer substantive evidence of the trap's hold. But the problem in this sphere is that liberalism's conceptual triumph can prop up a particular mode of inquiry, which imposes limits on how scholars address perennial questions and contemporary problems. Pressing political concerns—from structural inequality to democratic malaise—are presented as subjects of liberalism's rise, decline, evolution, and so on. Escaping the liberalism trap is thus a disciplinary problem with political ramifications.

Imagine that the very efficacy of political science is seen as tethered to "the consequences of liberalism's fate in the polity at large."[15] Disciplinary historians have argued that professional political science is and always has been a "species of liberalism" that responded to demands for revising or reconsidering the "liberal visions" at its foundation.[16] Disagreements over liberalism are understood to have reoriented the intellectual identity and relationships among the subfields of political science as a whole. Scholars document, for instance, how the "varieties of liberalism" that organized the US discipline became targets of censure for European émigrés like Leo Strauss, Hannah Arendt, Theodor Adorno, and Max Horkheimer.[17] Having experienced political upheavals across the Atlantic, these thinkers took a largely critical view of liberalism's intellectual purchase in US political science.[18]

Yet even these challenges to liberal visions of the discipline have helped to perpetuate scholarly preoccupations with the idea. The process of perpetuation-through-critique marks one of the most influential confrontations with liberalism's role in US intellectual and political life, from scholar Louis Hartz. Published in 1955, Hartz's *The Liberal Tradition in America* contributed to the disquiet of the postwar era. In his view, liberalism had so fully captured the US mind that neither its citizens nor its intellectual leaders were equipped to rethink US political identity, nor its response to a rapidly changing global context. These liberal foundations made for a future in which past would be prologue.

*The Liberal Tradition* has haunted studies of US political thought and development since it appeared. Generations of scholars after Hartz have worked either to prove or debunk his central thesis about the United States' liberal origins, arguing for the elasticity of liberal ideas and their openness to contestation, or for competing ideologies which have prevented the kind of liberal indoctrination Hartz described.[19] His intervention effectively organized a scholarly tradition of investigating liberalism in studies of US political thought. In ways they may not have expected, then, the legacy of the postwar émigrés and critics like Hartz has been to sustain the conceptual power of the very idea they aimed to disrupt.[20]

As in the public sphere, liberalism's dominance in political scholarship is an achievement of twentieth-century contestations. Consequently, John Gunnell observes,

> the literature of political theory is, and since the late 1930s has been, saturated with discussions about liberalism and its tradition—rise and decline—faith—dangers, limits, collapse, challenges, agony, paradox, irony, spirit, development, end, poverty and crisis and its relation to innumerable things, individuals and other political concepts.[21]

For Duncan Bell, liberalism has simply become the metacategory of contemporary political discourse.[22] Without question, attention to this metacategory has been incredibly generative. Evaluations of liberalism have underwritten arguments over the role of the state in the provision of social goods, the relation between the individual, family, and community, policies concerning colonial and postcolonial contexts, and minority claims to representation and justice.[23] These debates have fruitfully proposed ways of thinking differently about liberalism in relation to social and redistributive justice, the nature of personhood, the challenges facing modern multicultural societies, and international relations.

But the broader interpretive effects of disciplinary preoccupations with the idea ought to give scholars pause. In attending to liberalism across various sites of analysis, we can transform the idea from a *subject* of study into a *condition* for study. The metacategorical effect of our investments in this idea is thus a methodological practice which puts liberalism first, so to speak. Now, preoccupations with liberalism can mark the boundaries of our interpretive work. And we can become trapped by them. Working within these interpretive boundaries can limit how we approach particular debates and problems, setting up divisive labeling practices in place of real conversations and ideological disagreements in place of political negotiations.

## A Caveat on Scope

An objection to this argument worth addressing at the outset involves the scope of the problem concerning liberalism. Readers might take my intervention against the liberalism *trap* to constitute an intervention against liberalism writ large. The distinction between these points is critical and goes to the heart of my departure from existing studies of liberal thought: I am not making a case for abandoning ideological frames per se (if such a thing is even possible). My intervention does not, therefore, dismiss the conceptual utility of liberalism in toto or its historical significance to the development of political thought. For these reasons too, I do not engage in already well-tilled debates over what liberalism is, does, or fails to be. This is not a book that tries to "pin down" liberalism and its notoriously elastic definitional history, nor is it interested in disparaging liberalism or saving it from attack.

What this argument *does* attempt is to unsettle the custom of examining politics through these questions. The problem I identify has little to do with the liberal idea and everything to do with how and why we *deploy* this idea in political discourse. By and large, liberalism's conceptual triumph has begun to infiltrate the practice of political theorizing rather than remaining subject to that practice. Put another way: scholars are not just thinking about liberalism; liberalism, or more particularly preoccupations with it, are shaping the way we think about politics. An examination of our reliance on this idea is therefore imperative. And nowhere is that reliance on better display than in the reception of liberalism's quintessential representative: John Stuart Mill.

## J.S. Mill, The Iconic Liberal

No doubt J.S. Mill will appear to be a counterintuitive choice for this project. Most students are introduced to his thought through its association with liberalism. They first encounter *On Liberty* as one of liberalism's essential texts. Beyond the classroom, too, Mill's name is referenced almost daily across dozens of articles concerning liberalism from issues of education to debates about pornography.[24]

So why pursue an assessment of our investments in liberalism through one of the idea's most iconic representatives? The argument that our relationship to liberalism has come to constitute an interpretive trap might be more apparent with figures like Hobbes or Locke, thinkers who predate liberalism's political emergence. Here, at least, the charge of anachronism could be applied and would clearly outline the interpretive latitude we take in making liberalism central to analyses of thinkers or texts. As Chapter 2 notes, there is certainly room for investigating the role liberalism plays in receptions of these canonical figures and others like them. Laying the groundwork for such inquires, however, is most effectively done in relation to Mill. My concern is not simply that we are applying the "wrong labels" to the "wrong thinkers." It is not about correct labeling practices, but about the *politics of labeling*. The application of ideological labels to a text or thinker has interpretive and political consequences for how we perceive them going forward. It is, therefore, Mill's paradigmatic status that can best illustrate the methodological effects of political theory's affair with liberalism. The thinker we are most comfortable with reading under the liberal label can illustrate the consequences of centering liberalism in general.

Chapters 2 and 3 focus on Mill's ideological status, and what it has cost us in terms of our engagement with his thought, while Chapters 4, 5, and 6 illustrate how his tenure as "the liberal" negatively impacts the way we treat his work on questions of gender, class, and empire. As an iconic liberal, Mill exemplifies the interpretive problems that arise out of our relationship with liberalism. After all, reliance on settled opinion, *On Liberty* tells us, can undermine critical thought. And because Mill's association with liberalism is so often relied upon, little consideration is given to how that association has directed the way scholars understand and appropriate his political writings.

Mill is hence a critical test of the book's central premise. That our attachments to liberalism might limit engagement even with one of its paradigmatic figures would indicate that something has gone awry. It is my contention that Mill's exemplary status within the liberal canon can lead us to read his theories as if they speak to ideological certainties and to style particular elements of his texts to fit whatever version of liberalism is under review. Trapped within the confines of this idea, readers substitute Mill's now canonical *status* as a liberal figurehead for his political *arguments*. The thinker is being drowned out by the very tradition he is supposed to captain.

Considered by many to be the father of modern liberalism, Mill is ideally placed to illustrate how our preoccupations with the idea shape the practice of political theorizing.[25] Drawing inspiration from Mill's concerns with habituated learning, we ought to ask whether our focus on liberalism has itself become habitual, and to what extent it closes us off to alternative resources for, or approaches to, political theorizing.

As I argue, emphasizing Mill's exemplarity as a liberal has obscured a key element of his political thought: the *uncertainty* he employed as a political thinker and actor. Untethered from his now customary identification with liberalism, Mill's political writings on human nature, individuality, and social progress give evidence of a cautionary radical, a thinker driven not by ideological certainties but by the challenges and the possibilities of doing politics without any guarantees of success. I develop this reading by re-centering Mill's oft-overlooked *Autobiography*. A text avidly read and commentated on by Mill scholars working in the tradition of intellectual biography, Mill's self-reflective study is rarely drawn into contemporary appropriations of his more famed political discussions concerning individuality, harm, or the conditions for individual and social development.[26]

The separation of Mill's self-assessments from his political writings is a mistake. The *Autobiography* is an essential primer to Mill's thought, an argument I make in Chapter 3. Written and revised over seventeen years, the text details Mill's evolution as a public intellectual with a mind "always pressing forward, equally ready to learn and unlearn either from its own thoughts or from those of others."[27] It is a text which shows Mill turning many of his observations about political life—the dangers of customary knowledge, the connections between individuality and community, and the challenges of social progress—upon himself as he examines the effects of his education, his relationship with his father, James Mill, and his pivotal mental crisis. Mill's experiences lead him to appreciate the role of uncertainty in political life, and his own politics are very much instructed by that appreciation.

## A Caveat on Mill

My profile of Mill might rankle some readers who will protest the focus on his relation to liberalism. Why not consider his identification with utilitarianism, democracy, or socialism? After all, Mill explicitly wrote on these ideas, and scholars have attended to those writings.[28] In response, I would argue that the liberal identifier has claimed a greater hold on Mill's legacy, and I would not be alone in noting this. Though Mill scholars have examined his engagements with other traditions of thought, his almost parental relationship to liberalism is rarely questioned. Even as he warns us away from labeling Mill too narrowly, historian Richard Reeves lists liberalism as being decidedly ahead of Mill's democratic or socialist identifications.[29] That narrative is reinforced by the way we are introduced to Mill in the first place. In their volume on Mill's political thought, Nadia Urbinati and Alex Zakaras point out that the first thing a student learns about Mill is that he is the exemplary liberal philosopher.[30] This description will hardly surprise anyone familiar with introductory political theory textbooks; it reflects an opinion shared across generations of readers of Mill's thought.[31] To say that the association of Mill with liberalism is a customary practice in the modern world is thus not an argument for how he should be read, but a statement about how he *is* read.

## Cannon Fodder

That Mill himself was a critical observer of the dilemmas of customary knowledge and is now subjected to the practice of being read as a canonical liberal is both ironic and illustrative of what can happen when our political imaginations are held captive by an idea like liberalism. As subsequent chapters argue, Mill's iconic status has suppressed the importance of his self-reflections and thus missed the role uncertainty plays in his political thought.

In drawing these omissions out, the argument made here also taps into contemporary debates about canon construction and deconstruction.

Discussions about the politics of canons are increasingly widespread, not only in political thought but across different academic disciplines. Driving those discussions are concerns with how canons can be both productive and exclusionary at the same time.[32] On one hand, canons serve useful organizing purposes because they "set up paradigms to govern work in their disciplines"; on the other, those governing paradigms will necessarily privilege and exclude.[33]

For these reasons, political theory and its tradition of great texts has garnered criticism in the twentieth century from scholars who point to what that tradition has left out and actively rendered invisible.[34] As Penny Weiss argues:

> remote and academic as they sometimes appear, debates about what to include in the canon ultimately touch almost everyone: students handed texts from lists of "great books" to guide them, for example; members of groups whose history and literature is more or less available or widely known; and citizens whose governments justify their actions with ideas from political texts deemed classic.[35]

Canons and canonizing processes are evidently political. Feminist scholars note that the history of political thought as it has been constructed within academic political theory consistently marginalizes the varied contributions of women to the development of political thought and practice.[36] Race and ethnicity constitute sites of exclusion as well—even as work produced by scholars of color has been appropriated by the field at large.[37] From a global perspective too, critics argue that efforts to take up non-western works still employ western canonical themes and authors as evaluative standards, while studies in comparative political thought can reify, rather than disrupt, east/west dichotomies and the divisions they sustain.[38]

Notably, such concerns are not aimed at removing traditionally dubbed canonical thinkers from political theory rubrics, but at adapting our reliance on them to reflect "an awareness of their social and historical limitations and an appreciation for other kinds of work."[39] Challenges to canon construction recognize that "political theory is about human and not merely Western dilemmas"[40] nor, we can add, merely male or white subjects. Interrogating the canon is vital to ensuring reflective rigor in how the field defines itself and for brokering new ways to read and do political theory, not only outside the traditional canon but also alongside and in contestation with it.

My argument is a companion to these examinations of canons and their exclusionary politics. But I reorient the critique of canon construction to consider how *canonization* itself can pose challenges for scholarship. Alongside canonical omissions, we need to consider how being contained within (even restricted to) canons can shape texts and authors, as well as the ways we draw upon them to organize and resolve our own political challenges. The rereadings of Mill presented in Chapters 4 through 6 in fact suggest that canonical inclusion can direct the reasons we turn to particular texts and authors, as well as the conversations we draw them into. This is the problem I identify with receptions of Mill's work on gender, class, and empire. A thinker whose intellectual legacy has been captured by the liberal label, Mill's writings have become cannon fodder for debates about how and where liberalism interacts with these issues.

Together with the pedagogical utilities of canons, a point discussed in Chapter 2, scholars ought to be attentive to the methodological effects of canonical identification. Those identifications, as in the case of J.S. Mill, can restrict from the outset the parameters within which texts and authors are read and applied. To confront the liberalism trap is, in part, an intervention against the limits imposed by disciplinary canonization.

## Plan of the Book

From interpretive habits and their textual effects to the politics of canon construction, the scholarly convention of making liberalism a necessary frame for contemporary inquiry is apparent. The book takes several steps in its assessment of this tumultuous affair with the most dominant idea of the modern age. The first step is *identification*; the second, *refusal*; the third, *recovery*; and the fourth, *discovery*.

Chapter 2 offers a close examination of the evolution of liberalism's conceptual dominance in political theory and of its disciplinary effects in the field. As I suggest, scholarly preoccupation with the idea has shaped not only the parameters of our debates and contestations, but more broadly, it is conditioning the field's pedagogical practices and organization. That conditioning influences the ways in which students of political thought are introduced to canonical "liberal" thinkers and ideas. Turning to scholarly receptions of

J.S. Mill, I identify how our pedagogical practices involving liberalism have *modified* those thinkers and ideas in troubling ways. Once "canonized" by liberalism, figures like Mill become fixed resources to which contemporary narratives about liberalism can easily turn.

Having identified the dangers of entrapment, the next step is to confront those dangers by refusing liberalism's interpretive claim on textual analysis. Chapter 3 offers an account of Mill's politics untethered from his liberal status. Focusing on Mill's intellectual development, which took a sharp turn following his experience with depression, I examine his move from a "manufactured" mind under the tutelage of his father and Jeremy Bentham to his intellectual revolt and turn to uncertainty. Uncertainty channels the intellectual flexibility and caution fostered by Mill's embrace of "eclecticism," "half-truths," "many-sidedness," and "fallibility," terms he employs in the *Autobiography* to describe his changing intellectual orientation. I catalogue these changes in terms of "uncertainty" to provide a structured way of tracing Mill's self-described shifts away from dogmatism, and the growing discomfort he develops in his early twenties with determinative ideological platforms. As I argue, Mill's appreciation for uncertainty not only generated the distance he needed to reassess his early education under Bentham and his father, James Mill, it also angled him toward a more capacious approach to political thought and action.

Pursuing these shifts in Mill's development enables recovery of the political strategies Mill's uncertainty sustains in relation to questions of social reform, strategies which have been occluded by reading him through liberalism. From *radical* critiques to *gradualist* and *paternalist* precautions, Mill's uncertainty not only shaped his intellectual orientation but also underwrote his political proposals regarding gender, class, and empire. Recovery of those strategies and their effects are taken up in Chapters 4, 5, and 6.

Chapter 4 attends to the limitations of treating Mill's gender politics as a cipher for liberal feminism. Looking at prominent feminist receptions of Mill's gender politics, I argue that much of the literature assesses his politics with a prior investment in assessing liberal feminism. Against this practice, I highlight the complexities of Mill's feminist politics, apart from concerns with defining the ideological label he is so often read under. The chapter shows that uncertainty generates a particular set of political anxieties for Mill, revolving around a desire to expand (rather than contract) the possibilities for "man as a progressive being"; but it also prohibits Mill from taking a determinative approach toward obtaining such possibilities.[41] Thus, though Mill offers a radical critique of gender inequality in the nineteenth century, calling for the political enfranchisement of women and their emancipation from the confines of the household, he simultaneously enacts cautionary caveats, even reversals. On issues of divorce and women's employment for instance, Mill's fears about the unintended consequences of women's social and political liberation take root. In effect, despite Mill's support for gender equality, his approach to reform is inflected by uncertainties about the direction and consequences of making broad structural changes to achieve it.

Recovery of Mill's uncertainty and its political consequences can and should be traced comparatively. As Chapter 5 outlines, Mill's strategies for political reform concerning gender interact with his discussions of class inequality and representation in England. His cautions regarding women's emancipation are in fact exacerbated by his class politics, such that his defense of women's emancipation is mediated by the economic classes to which they belong. Mill's support for removing sex and class-based distinctions for suffrage took account of how changes to the electoral body would draw in new and diverse political interests and groups. His response to those challenges again reflects his uncertain mode of political theorizing. The radical, gradualist, and paternalist strategies he employs in relation to women's emancipation gain traction and become further institutionalized in his policies regarding class and representative politics. From excluding the poor to advocating plural voting for enlightened citizens, Mill's insightful critiques of class inequality are attended by efforts to slow, if not forestall, the effects of universal suffrage and its impact on parliamentary representation.

Building upon these applications of Mill's uncertainty, Chapter 6 draws the comparative assessment of Mill's political interventions into his writings on empire. Contrary to the now dominant refrain citing Mill as an unwavering "liberal imperialist,"[42] I argue that we do in fact find the same radical critiques and gradual and paternalist reforms in Mill's view of the British Empire. Yet, as with his feminist and class politics, Mill's imperial writings are often read through his liberal status. For scholars interested in the imperial roots of liberal political thought, Mill's iconic position within that tradition makes him the model for studies of liberal imperialism.

Importantly too, readings of Mill on liberal empire have tended to keep his writings on empire at a distance from his domestic considerations, such that his "radicalism" at home is contrasted with his "imperialism" abroad. But following Mill's uncertain mode of politics enables a clearer comparative view of his writings across these issues. Even as Mill defends the imperial project and refutes the right of self-determination for colonized subjects, he is never wholly comfortable with the realities of colonial rule, a discomfort that has been almost entirely obscured in the now standard reading of Mill in the context of liberal empire. That discomfort leads him to make some striking critiques of the British Empire and its colonial administrators, on issues of violence, education, and the demands of justice for colonial subjects. That he could both defend and doubt empire is an effect not of ideological certainty but of political uncertainty.

The book concludes by outlining the new terrain we might discover for engaging with the full scope and nuance of Mill's arguments regarding women's emancipation, class reform, and British imperial practice. Beyond the convenient labels of liberal radical, liberal elitist, liberal imperialist, etc., which are differentially applied to him, what Mill's politics reveal is a complex and interactive set of strategies that recognize the necessity of political critique and reform, while remaining wary of their uncertain possibilities. Understanding the generative tensions of Mill's uncertain mode of theorizing can be an informative resource for contemporary political thought.

To illustrate this point, I focus my discussion in Chapter 7 on three areas: contemporary feminist studies of gender in transnational perspective, studies of empire and imperialism today, and the challenges of a critical interpretive practice. Scholarly preoccupation with liberalism in these areas bears the same methodological and political risks that attend treatments of Mill as a liberal exemplar: namely, a narrowing of our interpretive horizons and by extension, of the political possibilities we envision. Moving beyond those preoccupations uncovers alternative avenues for cross-cultural collaboration on issues of gender equity, as well as for a more expansive and comparative analysis of empire and the legacies of imperialism in the modern age. My concluding remarks reimagine contemporary interpretive practices through Millian uncertainty, and beyond the trap of liberalism.

With Mill as its guide, the book highlights how liberalism gets deployed to decode historical texts and contemporary questions. From pedagogical practices to scholarly debates, there is a discernible proclivity for assessing political developments and arguments according to the various aspects of liberal thought that scholars presume must be critiqued (or defended). Thinkers, texts, social and political problems are thus forced into "nominalist cubbyholes,"[43] molded to suit the conceptual boundaries of a field disciplined by liberalism. The perpetual danger facing interpretation, Quentin Skinner notes, is that established frames of reference might prepare the scholar to perceive or react to their subject of study in particular ways.[44] To defend against that danger, political thinking must involve an effort to ensure that our preconceptions do not determine how we encounter a text or problem, nor exhaust the dialogue surrounding them.

The problem is that we have become complacent about how easily we impose liberal identifiers on political texts and issues and are thus losing an important degree of critical perspective in studies of political thought. We are in effect transforming what might be a *particular* lens into a *general structure* of inquiry, allowing our attachments to liberalism to fix in advance the terms of political theorizing and the politics it makes imaginable.

My hope is that bringing these issues to light will not only shift how we approach Mill's work but also encourage critical reflection about the authoritative role our attachment to liberalism occupies in political inquiry today. What follows is thus a preliminary step toward confronting the dangers of the liberalism trap—to exchange established understandings for the invigorating challenges of uncertainty.

# 2
# Disciplined by Liberalism
## Contestations, Pedagogies, and the Exemplary Mr. Mill

> *It is not to be denied that Mr. Mill had many followers who were more inclined to close the mouths of their opponents with the mention of his great name than to face the logical consequences of their own views. But this happens to all leaders. Nothing was further from Mr. Mill's own habit than to rest upon mere authority.*
>
> Mill's Obituary, The New York Times

Debates about liberalism are, arguably, one of the few areas in which the discursive habits of public and scholarly spaces intersect.[1] Disputes over the liberal idea among G20 members, political pundits, and legacy media are ever present in the scholarly world of political science. Liberalism's sustained dominance in studies of political thought, however, is particularly striking given the diversity of contestations over the idea's meaning and roots. While defending or demeaning the liberal idea has marked much discussion in the public sphere, debates within the academy have also been mired in disagreements over *what* liberalism is.

Even while scholars generally recognize a liberal family of values—a commitment to the rule of law, individual rights, free press, and religious tolerance, among others—"no one settled concept *liberalism* or *liberal*" has prevailed.[2] Instead, liberalism is "marked by disjuncture, competing and often-incompatible values, and a breadth of social, political and moral ideals—some in tension, others in outright contradiction."[3] The family of values attached to liberalism "can be defined, related, and integrated in several different ways."[4] In effect, the hallmark features of liberalism are essentially contested. Between its disjunctures and its variations, liberalism emerges in scholarship as a "squabbling family of philosophical doctrines, a popular creed, a resonant moral idea, the creature of a party machine, a comprehensive economic system, a form of life . . . all of these and more."[5] For scholars to attempt an authoritative definition of the liberal idea might thus be "impossible and probably counterproductive."[6]

However, these definitional disagreements explain why our preoccupations with liberalism in the academy have been phenomenally *productive*. Liberalism's elasticity affords scholars of political thought space to interpret and deploy the idea in wide-ranging ways. And that range generates a set of interpretive possibilities—and problems—which have substantively shaped the field. Concerns with liberalism have infiltrated political theory's contestations within the academy, the field's interpretive practices, and its organization of canonical texts and authors. Those concerns have also shuttered alternative interests and approaches to texts or issues that get caught within liberalism's orbit. We have become disciplined by our attachment to liberalism and are now prey to the disciplinary repercussions of that attachment.

This chapter identifies three aspects of liberalism's authoritative position in contemporary political thought: (1) the discipline's organizing *entanglements* with liberalism; (2) the *expansion* of those entanglements through interpretive and pedagogical practices; and (3) the *effects* of both on a model case: receptions of John Stuart Mill.

Considering first how the identity of the discipline has become entangled with liberalism, I discuss the merger between liberalism and the development of the discipline in the west documented by historians of political science. But while the close connections between the discipline and doctrine are recognized, little attention has been given to the impact of their merger on the actual practice of political theorizing. The chapter thus turns to those impacts by following how attentiveness to liberalism has expanded in the field of political theory. I look specifically at Duncan Bell's helpful analysis of liberal "conscription" and "retrojection," processes which work to widen liberalism's conceptual reach.[7] Those processes indicate how texts and thinkers are variously drafted into an ever-growing liberal canon. But the real challenge, I argue, lies beyond who and what gets labeled as liberal; rather what scholars have to watch for is how that label *modifies* the thinkers or themes under study. And indeed, the label's modifying powers are visible in the field's pedagogical practices. Introducing students to particular ways of reading texts and authors as members of liberalism's squabbling family inevitably helps to nurture the idea's interpretive grip.

The chapter's third move is to examine the effects of these processes of entanglement and expansion in the case of John Stuart Mill. Looking at the evolution of Mill's reception in the twentieth century, I note that his iconic status has been especially important in an era where liberalism became its own category of analysis. Mill, in this context, has become a standard bearer of a tradition under constant scholarly review. And once canonized as such, figures like Mill become fixed resources to which reviews of liberalism can turn. Even as focus has shifted to different aspects of Mill's political writings, what those writings say about liberalism has remained a permanent feature of how and why scholars take up his works. Notably too, evolving receptions of Mill show how his status as a liberal icon has allowed for interpretations which are, at once, limiting and curiously diverse. Limiting because wherever liberalism is under review, Mill is called in as a representative case; diverse because the "liberalisms" he is tasked with representing are sometimes so different as to be incompatible. The danger across these instances is that Mill's politics are lost to our preoccupations with liberalism.

I close the chapter with two important notes about the conceptual shift this argument is pushing for. First, there are alternative approaches to the "liberal icon" reading of J.S. Mill, which attend to his political career and to his own observations about his ideological bearings. These alternatives show us not only what his liberal canonization risks, but just as importantly, what we might recover from Mill by suspending focus on his liberal status. The second concluding note of the chapter posits that such alternatives help chart different directions for the practice of political theorizing. By tracing the methodological effects of the liberalism trap, and reconstructing Mill's thought beyond its tethers, this and later chapters argue that new textual insights and political opportunities await discovery.

## Entanglements: Liberalism's Disciplinary Evolution

Dating the birth of academic political science is not without challenges. Erkki Berndston points out that while professorships on the theme of politics were established in Europe as early as 1622, scholarly appointments to the study of politics appeared only in the 1840s.[8] As late as 1949, only four countries had formal political science associations, and while many nations had scholars who researched in the area of politics, "the United States alone had an established institutionalized political science profession."[9] That fact led some to characterize the discipline as US in origin.[10] But the US roots of political science have since been complicated, if not altogether refuted. As Dorothy

Ross notes, the origins of US political science actually reflects a "multinational conversation that contributed German, French, and British political ideas to America's own blend."[11]

The discipline's multinational evolution was the subject of a series of studies commissioned by the International Political Science Association in 1988. Looking for connections and variations in the development of political science across nations, some studies took a comparative historical approach following new methods of inquiry and their shifting popularity across different national contexts.[12] Others worked "forensically" to trace critical "arguments and debates."[13] Robert Adcock's history of the discipline pursues a more genealogical account of political science that focuses on shared ideas. Arguing that European scholars directly influenced the field's emergence in the United States, Adcock observes that those international influences have clearly placed liberalism at the core of US political science.[14]

The influence of European transplants like Francis Lieber (the first formally titled political scientist in the United States), as well as conversations between "specifically liberal writers," resulted in the emergence of a discipline organized by "varieties of liberalism."[15] While noting critical philosophical differences between the writers he nets under the label (from men like J.S. Mill and Alexis de Tocqueville to William Graham Sumner and Franklin Delano Roosevelt), Adcock finds that transatlantic contributions to a liberal tradition of thought shaped the broadly "liberal visions" of political science in the west.[16] In this telling, professional political science was and is a "species of liberalism," a characterization largely shared by disciplinary historians.[17] But so too was its development linked to perceptions of liberalism in the public sphere. As David Ricci suggests, political science in the postwar period "strongly supported the existing institutions and practices of liberalism."[18] In the US context, Raymond Seidelman observes that the efficacy of the discipline was thought to be bound to "the consequences of liberalism's fate in the polity at large."[19] Discipline and doctrine appear intertwined on multiple levels, with investments in liberalism written into the founding concerns of political science in the west.

But this history was not a smooth one. Rather, liberalism's merger with academic political science in the twentieth century was timed in an era of crisis: the authoritarian fevers that swept Europe following the Great War, persistent racial and ethnic tensions, and attendant conditions of social and economic inequalities seemed to fly in the face of what scholars and civilians alike considered to be the "liberal promise" of liberty, equality, and self-government. In view of these tensions, the leaders of an academic field already engaged in studies of liberal thought wondered whether liberalism was to be rescued as a universal doctrine or relegated to an artifact of history.[20]

## The New Political Science

Worry about liberalism's future stimulated serious debate over its role in both the practice and study of politics in the postwar period, a debate sharpened by the "behavioral revolution" of the mid-twentieth century. Commonly understood as a shift toward positivist methodologies, the behavioral revolution is widely seen as a critical moment in the evolution of the discipline in the United States and, some argue, across the Atlantic as well.[21] Notable too is the central role liberalism occupied in discussions of the movement's aims and effects. James Farr suggests that the behavioralist's call to focus on more scientific methodologies were made alongside a "political message about liberal pluralism."[22] And those political scientists who adhered to the movement's "proclamations about behavior, science, and liberal pluralism were also those who were (or were to become) the most influential authors of scholarly texts and the highest office holders in the professional associations."[23] For John Gunnell, the behavioral turn "was less a revolution" than it was "a recommitment to the visions of both the scientific study of politics and liberal democracy that had informed the discipline for nearly a half century; it was also, in part, a response to the first significant challenge to those visions."[24] Indeed, the professional successes Farr notes developed alongside criticism from scholars who questioned the quantification of political science research and also, quite vocally, from those who questioned the movement's liberal conceits in view of behavioralist claims to be value-neutral. The convergence of these criticisms was significant for the development of academic political theory.[25] A conflict over growing "antiscientific and antiliberal sentiment in political theory"[26] targeted the apparent "consensus on the values of liberalism" animating political science.[27]

Varied critical reactions came from those trained in the US academy, like Louis Hartz and Theodore Lowi, as well as from a generation of postwar European émigrés who rejected the cozy symbiosis they saw between liberalism and the discipline. Leo Strauss famously chastised the "new political science" for failing to recognize that the war and its effects had revealed why liberalism needed challenge: "This almost willful blindness to the crisis of liberal democracy is part of that crisis."[28] Strauss lamented that the discipline merely "fiddles while Rome burns," and yet "it does not know that it fiddles, and it does not know that Rome burns."[29]

But scholars may have been more attuned to the crisis than Strauss implies. The tensions disciplinary historians identify with the behavioral turn generated internal strife within US political science for years to come.[30] And messages about liberalism were ever present. In 1967, for instance, the Caucus for a New Political Science formed to return the discipline to a "study of politics relevant to the struggle for a better world."[31] Among their members were political theorists intent on drawing the "critique of U.S. liberal democracy into the disciplinary center."[32] That critique and responses to it continue to inform professional reflections about the discipline's identity and aims—with efforts to complicate narratives about the "uniformly liberal"[33] character of US political theory, or to frame political science itself as a "product of liberal modernism."[34]

All told, the discipline has been, and in fact remains, acutely attentive to the liberal idea. From its transatlantic influences onward, the varied negotiations over liberalism which disciplinary historians attach to the development of political science in the west, and in the United States particularly, have imprinted the field of political thought. That imprint has important methodological implications. As debates about liberalism expand, so to do the resources drawn in to fuel them. I argue next that preoccupations with liberalism have not just evolved with the practice of political theorizing. They have *restructured* that practice to grant more and more conceptual space to liberalism when it comes to defining who and what we study, as well as the terms upon which we do so.

## Expansions: Liberal Conscriptions and Liberal Pedagogies

With our disciplinary entanglements in play, it is no wonder that liberalism is a dominant subject of contemporary political scholarship. For political theory in the wake of the behavioral turn, questions about liberalism have been viewed as central to its revitalization within the academy. John Rawls's seminal *Theory of Justice*, for instance, is credited with sparking a new era of political thought in the wake of behavioralism, prompting a wide-ranging discussion about the substance and parameters of justice in modern societies.[35] *Theory* and subsequent scholarship took up that question in relation to narratives of liberalism. If sympathetic readers aimed to refine *Theory* to strengthen liberalism's premises, critical readers saw in the text proof positive of liberalism's weaknesses.[36] In that sense, the book's intervention offered a revival and recentering of liberalism for contemporary political theory.[37]

Rawls's *Theory* and its receptions are just one example of how the liberal idea has held as the center of scholarly focus. As Seidelman suggested, the politics of the discipline are still tied into the study of liberalism in the polity, and the late twentieth and early twenty-first centuries bear witness to an expansion of preoccupations with liberalism and its merits, its meanings, and its prospects in feminist and postcolonial interventions, histories of empire, multicultural politics, postmodern hesitations, and much more.[38]

In his informative piece "What is Liberalism?" Duncan Bell observes:

> Today there is little that stands outside the discursive embrace of liberalism in mainstream Anglo-American political debate (and perhaps especially in academic political theory), and most who identify themselves as socialists, conservatives, social democrats, republicans, greens, feminists, and anarchists have been ideologically incorporated, whether they like it or not.[39]

Regardless of one's stance on liberalism's merits, in other words, working within liberalism's embrace is a condition of contemporary political scholarship. As Bell continues, the challenges involved in defining liberalism have led to a practice of using risky shortcuts, definitional fiats, reductive portrayals of canonical figures, and arbitrary timelines to outline the parameters of our positions vis-à-vis liberalism. To minimize those risks, he argues for greater precision in explaining how and why certain thinkers or ideas have been moved under the liberal umbrella. Taking the case of John Locke's relatively recent ascension into the liberal canon, Bell points out that Locke was not regarded as an ideological ally of liberals until nearly a century after liberalism's political founding. Indeed, Locke worked well before the term, much less the tradition, had come into being. Today, however, Locke is understood to be comfortably located in the liberal canon by many contemporary thinkers.

What mechanisms were involved in bringing Locke into the folds of a tradition that emerged well after his time? Bell shows that Locke "*became* a liberal during the twentieth century. As part of a process of *retrojection*, Locke's body of work—or at least some stylized arguments stripped from it—was posthumously conscripted to an expansive new conception of the liberal tradition."[40] And thanks to that conscription, in the "shorthand history of political thought" Locke's name now reads as "the grandfather of liberalism."[41]

## Conscripting the Canon

We should work carefully through this process of conscripting authors to the liberal canon. What implications run through the assertion that stylized arguments can be stripped from a work and enlisted in service of an ever-expanding liberal tradition? Retrojection expands liberalism by retroactively claiming thinkers and issues into ongoing scholarly debates about the liberal tradition. It does not constitute a problem so long as we understand that liberalism amounts not to one thing in perpetuity, but to "the sum of the arguments that have been classified as liberal, and recognized as such by other self-proclaimed liberals" over time.[42] This again points to the immense productivity of liberalism's definitional elasticity: the disjunctures and variations that attend scholarly contestations over liberalism's meaning create room to recruit Locke's body of work, or stylized versions of it, into liberalism's ever-expanding camp.

Retrojection provides a compelling measure of how and why the liberal label now governs so much of the discourse of contemporary political theory. As questions about liberalism emerge, expand, and transform—so too will the persons and places we turn to in order to address those questions. For instance, Jennifer Pitts notes that while liberalism might be applied strictly to theories developed after its political origins in the nineteenth century, it has been "more broadly but conventionally" applied "to the languages of subjective rights and self-government stemming back to the early-modern period."[43] With liberalism's elasticity widely recognized, the charge of anachronism in such cases can be sidestepped with a few well-placed clarifications about the themes or general values the liberal canon might reach back to claim. Careful scholars will acknowledge their participation in liberal retrojections when appropriating thinkers and ages who fall outside (sometimes far outside) the temporal parameters of liberalism's emergence.

Together with the definitional challenges surrounding the liberal idea, retrojection accurately describes the phenomenal conceptual reach the idea now has on the past and present of political thought. Not only Locke, but also Burke or Hobbes may fall under its sway; and not only seventeenth or eighteenth century thinkers, but even the Ancients might be brought into discussions of liberalism.[44] Conscription into the liberal canon requires only that elements of the past pertain, in some way, to the sum of the arguments we identify with liberalism *now*. Theoretically, one might suggest that the idea's canonical boundaries are boundless.

For Don Herzog, we ought to consider what such umbrella categories are tasked with doing: are "they bearing too much weight? or being asked simultaneously to perform contradictory tasks? Or silently shifting their meanings?"[45] And to those questions we should add: what happens to the ideas, texts, and thinkers that are marshaled as evidence of those meanings at work? Greater attention needs to be paid not only to how study of liberalism has grown—but also to how its morphing over time informs interpretive work. How, particularly, does the process of liberal expansion change the way we learn to read and identify these texts or thinkers once the label has been put in place?

## Pedagogical Foundations: Establishing Liberalism

Answers to that question can be found in the way theory is taught. Looking specifically at how liberalism and its presumed architects are presented in general politics textbooks and instructional surveys of the liberal tradition offers a useful snapshot of how scholarly practices expand liberalism's metacategorical power over the field.

In their introductory textbook to ideologies, Terence Ball and Richard Dagger suggest to students that liberal ideas "are so much a part of our lives and our thinking that they seem natural. But that is because these liberal ideas are so much a part of our heritage throughout Western civilization in general."[46] Ball and Dagger here remind students that liberalism is a constructed political category, which only appears natural because we have become accustomed to its presence in our discourse. Nevertheless, the authors point out, once established as familiar, ideologies like liberalism function to "provide people with some sense of identity and orientation—of who they are and where and how they fit into the great scheme of things."[47] Put another way, liberalism's "history carries a crucial heritage of civilized thinking, of political practice, and of philosophical-ethical creativity."[48] Ideological perspectives map out our conceptual world, organizing our engagements with it—and liberalism is *the* map for our contemporary experience.

Despite, or perhaps because of, liberalism's resistance to definitional consensus- narratives about its heritage and place within political thought inevitably turn to a "family of values," and the thinkers or texts related to them, to give students some sense of the idea's ideological borders. Here, the interpretive effects of our confidence in liberalism's orienting labors becomes apparent. Instructing the "common reader" on the life of the idea, Edmund Fawcett attaches several themes to liberalism including a recognition of conflict, distrust of power, faith in progress, and respect for the rule of law.[49] Those themes might be ferreted out in quite a few places, as Michael Freeden points out, such that scholars have looked for the prehistory of liberalism in the "proto-liberalisms, or segments of what was to mature into a full liberal credo, from the end of the Middle Ages onwards."[50] Figures like Machiavelli and contexts like Renaissance Florence might thus be included among the sites to excavate for the "embryonic form of liberalism."[51] As Fawcett says, "Liberalism has no foundation myth or year of birth. Its intellectual and moral sources go back as far as energy or curiosity will take you."[52] In effect, if you are motivated enough to find it, all roads can lead to, or from, liberalism.

In Ball and Daggar's textbook, it is concepts like individual liberty, equality, self-interest, or private property that constitute the "hallmarks" of liberalism.[53] With that rubric, the authors turn to the seventeenth-century writings of Thomas Hobbes as the "first major work of political philosophy to bear the distinctive stamp of liberalism" in a lineage that extends to President Barack Obama's 2008 campaign.[54] Though Hobbes, they acknowledge, worked well before liberalism appeared as a political category in the nineteenth century, they suggest that his discussion of individual liberty and political consent "articulated the main premises of an emerging liberal ideology."[55] Some accounts go even further to make Hobbes the true "founder of modern liberalism."[56] Also shoring up John Locke's posthumous recruitment into the liberal tradition, Ball and Dagger suggest that Locke's defense of "life, liberty and property" via the social contract follows Hobbes as the next "milestone in the development of liberalism," and so too does Adam Smith's interest in laissez-faire markets, and Jeremy Bentham's utilitarianism. Even as variation and disagreement are tracked among these representatives of the liberal tradition, those differences are seen as "matters of emphasis and disagreement about means, not ends," signaling to students that despite the varied texts and contested meanings used to define it, liberalism can function as a stable, orienting horizon within which the "great scheme of things" may be mapped out.[57]

In many ways, these processes of retrojection and conscription reveal more about our changing relationship to liberalism and its meanings over time than they may reveal about the texts or authors we choose to label as "liberal." But the key concern is that retroactively conscripted thinkers can be trapped by the label, as can the readers who rely upon it. And so too can those we have come to regard as liberal exemplars.

In J.S. Mill's case, as I detail in the next section, liberal canonization becomes a justification for drafting a now iconic liberal to represent whatever aspect of the idea is in question. Unlike Locke and others who have been adopted into a tradition that arose after their time, Mill wrote and worked during liberalism's emergence in western political discourse. There can be no charge of anachronism applied to the liberal status given to him. However, for the same reasons, Mill offers the most damning indictment of our scholarly preoccupations with liberalism in studies of political thought. Because he wrote and practiced politics in "liberalism's time," his iconic status is largely unquestioned. Mill is easily recruited to represent the liberal tradition, and all that scholars want to say about it through him.

This is the making of a troubling interpretive method in political theory. Troubling because, as we have become more invested in centering liberalism as a condition of analysis, an investment aided by its flexible boundaries, we have lost sight of how those investments are shaping our own interpretive practices.

## Effects: Reading J.S. Mill through Liberalism

On the bicentennial of Mill's birth, a volume celebrating his work noted that the "first lesson one typically learns about Mill is that he was a liberal philosopher, perhaps *the* exemplary liberal philosopher."[58] For a thinker once described by his contemporary as being innately suspicious of ideas, Mill today might be rather amazed to find his name authoritatively bound to one of the most written about ideas in the world.[59] But, as his obituary in the *New York Times* suggests of leading thinkers, the fame of their name can overtake the deeper complexities of their thought.[60] Even so, it is surely troubling that a man whose *Autobiography* took pains to give evidence of a "many-sided" mode of thinking, which privileged the process of understanding over the authority of any system, has nevertheless been hitched to the powerful tradition his name alone has come to signify. But this is the legacy ascribed to Mill in the years since his death in 1873.

Mill is now one of the first figures described in introductory textbooks or surveys of political thought whose work falls within the period of liberalism's ascendance as a political concept. *On Liberty*, Ball and Dagger suggest, was published at a time "when liberalism seemed to have triumphed." However, Mill remained "alarmed by what he took to be a new threat to liberty in the growing power of public opinion," and his response in *On Liberty* made Mill the "leading liberal philosopher" of his time.[61] They are not alone in this view. Across surveys of liberal political thought, Mill's name appears in vaunted terms. For some, Mill alone remains "a paradigm and pure liberal."[62] Isaiah Berlin remarked in 1959 that through his defense of principles of tolerance, Mill had effectively "founded modern liberalism."[63] Mill now operates as "a major, if not the major, point of reference"[64] for liberalism so that, according to the *Economist*, he is simply "an inevitable citation in debates about liberalism."[65]

With Mill's paradigm liberalism taken as given, we should expect his seminal political text *On Liberty* to make much use of the political language of liberalism. But this is not the case. Rather, while Mill was indeed concerned with the threat of social tyranny to individual liberty, it is not evident in the text that Mill meant to conflate his theorization of "liberty" as a virtue of social and political life with "liberalism" as a political philosophy or ideology. He uses "liberal" or "liberalism" in fact only four times in *On Liberty*: First, Mill discusses the notion that where rulers were identified with the people, the nation did not need to be protected against its own will. He presents this as being a commonly held view "among the last generation of European liberalism, in the Continental section of which it still apparently predominates."[66] Mill, however, argues against this view, suggesting instead that those who "admit any limit to what a government [of the people] may do . . . stand out as brilliant exceptions among the political thinkers of the Continent." Hardly a ringing endorsement, Mill's first reference to liberalism is neither self-reflective nor politically prescriptive, but entirely critical in nature. He uses the term politically again in a scathing footnote about an English official who was "deemed fit to fill a high office in the government of this country, under a liberal Ministry," despite asserting "the doctrine that all who do not believe in the divinity of Christ are beyond the pale of toleration." Who, Mill asks, "after this imbecile display could suggest that religious persecution has passed away?"[67] In its second textual appearance, liberalism is again associated with an object of Mill's political censure, not praise.

The term appears twice more in *On Liberty* as an adjective: Mill first describes the "liberal and large-minded man" for whom "anything so comprehensive as his own country or his own age" forms the context of his judgment, and again, the "large and liberal mind" that cannot do without freedom.[68] These are hardly the extensive references one would expect in one of liberalism's founding texts, written by a thinker alive and well during the idea's establishing era. Mill's writings on *liberty* are seen as evidence of his *liberalism*; but nowhere does Mill categorize the argument being made in *On Liberty* in ideological terms.[69]

A man who was elected as a member of parliament for the Liberal Party and has since become a symbol of liberal political thought did not think to identify what he knew to be one of his most important political works with liberalism. Moreover, as Chapter 3 illustrates, he was decidedly wary of working under the sign of any particular system. By tethering "liberty" to "liberalism," however, these facts are easily supplanted. It is, instead, the liberal label that gives us entry into Mill's work, and which marks out the political content of *On Liberty* and of the author's place within the canon of political thought—not only for students in the classroom but for scholars well.

In the prologue to an extensive biography of Mill, Richard Reeves finds that Mill has been claimed by pretty much everyone, "from the ethical socialist left to the laissez-faire, libertarian right."[70] But, Reeves points out, questions about whether Mill is on the "left" or "right," a "progressive" or "conservative," "elitist" or "democrat," etc., will not get us very far both because Mill's work offers evidence to support many sides,[71] and because such questions eclipse the nuances of his arguments.[72] Put simply, Reeves says, "they are the wrong questions" to ask.[73] So, one is naturally struck by the fact that in the introductory pages, Reeves himself associates Mill with liberalism eight times. And if the first seven need reinforcement, the eighth reference emphatically provides it: "Mill was a liberal, a democrat and a socialist—in that order."[74]

My intent in noting this is not to undercut the quality of Reeves's biography by any means. A nearly 500-page exposition on Mill's intellectual and political evolution, Reeves's biography is impressively researched and wonderfully compelling. But it does illustrate how deeply rooted liberalism is in the academic psyche. Though Reeves rightly questions the merit, much less the utility, of pigeonholing figures like Mill given the eclectic quality of his work and its reception, that questioning is not applied to Mill's association with liberalism. It is as if the interpretive grip of liberalism is so encompassing, the labeling politics surrounding it escapes scrutiny.

Reeves follows what is now a scholarly custom of reading Mill through concerns with liberalism. C.L. Ten insists that any temptation to "reject, or radically modify, the traditional picture of [Mill] as the great liberal... would be a grave error."[75] That we can be issued such a warning indicates something of the power that we have given over to liberalism as an entry point into political texts. But Ten accurately describes the way Mill has been bound to liberalism—or more appropriately, to different liberalism*s*. Consider Mill's extensive corpus: it offers an array of political commentary concerning, for example, education; the origins and evolution of government; gender equality; slavery; class and economic redistribution; colonialism and empire; cultural pluralism; the dangers of public opinion and uniformity; human nature; and social progress. However, scholarship on these and other elements of Mill's work is often caught up with efforts to describe, challenge, justify, or reclaim them within the context of debates about liberalism. While some have taken a more direct route through Mill's texts to contrast his liberalism with other versions, others have rather claimed him as a representative of a particular mode of liberal politics.[76] In either case, studies of Mill often seek to raise "questions about the nature and implications of Mill's liberalism and invite us to see it in a new light."[77] Mill scholarship invariably accepts his liberalism, though it may be interpreted in different ways. Is it any wonder then that Mill's liberalism has been variously identified as "classical," "radical," "socialist," "conservative," "individualistic," "democratic," "comprehensive," "developmental," "perfectionist," and so on.[78]

Nicholas Capaldi accurately notes that "How one understands Mill's *On Liberty* reflects not just one's interpretation of a particular philosophical work but one's engagement with modern liberal culture."[79] Across the many iterations of liberalism presented by its defenders and critics alike, Mill functions as a tool to ground claims about *the idea*. Even as interest in his work has shifted to different aspects of his thought, from questions about its internal tensions, to its defense of imperialism, Mill's status as "the liberal" remains an orienting frame for how we learn to read and use him in political scholarship.

## Deploying the Exemplar

Mill's text serves as a conduit for working out our relationship to liberalism. And precisely because of this, Ten suggests, "Whenever liberalism is attacked today, John Stuart Mill's name will almost certainly be mentioned. Often indeed the conservative and radical critics of liberalism have seen in Mill's essay *On Liberty* the embodiment of all the liberal errors and vices they wish to expose."[80] Mill scholarship over the twentieth century does offer a striking illustration of these patterns of association. It is not simply that Mill is popularly identified as a liberal within contemporary studies—but rather, this identification has dictated how and why Mill is studied in the first place. Akin to the processes of retrojection that make someone like Locke a founding liberal, the turn to Mill as an exemplar also involves appropriating his work to support a larger consideration of liberalism in a given moment. The wide-ranging applications of his work in evolving debates about liberalism are also indicative of how much this idea frames contemporary inquiry.

Some of the early twentieth-century receptions mined Mill for what his internal tensions and inconsistencies might suggest about the tensions and challenges of liberalism. In 1927, for example, Ludwig von Mises argued that Mill was the "epigone of classical liberalism . . . [and the] originator of the thoughtless confounding of liberal and socialist ideas that led to the decline of English liberalism." In Mises view, that thoughtless confounding of ideas that ought not to meet could not be understood without first becoming "acquainted with Mill's principal writings."[81] Concerned to recover a better liberalism from the social "decline" she perceived in the 1960s and 1970s, Gertrude Himmelfarb found in Mill's corpus the competing trajectories of modern liberalism. Those opposing liberalisms played out through the conservatively liberal younger Mill who, influenced by Coleridge, blended liberty with the importance of history and social traditions, and the radically liberal later Mill of *On Liberty*. The latter of the two Mills, argues Himmelfarb, made possible the moral and cultural permissiveness she associated with the liberal social movements of the 1960s and 1970s.[82] But there was, Himmelfarb proclaimed, "no better corrective to the Mill of *On Liberty* than the "other Mill."[83] Of course, not everyone agreed that there was anything to be redeemed in Mill, or more particularly, in what Mill *did* to liberalism. For economist Murray Rothbard, Mill was a "woolly minded man of mush" whose thought was a "vast kitchen midden of diverse and contradictory positions." Consequently, Rothbard despaired, Mill was able to "change the face of nineteenth century British liberalism" for the worse.[84]

Revisionist accounts argued for a more consistent reading of Mill, but a consistency which reflected liberalism's core challenges. Maurice Cowling described Mill's defense of individual liberty as a form of moral totalitarianism. Mill, Cowling says, was no "fumbling liberal," rather his liberalism was "a socially cohesive, morally insinuating, proselytizing *doctrine*," based on the belief that individual freedom must be maximized in order to reach Truth.[85] Offering a somewhat gentler take, John Gray argues that Mill's "liberalism has a relevance which transcends the conditions of the age in which he wrote," but part of that relevance stems from where Mill's liberalism fails. Most problematically, for Gray, Mill's liberalism invokes a "strong conception of autonomous choice, distanced from convention, it condemns as devoid of individuality all traditional forms of life."[86] Mill's understanding of individuality in this reading dismisses the conditions of sociality within which we live such that any account of progress derived from it must rely on an "abstract-individualist distortion."[87] Allan Bloom extends this point to suggest that the kind of individualism Mill's liberalism constructs pays no attention to "the fundamental principles of the moral virtues that inclined men to live according to them." Bloom continues, "this turn in liberalism is what prepared us for cultural relativism."[88]

Reading Mill's liberalism as a coherent whole was also taken up in the intellectual struggle between "liberalism" and "communitarianism" in the later twentieth century.[89] Both John Rawls and Michael Sandel, respective leaders of this debate, sought to identify Mill as a "comprehensive liberal" for whom moral ideals about autonomy, individuality, and self-reliance must hold sway over other values. But where Rawls moved to distinguish his own "political liberalism" from Mill's comprehensive variant, Sandal countered that no real distance existed between his contemporary and Mill.[90] Scholars more sympathetic to Mill have sought to reconfigure the parameters of this debate altogether through a reconfiguration of Mill's liberalism. Some located in Mill—and thus within the liberal tradition—a more democratic (rather than individualistic) political spirit and a more holistic account of the relation between liberty and authority, individuality and society.[91] In Will Kymlicka's view, "modern liberals from J.S. Mill through to Rawls and Dworkin" represent a misunderstood class of liberal thinkers. Contra Rawls's own assertions, Kymlicka argues that Mill *with* Rawls has a coherent account of political morality that takes seriously the role of culture and the necessity of community in the development of the individual.[92] Others instead turned Mill *against* contemporary liberals. For Bruce Baum, Mill's "liberal theory of freedom" parsed out a necessary challenge to the more conventional liberalisms of Rawls, Isaiah Berlin, or Robert Nozick, while also generating "an effective liberal response to contemporary communitarian critiques of liberalism, such as that of Michael Sandel."[93]

The coherent Mill has more or less won out in the contemporary literature, with efforts to read Mill's politics as a cohesive statement about "liberal culture" and its various limits. One prominent strain of that approach can be found in the return to Mill's writings on gender equality. Scholars like Carole Pateman, Susan Moller Okin, Catharine MacKinnon, and Saba Mahmood among others invoke Mill to interrogate the structure of liberal feminism. I discuss this at length in Chapter 4, but the general trend in this literature has been to stake either critiques or defenses of "liberal feminism" on Mill's arguments about gender. If for Mackinnon, Mill embodies the essential traits, and therefore the limits, of liberal feminism, for Maria Morales his "egalitarian liberalism" is an effective counter to "contemporary communitarian and feminist criticisms," even though he "did not hold the positions that most critics take to be essential to liberalism."[94] Indeed, for many readers the form of feminism we find in Mill will reflect debates about what kind of feminism *liberalism* enables. Because "the orthodoxy has been to construe Mill's moral and political thought as (more or less narrowly) liberal, the tendency has been to interpret his feminism as liberal feminism,"[95] with all the attendant disagreements over what that designation means for understanding Mill's views on gender and the family.

While different aspects of Mill's politics have been the focus of scholarly review in different moments, one area that draws consistent attention concerns Mill's political economy. In this arena, notably, Mill's liberalism has sometimes been called into question—or at the very least troubled, though primarily because his self-proclaimed sympathies with socialism seem to disrupt narratives which oppose these traditions (or their leading figures). Lively debate has thus ensued over the extent to which Mill's socialist affirmations ought to be read seriously. Revealingly, responses to that question line up with efforts to preserve (or refute) his "liberal credentials."[96] As Helen McCabe argues, it is those credentials that dominate conversation about Mill's socialist politics and which have, as a result, diverted attention from what his socialist claims might *actually* entail.[97]

But perhaps the most sustained attention to Mill's thought moving into the contemporary era has been in studies of empire. Mill's work with the British East India Company alongside his status as the exemplary liberal are in perfect alignment with the study of liberal imperialism that shapes much discussion of empire and colonial politics. The scholarly consensus seems now to be that imperialism is "intrinsic to the articulation of liberal political theory," such that to study one is to study the other.[98] Some of the most compelling examinations of empire and its legacies have, almost without fail, found in Mill's colonial writings the very embodiment of liberalism's imperial conceits in its encounters with non-Europeans. Mill here represents the imperialist origins of modern liberalism, the ethnocentrism behind liberal notions of individual freedom and progress, the limitations of liberal rights discourses for resolving gendered, racialist, and classed conditions of inequality, and the asymmetries of power involved in the geopolitics of a postcolonial, liberal order.[99] He has become an inevitable citation in studies of "liberal imperialism."

The evolution of Mill's reception shows a fascinating and wide-ranging engagement with his work, from questions about the tensions of individuality and community to assumptions about the relationship (or opposition) between liberalism and socialism, or to the fraught politics of empire and its legacies. But what has tied these evolving interventions into his thought together is their operation *under the sign of liberalism*. Across these receptions, liberalism marks both the interpretive frame for reading Mill and, ultimately, the object of scholarly analyses. But grafting Mill's thought in these ways onto the assumption that he always already represents the varied liberalisms we need him to has risks. We pay for our preoccupations with the idea, not only by limiting the way we study and deploy Mill but also by limiting our own interpretive perspectives as well. It is time to reconsider these costs.

## Rethinking the Liberal Narrative

Studies which strain focus on Mill's liberal status do exist. And their existence suggests something important: our investments in liberalism need not exhaust our encounters with Mill. Sometimes alternative narratives have not so much abandoned Mill's liberal legacy but have worked alongside, instead of through it. Baum, for example, provides a more complex approach to Mill's notion of freedom and power, to offer "a new perspective on the emancipatory possibilities of the liberal tradition."[100] But Baum focuses on Mill's own view of power and freedom to suggest that his theory accommodates an interactive and complementary politics, where freedom denotes not the absence of social or governmental power (which critics of liberal freedom attribute to Mill) but the range of possibilities open to agents situated within different power relations.[101] Nadia Urbinati steps around Mill's liberal legacy to offer a reading of his distinctly democratic politics, through the emphasis he places on political participation. This, for Urbinati, points to the explicitly participatory orientation of Mill's thought and contrasts with the de jure or perfectionist notions of citizenship that have been associated with more individualistic accounts of his liberalism.[102]

Dennis Thompson's study of Mill in Parliament considers how Mill navigated his philosophical interests and his role as an elected representative. Thompson finds that although "[Mill] ran as a Liberal, he did not toe the party line once in office. His defeat in 1868 after only three years in Parliament is sometimes attributed to [his] radical enthusiasms and political reluctances."[103] Similarly, in his case analysis of the Contagious Diseases Acts, Jeremy Waldron explores the relationship between Mill's political thought and his work as a public intellectual.[104] Waldron tries to discern the practical significance of Mill's Harm Principle, as it was applied to the issue of prostitution and public health in his time; the meaning and limits of liberalism are not central to the analysis.

Though they may leave to the side the question of how or whether reliance on liberalism governs Mill's significance to political thought, this kind of scholarship has the benefit of not *privileging* liberalism in analyses of Mill's politics. And that they take this route is well supported by the fact that Mill himself strained against ideological moorings. His remarks on his role as a public official are notable for the distance they put between Mill and ideological or partisan labels. Mill signaled a willingness to withstand the demands of public office without compromising his principles about representative politics, or his willingness to speak bluntly on political issues. As he says of his time in parliament: "As I therefore in general reserved myself for work which no others were likely to do, a great proportion of my appearances were on points on which the bulk of the Liberal party, even the advanced portion of it either were of a different opinion from mine, or were comparatively indifferent," and further, "how few occasions there had been on which the line I took was such as could lead them to attach any great value to me as *an organ of their opinions*."[105]

That independent spirit is again confirmed in his essays on Bentham and Coleridge: "I was writing for Radicals and Liberals, and it was my business to dwell most on that in writers of a different school, from the knowledge of which they might derive most improvement."[106] In other words, Mill saw his role not as grounding the premises of "Liberalism" or "Radicalism," but as ensuring that an audience who identified with either was confronted by different approaches to political questions. Mill's willingness to break party lines comes to the fore in 1871, when the Liberal government kept a previous Tory promise to pay the legal fees of Governor Eyre, whom Mill had attempted to bring to trial for his leadership in the violent massacre of opponents in Jamaica. In reaction, Mill wrote: "After this, I shall henceforth wish for a Tory government."[107] With such statements in view, Stefan Collini observes that principled perspectives provide a better way to understand Mill's career than "do any of the conventional political labels."[108] What Mill himself suggests is that our custom of identifying him with liberalism does not go far in telling us much about Mill's political thought.

Why then does the custom of interpreting Mill via liberalism dominate academic political theory? As we have seen, even readers like Reeves or Collini, who explicitly point to the inadequacy of that ideational label for Mill, nevertheless return to it. Collini, who eschews conventional political labels for Mill's politics, identifies "the essential moral basis" of liberalism in the modern world with *On Liberty*.[109] As Chapter 1 argued, the inability to move beyond liberalism is partly due to our zeal for assessing the idea and our positions in relation to it. We have not been consistently reflective in questioning how that zeal conditions theoretical work. The very assumption that Mill's philosophy is quintessentially liberal can make Mill, and the potential insights his work might lend students of political thought, *incidental* to a prevailing interest in liberalism.

We know that liberalism's definitional elasticity has been exceptionally productive for scholarly appropriations of Mill. Though he may be called many things—an individualist, a radical, a conservative, a democrat, even a moral totalitarian—Mill can remain, always, a liberal. Even when it seems he will not fit a given liberal mold, he is simply recast as the representative of "another kind of liberalism." This has been the consequence of our disciplinary attachment to liberalism. Alan Ryan illustrates the problem best when he says of *On Liberty*: "*That* it is a liberal manifesto is clear beyond doubt; *what* the liberalism is that it defends and *how* it defends it remain matters of controversy."[110] Much like Hartz assumed that US politics was so inherently liberal it was limited to an interminable debate over liberal values, Ryan classes studies of *On Liberty* as being limited to controversies over what those liberal values are. But what kind of leverage, if any, does liberalism give us in making sense of the complexity of Mill's work? I suggest that we are losing opportunities for more fruitful political inquiries in the move from thinking about Mill's texts and their theorization of concepts we might associate with liberalism, toward allowing an identification of Mill with liberalism to constitute the reason we engage with his texts.

## New Directions

Let me pause here to consider some objections to the argument. Does liberal exemplarity *necessarily* draw us in the direction I am suggesting—that is, toward imposing an undue burden of meaning upon a thinker or text? Going back to pedagogical practices—though *On Liberty* might not reference liberalism per se, is there really any danger in associating its key arguments with a tradition of thought which, as scholars everywhere acknowledge, is wide-ranging in its meaning and applications?

In response, I should note first that my contention is not with whether values like liberty or discussions of individuality and self-determination *are* liberal. These concepts have long been imagined within the expansive family of values contemporary scholars associate with liberalism—and whose meanings have also been contested within that tradition. In pointing out that *On Liberty* does not conflate liberty with liberalism, however, I am not making a semantic argument; I am making a methodological one. Beyond the idea's conceptual affiliations, it is the *act of ideological claiming* which uses those affiliations that requires consideration.

As a "label that attaches both to a history of a fairly diverse set of political movements, and to the ideas and arguments associated with those movements, and to an ongoing research program in contemporary political philosophy,"[111] liberalism's interpretive reach is enormous. When broad political concepts become evidence of ideological titles, the move from thinker to tradition is too easily taken, and in Mill's case that move forces him to take on a paradigmatic role in conversations about the various iterations of liberalism that come before us. In turn, texts like *On Liberty* become mere descriptions of liberal culture, however we seek to define it. Learning about

Mill through the lens of liberalism has already harmed how and why we turn to him in discussions of political thought.

The act of ideological claiming we see even in introductory narratives about liberalism generates a secondary path through a thinker's body of work, not by way of the concepts they engage—which may well be part of that liberal family of values—but through the *categorization* of authors or texts within a larger tradition. Where taking the first path involves a primary engagement with Mill, taking the second makes Mill a project (and casualty) of our primary engagement with liberalism. This is especially problematic for a thinker identified as its paradigmatic representative. How much labor can Mill be made to do in service of this manifestly multiform, shifting, contested idea? The evolution of Mill scholarship I have outlined suggests that he can be made to do quite a lot. Taking him for granted as "an inevitable citation" in the literature of liberalism[112] shifts readers from considerations of what constitutes Mill's politics to applying Mill as a placeholder for liberalism.

Nevertheless, the practice of reading through liberalism need not be inevitable. Customs can be challenged. Refusing liberalism's interpretive claim on Mill, the next chapters instead recover a thinker who displays a remarkably uncertain intellectual attitude—an uncertainty that shapes his politics. In the case of his proposals for women, class representation, and imperial rule, Mill's politics are not indecisive but open; they are not ideologically constrained, but politically experimental. But as a critical practice, the results of Mill's uncertain politics are complex and sometimes troubling. To see how this is so, however, we must turn first to Mill's *Autobiography* and the account it provides of his intellectual development. In that narrative we find the origins of what I call Mill's politics of uncertainty.

# 3
# Mill Reconsidered

From a Crisis of Certainty to a Politics of Uncertainty

> *The importance of Mill's own autobiographical statements has been largely lost amidst the endless flow of books and articles that identify John Stuart Mill as the father of modern liberalism.*
> Richard Ashcraft in *Mill and the Moral Character of Liberalism*

Introduced to generations of students as one of liberalism's founding fathers, it is hardly surprising that Mill's name is now synonymous with the term.[1] And yet there is little consensus as to what *kind* of liberalism Mill represents. While for some his work outlines the socially embodied quality of liberal theories of character, or the value-pluralist sensibilities of liberalism, for others he defines the abstract nature of liberal citizenship and the Western cultural norms that permeate liberal pretensions to universalism.[2]

That he is often deployed to represent all these variations and more poses problems. Now emerged is a habit of calling upon Mill to substantiate scholarly investigations of an idea increasingly associated with "whatever aspect of modernity or western societies one happened to dislike."[3] Even where the association is positive, the processes of conscripting Mill discussed in Chapter 2 can prime particular elements of his texts to fit the investigation underway. Our relationship to this idea is dictating the terms of our engagement with Mill's political thought. Consistent across the different and sometimes conflicting versions of the "liberal Mill" on offer, we find his status within a liberal tradition presented for argumentative leverage: Mill's liberal exemplarity grants canonical force to varying debates about the idea. When we privilege our preoccupations with liberalism—our various investments in ferreting out its true meaning, successes, or failures—Mill can become mere cannon fodder in our battles, his thought trapped within "nominalist cubbyholes."[4]

But we can refuse to participate in the liberalism trap. And we can find resources for that refusal in Mill's own struggles with limiting intellectual frameworks. In what follows, I rebuild and deepen an account of his intellectual biography as a basis for understanding his political thought and practice. Notably, the contemporary custom of reading Mill within ideological narratives stands in distinct contrast to a tradition of Mill scholarship that pays close attention to his self-reflections in the *Autobiography*. Scholars in that tradition, like John Robson, Nicholas Capaldi, John Skorupski, and others, note that reading Mill's politics through the lens of biography requires the reader to account for his many-sided approach to argument, his rejection of absolutist claims, and his recognition of the fallibilist quality of social and political knowledge. As Robson observes, these qualities coalesce to form a thinker driven by an "unceasing play of thought about ideas and institutions."[5] But Mill's self-described intellectual eclecticism, and subsequent examinations of it, have been sidelined in contemporary studies which focus on his place within the liberal tradition.

Reconnecting Mill's self-examinations in the *Autobiography* with his politics, however, allows us to take account of what I call Mill's appreciation for *uncertainty* as a necessary quality of social and political life. The chapter lays out how that appreciation created the distance Mill needed to reassess the dictates of his early education and angled him toward a more capacious approach to political thought and action. Uncertainty captures Mill's embrace of "eclecticism," "half-truths," "many-sidedness," and "fallibility"—terms he variously employs in the *Autobiography* to describe his evolving intellectual disposition. Millian uncertainty is an epistemic and normative orientation. It describes an intellectual attitude for which imperfect information (for Mill, the sine non qua of political life) elicits an antifoundational philosophical disposition and a cautionary political radicalism. Uncertainty is the expression of the intellectual flexibility and restraint fostered by Mill's self-described shifts away from dogmatism and by his discomfort with determinative ideological programs. To trace how uncertainty operates in Mill's thought is, effectively, to follow his method of political critique and analysis.

In an interesting sketch of Mill's reception history, John Gray concludes that readers ought not to look for "an integrated and comprehensive philosophy" in Mill's work; we should instead recognize his "tolerance of uncertainty, and reverence for diversity, which is the distinctive feature of Mill's intellectual personality."[6] That Mill's uncertainty is a distinctive feature we ought to recognize is a point on which I concur. But my understanding of

Millian uncertainty departs from Gray's account in important ways. First, I suggest that uncertainty ought to be the premise, rather the concluding note, of an analysis of Mill's thought. More than a descriptive label for Mill's personality, as an *essential* feature uncertainty constitutes a principled perspective from which Mill's politics begins. Second and directly following, I contend that uncertainty is not something Mill was merely tolerant of. Rather, I find in Mill a deep *appreciation* for uncertainty. It is an appreciation, moreover, that substantively shapes an intentional political practice beginning in Mill's youth, and which informs his later work as a public intellectual.

As a political orientation, Millian uncertainty considers, as best one can, the myriad knowns and unknowns that shape both existing social realities and efforts to change them. Mill tells us as much in his *Autobiography*, when he says that his guiding principle was not any one system of thought, but a practice of thinking critically in view of human fallibility. That practice enables his interventions into social and political life while bracketing any guarantee of success. Precisely because of this, uncertainty operates in Mill as a condition of possibility and of risk. With that dual function, it generates the kind of normative tensions we find in Mill's political arguments, for instance, between his sharp critiques of inequality, as in the case of women, and his problematic deferral of liberty, as in the case of colonial domination. Recovering Mill's appreciation for uncertainty thus allows us to identify a *consistent approach* to political questions, without sacrificing attention to the various difficulties it produced in Mill's proposals for addressing those questions.

And indeed, as subsequent chapters detail, Millian uncertainty is not without problems. Mill's political investments in bringing about equality and liberty as a condition of justice and of human progress are fractured by his doubts about the means for achieving such goals. This is particularly evident in his hesitations regarding women's work beyond the home, class-based politics, and certainly empire. But we should understand those investments and their ruptures as being part of Mill's overall political practice. Uncertainty facilitates even as it tempers Mill's political radicalism.

Understanding those intellectual negotiations requires attention to Mill's intellectual development, which his *Autobiography* has preserved for posterity. The conceptual nuances which attend his development are something that Mill's canonization within the liberal tradition blocks from view. Whether we read him as a "liberal universalist" or a "liberal relativist," whether we find in him arguments for "liberal pluralism" or "liberal universalism," each of these "Mills" is offered as a blueprint of a particular kind of liberalism. Branding Mill with any one of these liberalisms risks superimposing ideological certainty upon a thinker who actually embraces an uncertain mode of political theorizing. What we lose in our readings of Mill through the lens (or lenses) of liberalism are precisely the *politics* of his thought—the ways in which he navigates the challenges of his age.

In contrast, identifying the role uncertainty plays in Mill's thought can bring us back to a thinker who was inspired by the provisional nature of political claims and who took an experimental approach to political problems. But to fully appreciate Mill's uncertainty requires a move beyond our reliance on his status within the liberal tradition. I make this case knowing that refusing the discursive embrace of liberalism where John Stuart Mill is concerned might require us to commit something like canonical patricide. But in killing "*the* liberal" we might breathe new life into Mill as a political thinker and actor, and into our own engagements with his work. That is a revival worth pursuing.

## Lessons from an "Uneventful" Life

The *Autobiography* opens in exceedingly modest terms: "I should prefix to the following biographical sketch, some mention of the reasons which have made me think it desirable that I should leave behind me such a memorial of so uneventful a life as mine."[7] Yet what the text delivers is an extraordinary portrait not just of Mill's life but of his assessment of its meaning. Mill's *Autobiography* has been, consequently, a rich text for scholars interested in his mental and moral growth. In it, readers have found a cogent elucidation of the value of experiments in living; revelations about what role pleasure and pain play in human development; and in its discussion of his own character, an important contribution to Mill's work on ethology.[8]

There is good reason to list the *Autobiography* as a key political text in Mill's corpus. He wrote the "Early Draft" of the manuscript in 1853, revised and added to it in 1861, and revised it again around 1870, just three years before his death.[9] That the text developed over a period of seventeen years uniquely positions it alongside Mill's better known political treatise. The *Autobiography* collates Mill's evolving reflections about his youth and later life with the production of those other works. And Mill invites the reader to use its narrative as an example for discussions on education and transitions in thinking, of a mind that was "always pressing forward, equally ready to learn and unlearn either from its own thoughts or from those of others."[10]

That Mill wanted his life to be a resource from which lessons could be drawn is unsurprising, given that he considered learning by the light of other minds to be essential to social and political improvement.[11] The text then does more than simply recount the events of his life; it relates his interpretation of those events and of their utility to the minds of his readers.[12] For Mill, self-knowledge was a form of philosophy.[13] The *Autobiography* is therefore an invaluable guide to his political thought.

Much of the work is spent on the first thirty or so years of his life, reflecting upon his early childhood, his education, and on formative moments like joining the East India Company, recovering from his famed mental collapse, and of course meeting Harriet Taylor. This suggests that Mill recognized how much his experiences during those years cultivated the person he became. And those experiences lay out some early indications of the directions Mill would take in approaching the challenges of social and political life in his various roles as a career man of the company, a one term parliamentarian, and a life-long critical thinker. They sketch the development of an intellectual disposition toward uncertainty, which becomes a mark of his politics.

## Educating Mr. Mill

Mill's early education is one area in which we see his politics of uncertainty begin to take shape. A veritable experiment of his father and later of Jeremy Bentham, Mill's childhood was used as an opportunity to test their own theories of education and reasoning. Taking up the works of Herodotus, Xenophon, and the dialogues of Plato (in Greek) before most children have mastered reading, Mill's education was rigorous to say the least. Though we now know it was the foundation for one of western political thought's most recognizable thinkers, one cannot help but to conclude with Isaiah Berlin that Mill's unique education was an "appalling success."[14]

James Mill and Bentham certainly intended that Mill would be a receptacle and disseminator of their philosophical program—"a successor worthy of both of us" as his father wrote to Bentham.[15] But the form of Mill's training, perhaps inadvertently, laid cracks in that plan. Though Mill expressed regrets about his father's approach to his schooling in some respects, he also found much to value in it: "Mine was not an education of cram. My father never permitted anything which I learnt to degenerate into a mere exercise of memory."[16] In this, one might hear notes of *On Liberty*'s critique of dead dogmas. Whatever his faults, James Mill insisted on the practice of questioning as a measure not just of the subjects under study but of the minds engaged with them. And however much the father and Bentham anticipated molding the student in their image, that they trained him to work through the structure and implications of arguments also attuned Mill to a distinctly critical mode of thinking.

We see that in his recollections of the encounters that most struck him. His study of Plato, Mill tells us, "took such hold of me that it became part of my own mind." But it was the practice of *elenchus* outlined in the Socratic dialogues that he found most compelling. "I have felt ever since" he writes "that the title of Platonist belongs by far better right to those have been nourished in, and have endeavoured to practise Plato's mode of investigation, than to those who are distinguished only by the adoption of certain dogmatical conclusions."[17] What these readings impressed upon Mill was the value of a critical approach to inquiry, which perpetuates the "testing of all general statements by particular instances," and which might predispose a mind to press forward, learning and unlearning by experience and by the light of other minds.[18]

He recalls with particular enthusiasm a six-month tour of the continent at the age of fourteen, under the care of Bentham's brother, Sir Samuel Bentham. This "fortunate circumstance" in his education exposed him to the "free and genial atmosphere of Continental life" in which he began to feel the contrast between the "frank sociability and amiability of French personal intercourse" and the English way of regarding everyone "as either an enemy or a bore."[19] What Mill recollects here with fondness is perhaps his first experience witnessing the "friendly feeling in every one towards every other." It is a stark admission but one we might well understand from a child whose "father's scheme of education" governed the whole of his life, even keeping him "from having any great amount of intercourse with other boys."[20] Mill's travels also helped him recognize an error "always prevalent in England," and one from which even James Mill "with all his superiority to prejudice was not exempt," namely the error of "judging universal questions by a merely English standard."[21] His experiences on the Continent helped to ground the importance of that critical disposition his early education had inculcated.

The privileging of investigation over dogmatical conclusions continued to shape Mill's development in the years commencing what he calls his self-education. He formed the Utilitarian Society in 1823, to gather young men with "Utility as their standard in ethics and politics" in collaborative discussions, and he also took up public speaking more generally. Two years later, Mill would represent the "political economists" at debates held with the Cooperative Society of Owenites over questions of distribution and population. Mill speaks fondly of their "perfectly friendly dispute" and of his esteem for the Owenite champion William Thompson.[22]

These intellectual exchanges were flourishing around the same time as Mill began his three-decade tenure at the East India Company in 1823, at the age of seventeen. Interestingly, one of the faults Mill finds with his early education was that his father trusted "too much in the intelligible of the abstract, when not embodied in the concrete."[23] Like his travels, his work provided a experiential corrective to that flaw: the company was of "considerable value to me as a theoretical reformer of the opinions and institutions of my time."[24] Working in the office of the Examiner of India Correspondence under his father, Mill had his first taste of the practical side of public affairs. For Lynn Zastoupil, the impact of Mill's exposure to "thousands of pages of East India Company documents that were full of Indian ideas" has been underestimated. This period shows Mill not only taking a considered interest in the perspectives and practices of Indians under British rule, but also, Zastoupil argues, how his "public career as a major Victorian intellectual" was influenced in turn.[25] It is here, for instance, that Mill says he found "opportunities of perceiving when public measures, and other political facts, did not produce the effects which had been expected of them, and from what causes."[26] Mill was now able to observe that even the best laid plans can have unpredictable consequences.

Widely read, energized by travel, intellectual societies, and a career in the bureaucracy of public affairs—Mill was afforded multiple opportunities and resources to develop an interest in investigation and experimentation. But the tenor of his education under James Mill and Bentham, though not one of "cram," was nevertheless tuned to a set of programmatic opinions and ends. As a teenager, having already been raised on a "course of Benthamism," Mill remembers his father giving him a translation of Bentham's philosophy by Étienne Dumont. In that moment, he says, a feeling rushed upon him, he became a "different being" who "now had opinions; a creed, a doctrine, a philosophy; in one among the best sense of the word, a religion; the inculcation and diffusion of which could be made the principal outward purpose of a life."[27] Mill had found a direction for the course of his life. It was shortly after this episode that he made public debate—as a representative of Bentham's teachings—a cornerstone of his intellectual engagements. But this security of mind and purpose was not to last.

## The Crisis

Mill's discussion of his mental crisis is one of the most striking moments in the *Autobiography*. Though his path toward uncertainty as a mode of thinking was laid earlier, the crisis stands as a kind of symbolic account of *why* uncertainty became such an important feature of his politics.

At the age of twenty, Mill experienced a crisis of certainty. Between 1826 and 1827, Mill was struck down by the fact that his single-minded pursuit of Bentham's philosophy, which "formed the whole foundation on which [his] life was constructed . . . had ceased to charm."[28] Thus, Mill's mental crisis—"one of the best-known identity crises in history"[29]—marks the moment when he breaks beyond the political mold of his father and Bentham. The crisis begins when Mill asks himself "if the changes in institutions and opinions which you are looking forward to, could be completely effected at this very instant: would this be a great joy and happiness to you? And an irrepressible self-consciousness distinctly answered, 'No!' "[30] The creed that had "rushed in" on him just a few years earlier had begun to weaken.

The crisis in many ways allowed the elements of Mill's uncertain mode of thinking that had been planted in his childhood to flourish. The *Autobiography* also makes clear that Mill's interest in uncertainty was invigorated by his need to break away from the directed path that his mentors had laid out for him. Finding himself at odds with their doctrine, he develops an uncertain mode of theorizing as a way to both cope with the loss of his intellectual foundations and to generate a new sense of creative, intellectual freedom. In this, I argue, uncertainty reorients Mill's thinking in two key ways: first, it matures his investment in considering alternative and competing modes of examining social and political life; second, it generates both the creative potential and burden of doing politics without any guarantee as to the rightness of our judgments. I outline both these effects next, through a reconstruction of Mill's crisis and its aftermath.

## The Rebellion

Mill intended that his *Autobiography* make note of the successive phases of his intellectual, political, and personal development.[31] In doing so, the text offers a poignant, and occasionally peculiar, portrait of a man confronted with an existential crisis at the tender age of twenty. His reflections on that experience reveal a recurring anxiety about being fettered or limited by circumstances and powers beyond oneself. One might say that Mill began to flex his training in critical modes of inquiry *against* the certainty that his mentors had presumed, and which his own youthful politics absorbed in turn, about the nature of individuals and about the paths to human well-being.

One of his more curious low points during the crisis occurred while he was listening to the opera *Oberon*, during which Mill recalls being "seriously tormented by the thought of the exhaustibility of musical combinations. The octave consists only of five tones and two semitones, which can be put together in only a limited number of ways."[32] As such, he feared that "there could not be room for a long succession of Mozarts and Webers, to strike out . . . entirely new and surpassingly rich veins of musical beauty."[33] It is, perhaps, an odd thought to fixate upon. His concern with the compositional boundaries of the octave can be understood, however, as denoting the potential limit on the creative capacities of human genius more generally. This fear of being made to conform to a pre-set musical boundary corresponds to Mill's emerging concern for the scope of individual development and modes of living.

In an early draft, Mill comments that his father's penchant for "starving the feelings themselves" constituted "the most unfavourable of the moral agencies which acted upon me in my boyhood, that mine was not an education of love but of fear."[34] He felt the effects of this most deeply during the crisis. Much like the restricted composer he envisions, Mill thought he was "scientifically proved to be the helpless slave of antecedent circumstances; as if my character and that of all others had been formed for us by agencies beyond our control."[35] He recalls the deep terror of being a "made" or "manufactured man."[36] These thoughts weighed upon him "like an incubus."[37] Mill's fear that he was preformed or enslaved to external powers follows: "my circumstances tended to form a character, close and reserved from habit and want of impulse, not from will."[38] In a frank self-assessment that he and Harriet Taylor would later remove, Mill stated: "I was so accustomed to expect to be told what to do ... that I acquired a habit of leaving my responsibility as a moral agent to rest on my father, my conscience never speaking to me except by his voice." Consequently, Mill says he "acquired a habit of backwardness, of waiting to follow the lead of others."[39] In this moment Mill seemed to be caught by the implications of his father's wish that he become, as his father told Bentham, their worthy successor.

What Mill describes to us is in some ways akin to an attack of claustrophobia. A helpless slave of circumstance, a manufactured man, a habit of backwardness, all these self-impressions bore down upon him during this period of crisis. On one side he felt the pressure of his identity confronting him as an alien thing, constructed to *function* but not to live. On the other was the political foundation he had been constructed to uphold. But it now occurred to him that the objects—those "dogmatical conclusions"—he had been taught to pursue might not offer the best, or at least the only, path to human happiness. Putting his own self-reflections together with his reassessment of his teachers' program, Mill now wondered whether the exclusive importance James Mill and Bentham had attached to the ordering of outward circumstances came at the expense of a concern for the feelings and for the varied, internal development of the individual. Taught what to *know* instead of encouraged to *do*, Mill laments that their system of education focused on altering "people's opinions; to make them ... know what was their real interest," so they could then, "by the instrument of opinion, enforce a regard to it upon one another."[40]

That statement appears quite at odds with the status Mill would acquire as the nineteenth-century critic of public opinion and custom. But Mill laid the fault for this focus on Bentham and James Mill, whose reliance on a finite set of assumptions about human nature produced a uniform account of human well-being, and of the means which would secure it.[41] So, when Thomas Macaulay assails the father for assuming a priori from "certain propensities of human nature ... the whole science of politics," the son is willing to agree: "I could not help feeling," says Mill, that "there was truth in several of his strictures on my father's treatment of the subject; that my father's premises were really too narrow."[42] Mill, with Macaulay, questioned his father's presumption of a constant and uniform human nature upon which to develop a system of government. He began to view as suspect the "apriorism of the classical utilitarian approach."[43]

Similarly, in an essay published a few years following Bentham's death in 1832, Mill chastises Bentham for using "his own mind as a representative of universal human nature."[44] In Mill's view, Bentham lacked the imagination necessary to "conceive the absent as if it was present" or to consider "the mind and circumstances of another."[45] Imagination fuels the capacity to think beyond what we can see. Without it, we might adopt the false idea that what we see determines everything there is to know. Absent that creative capacity, Mill finds Bentham's knowledge of human nature to be "bounded," so that "other ages and nations were a blank to him . . . he measured them but by one standard," that of utility, and "recognised no diversities of character."[46]

In coming to terms with the finitude of his intellectual program, Mill observes that the Benthamites "had at this time no idea of real culture. In our schemes for improving human affairs, we overlooked human beings."[47] How then could the technocratic reforms sought by the Benthamite radicals hope to motivate new and surpassingly rich human pursuits or to secure perennial sources of human happiness? With such concerns in mind, it may hardly be surprising that when Mill asks himself if happiness would find him should all the objects of his youthful activity be obtained, an irrepressible self-consciousness answers: No!

The certainty his Benthamite roots once afforded him had been displaced by the cracks laid in the form of his early education. However much his father had intended Mill to follow a particular path, what ultimately won out was that feeling Mill remembered taking hold of him as a child, reading the Socratic dialogues. Having been nourished by a critical mode of inquiry, exposed to the variations of social and political life, and to the unpredictability of public affairs, Mill's early life inadvertently disposed him toward rejecting his father's directives. But the peculiar quality of a childhood under so dominating a figure as James Mill necessitated that this shift involve a profoundly emotional struggle. In Mill's case, however, the crisis was also an achievement. Recognizing the limitations of his foundations pushed Mill to break free, to approach political thought and practice in a way that could nourish the powers of imagination, by leaving the future unwritten.

## The Recovery

The *Autobiography* offers a far more complex account of Mill's intellectual struggles and concerns than is suggested in ideologically rigid representations of his thought. Indeed, in his move *away* from sectarian allegiances, Mill tells us: "I left off designating myself and others as Utilitarians, and by the pronoun 'we', or any other collective designation."[48] Working from the perspective of the *Autobiography*, then, any "view of Mill as doctrinaire overlooks this early manifestation of his desire for flexibility."[49] The crisis delivers Mill from his youthful sectarianism, into a frame of mind that explicitly emphasizes variation and diversity. Mill began to view as suspect those who would reject alternative ideas without considering what portion of truth or value might be in them, and so took a "most decided bent in the opposite direction, that of eclecticism."[50] Many-sidedness had become his motto.[51]

The skills Mill developed in his youth were now freed to test out numerous and varied approaches to politics and society, a test which frequently targeted as pure folly assumptions of certitude. His encounters with new and different schools of thought confirmed for him the error (which he found in Bentham and his father) of mistaking the "moral and intellectual peculiarities of an era of transition for the normal attributes of humanity."[52] St. Simonian socialism, which he favorably contrasted to the Owenite school, instructed him as to the "limited and temporary value of the old political economy, which assumes private property and inheritance as indefeasible facts, and freedom of production and exchange as the dernier mot of social improvement."[53] Mill's interest in romanticism further emphasized for him the importance of diverse circumstances in shaping the individual's capacity for self-definition—a capacity Mill's crisis saw him struggling to reclaim.[54]

Yet, these encounters did not resuscitate a different sectarian leaning in Mill; he remained receptive, but cautious. So, though the St. Simonians' aims seemed to him "perfectly rational, however their means might be inefficacious." As Robson notes, Mill was especially troubled by their "desire to establish immediately a supreme power, modelled on the Catholic hierarchy" to govern the "material, moral, and mental needs of each and every member of the community."[55] For parallel reasons, while Mill supported Auguste Comte's view that "the moral and intellectual ascendency, once exercised by priests must in time pass into the hands of philosophers," Mill's suspicions arose when Comte "exaggerated this line of thought into a practical system . . . organized into a kind of corporate hierarchy." In the end, for Mill, Comte "stands as a monumental warning to thinkers on society and politics, of what happens when once men lose sight . . . of the value of Liberty and Individuality."[56]

Mill began to hone this mental flexibility as he emerged from his crisis. He was convinced of the "importance in the present imperfect state of mental and social science, of antagonist modes of thought."[57] In his 1840 essay "Coleridge," Mill regards as utter folly the practice in England by "Conservative thinkers and Liberals" of regarding each other's "speculations as vitiated by an original taint, which makes all study of them, except for purposes of attack, useless if not mischievous."[58] Nineteen years following this observation, *On Liberty* systematically assails partisan approaches for assuming certainty, and thereby, fomenting dead dogmas. Instead, from the crisis onward Mill applied, to all that he encountered, "Coleridge's sayings about half truths; and Goethe's device, 'many-sidedness.'"[59] Indeed, Mill now thought himself superior to others in his "willingness and ability to learn from everybody."[60]

Mill's understanding of how and why this willingness became indispensable to his intellectual and political outlook gets lost when we work to stuff him into dogmatic cubbyholes. With such a rich biographical narrative available to us, the habit of reading him in rigid ideological terms is especially disturbing. And Mill himself cautions against such interpretations of his work, when he insists that no new structure of political philosophy had been erected in the place of the one he had abandoned:

> If I am asked what system of political philosophy I substituted . . . I answer, no system: only a conviction, that the true system was something much more complex and many sided than I had previously had any idea of, and that its office was to supply, not a set of model institutions, but principles from which the institutions suitable to any given circumstances might be deduced.[61]

As Terence Ball elegantly puts it, the *Autobiography* shows by example how "a manufactured man can revolt against his manufacturer."[62] In that revolt, the bounded composer that Mill once feared himself to be was finally free to compose anew.

## A Very Special Relationship

It was during this period of renewal that Mill embarked upon one of the most important relationships of his life. In 1830 he met Harriet Taylor, whom he regarded as a true intellectual partner nearly from the time they met until her death in 1858. Mill called Taylor the "inspirer, and in part the author, of all that is best in my writings."[63] In Taylor, Mill found an intellectual compatriot with a spine. Their letters and editorial exchanges show the wide range of issues on which they worked as if of one mind—but she was no mere mirror for his ideas. On questions of gender equality, the family, class politics, and considerations of human nature, Taylor's positions would not only differ but would push Mill to take stock of his own views. This is evident in their personal exchanges when Taylor questions the account Mill gives, following Comte, of the "differences in characters & apparent capacities of men & women," as well as her decidedly more critical views of domestic labor, the value of marriage, and the importance of divorce.[64] Mill had the great fortune of meeting, and later marrying, a woman who held her own in their personal as well as intellectual partnership; and Taylor had the great fortune of finding in Mill a man who recognized her value.

Despite Mill's own statements about her collaborative influences, successive generations of Mill readers have had a great deal of trouble understanding them.[65] The gender politics at play in debates over Taylor's role have been striking—providing what Carole Pateman described as "a fascinating glimpse into the patriarchal bastion of political philosophy."[66] However contested Taylor's influence is in contemporary scholarship, in Mill's estimation she was an essential interlocutor, editor, and indeed a co-author throughout the course of their special relationship.[67] I propose we take him at his word.[68] A growing body of work now does this, by shedding light on Taylor's contributions to Mill's thinking (both as an ally and as a critic of his views).[69]

One passage in the *Autobiography* is especially of note for what it imparts about the political awareness Taylor helped him to develop. Mill always held that his position in support of women's equality was one of his earliest opinions, which he grew only more convinced of over the course of his life. But until he met Taylor, it was a position held in the abstract. The "perception of the vast practical bearings of women's disabilities which found expression in the book on *The Subjection of Women* . . . was acquired mainly through her teaching"; it was only in conversation with Taylor that Mill began to perceive how "the consequences of the inferior position of women intertwine themselves with all the evils of existing society and with all the difficulties of human improvement."[70] We have seen this sentiment about the importance of practical considerations expressed in relation to the limits of James Mill's approach. The "practical bearing" Taylor's politics brought is thus a feature Mill credits with grounding his own political philosophy in a consideration of the everyday effects of the principles and relations which govern society.

## The *Autobiography* against the Icon

Taken together, Mill's experiences, his evolving relationships, and his embrace of intellectual eclecticism, half-truths, many-sidedness, and a respect for fallibilism helped to shape an investment in uncertainty as a critical condition of social and political thought. What consumed him during the crisis was the sense that the conviction he had long held regarding the rightness of his education and political pursuits left nothing to the imagination. Adopting uncertainty as a condition of politics reopened that creative possibility, as it moved Mill into a pluralist engagement with ideas and with their effects in the world he observed. Much like John Dewey, a future critic of philosophical quests for certainty, Mill came to recognize that there "is no knowledge self-guaranteed to be infallible, since all knowledge is the product of special acts of inquiry."[71]

Appreciating the uncertainties of social and political life allowed Mill to attend to "half-truths," to opposing views, and to the complexities of politics over and above a desire for streamlined answers. And that shift was a productive one: it gave Mill a sense of authorship and responsibility for his thoughts and actions. To be uncertain about the direction of social and political life created room for him to pursue political questions creatively instead of dogmatically. More personally, incorporating uncertainty into his political thought allowed Mill to address not only the limits of his early education, but also his deep anxieties about being his father's "manufactured man." Resolving those anxieties by rejecting predetermined models of human development, Mill comes to believe that "We are exactly as capable of making our own character, *if we will*, as others are of making it for us."[72]

Recognizing the appreciation for uncertainty embedded in his intellectual development makes ideological deployments of Mill in discussions of liberalism all the more perplexing. Inattentiveness to the politics of Mill's *Autobiography*, as Richard Ashcraft notes, is partly to blame for appropriations of Mill as the father of liberalism.[73] And so, Mill has become something of a scapegoat for whatever features of liberalism scholars are intent on decrying or defending. Two cases are worth looking at in closer detail: (1) Mill's theory of the individual, and (2) his so-called Harm Principle.

Scholarly appropriations of Mill in each instance highlight the ways in which his liberal *status* is called upon to ground claims about liberalism itself—or about the particular visions of liberalism being defended or challenged. In short, Mill is brought in as the exemplary case in arguments over what liberalism *is*. And yet, such cases rely on precisely that which Mill is not: a thinker driven by ideological certitude.

## Rethinking the Millian Individual

Critics interested in exposing the failures of liberal individualism have used Mill as a representative of both the social conformity they insist is central to the liberal subject or conversely, of the inescapably decontextualized understanding of subjects and societies inherent to liberalism. With respect to issues of conformity, scholars like John Gray, Bhikhu Parekh, and Eddy Souffrant have argued that Mill highlights how the liberal subject is tailored to reflect particular social norms and values. Parekh suggests that Mill had a culturally specific understanding of the individual that most people "had to be educated into and, until such time as they were ready, held in check."[74] Similarly, Souffrant argues that for Mill, only persons who have been indoctrinated with "the ascertained results of human experience" are allowed the protection of liberty, so that when Mill speaks of individuality, he is referring to a type of individual that "has already been coerced to conform."[75] For these reasons, liberalism cannot facilitate a toleration of different perspectives or values.[76]

Mill is a tenuous basis upon which to rest this case. We should not confuse Mill's claim that we cannot "isolate a human being from the circumstances of his condition" with a prescriptive *bias* toward conforming to those conditions.[77] Rather, the eclectic and fallibilist approaches that uncertainty generates in Mill keep him attuned both to the utility of established rules and customs and to their potential flaws. Mill does indeed acknowledge that we are always embedded in social and political conditions: "it would be absurd to pretend that people ought to live as if nothing whatever had been known in the world before they came into it." We should therefore be taught from our youth what are commonly held to be the "ascertained results of human experience." Customs, he continues, are evidence of what other people or generations have learned by experience, and insofar as they reflect that knowledge, they do "have a claim to [our] deference."[78] But Mill stops well short of suggesting that customs, simply by being customary, must therefore be accepted as universal truths.

This is why, alongside his nod to the utility of customary knowledge, Mill argues that we cannot deny "the privilege and proper condition of a human being, arrived at the maturity of his faculties, to use and interpret experience in his own way."[79] Exposure to customary knowledge and practices does not exclude one's own ability to learn (and learn differently) by experience. Contra Souffrant, for example, Mill does not assume that prior "social training" will preclude mature individuals from reflecting critically upon their societies.[80] Mill's personal ethology speaks to this point eloquently. The *Autobiography*, after all, recounts Mill's overwhelming fear of being a "made man"—a man whose conscience never spoke to him except by his father's voice.[81] Mill's turn to uncertainty helps him address that fear, redirecting him away from dogmatic assertions in favor of a willingness to learn from everybody. Adopting uncertainty as a condition of his thought was a means of reclaiming and remaking his own character, and its influence is reflected again in his exploration of customary knowledge and practices. Mill comes to see that the very existence of difference in society entitles us "to infer that a person encumbered by popular norms and beliefs is nevertheless capable of deciding to choose differently than the majority of his fellows."[82] What he sought for himself, and in his discussions of individuality and custom, were the conditions under which a capacity to choose differently could be exercised, even within the material reality of existing social relations and influences.

*On Liberty* lays out several reasons that the customs resulting from experience must be subject to further consideration or critique: first, existing customs may be too narrow, and second, customary knowledge might be faulty. Third, and more perversely, an unthinking adherence to social customs can negatively impact the development of individual capacities and social interests.[83] As his discussions of the "hothouse woman" and the "household sultan" in *The Subjection of Women* make clear, women are so constrained by existing gender norms that they are bred solely to see themselves as servants to the interests of others, while men gain their elevated position among women not by merit but by habit. Social norms regarding gender help to promote schools of despotism within the family, a condition that expresses the corrupting influence of customary power.[84] Consequently, while Mill may regard the ascertained results of human experience to be a significant resource for mental and moral development, he does not consider us to thereby be beholden to those results.

Though discussed at length in Chapter 4, I should note here that the same aversion to unexamined customary powers or relations that makes Mill unsuitable to a "liberal conformist" reading makes him unsuitable to the "abstract liberal" reading offered by scholars like Catherine MacKinnon and Wendy Brown. For Brown, Mill stands in for liberalism's inability to engage with substantive conditions of inequality in social and cultural life, while MacKinnon cites him as the source of liberalism's problematic treatment of thinking as a transhistorical exercise, separated from context and audience.[85] These may be compelling critiques of particular authors who have been identified (or self-identified) with the liberal tradition. They are not, however, appropriately applied to Mill.

The *Autobiography* highlights the emphasis Mill places on social conditions and relationships as constituent elements in the formation (and transformation) of character. His uncertainties about his early education gave Mill the mental distance needed to rethink those conditions and relations, and to rework his approach to politics as a result. Thus, "both his own life and the political issues arising in the life around him are understood and addressed historically."[86] Further, drawing upon the uncertainties that Mill develops in relation to his own upbringing, we can see why his political thought treats as suspect claims or beliefs that attempt to shield themselves from interrogation. We find these suspicions in his writings concerning the status of women, of the working and poor classes, and of slavery, all of which question the assumed inevitability or rightness of relations of authority and existing social customs.

Mill's autobiographical and political writings display a clear sensitivity to historical contexts and to existing social conditions. His personal and political examinations center uncertainty, and contend that even the beliefs "we have most warrant for" must always be subject to critical consideration.[87] Yet, these core aspects of his approach to politics and society are jettisoned in attempts to read him as an abstract "liberal individualist" or as a closet "liberal conformist." Such readings obscure the fact that Mill takes account of the social and political conditions into which we are all born, while remaining alert to the possibility that those same conditions, being contingent upon particular understandings and modes of living, might be otherwise.

## Deliberation and the Harm Principle

Circulating through the preceding discussion of individuality and customary knowledge are questions about the relationship between the individual and society and the interventions of authorities to balance it. Interpreted as the "scion of liberalism," it is not surprising that Mill's harm principle has received significant attention within debates concerning liberal grounds for intervention and regulation.[88] The harm principle (HP) is often invoked to defend or attack liberalism's ability to govern the line between liberty and authority. The principle itself states that the prevention of harm to others is the "sole end for which mankind are warranted, individually or collectively, in interfering with the liberty of any of their number."[89]

Debates over the HP focus on whether it provides too narrow or too wide a justification for intervening against practices that might constitute harm to others. While some scholars have found in the HP a liberal basis for defending state censorship in the form of anti-pornography laws, others argue that it provides liberal grounds for preventing such interventions.[90] The HP has also been jointly rejected by distinct political projects, and for directly opposing reasons. Scholars who favor coercive forms of paternalism chastise the HP for enabling too much liberty and reject the libertarian quality of "Millian liberalism," while libertarian readers find the HP to be too vague, open to speculation, and therefore incapable of protecting liberty against coercive practices.[91] For those concerned with liberalism's ability to encompass value-pluralism, the HP is too specific to account for the diversity of moral outlooks in a liberal society.[92] Others suggest that the HP is not specific enough, such that it highlights liberalism's inability to consider the socializing pressures of group membership among minority communities.[93]

As with other appropriations of Mill's thought, these readings are motivated by orientations toward liberalism. They treat the HP as a reflection of the categorical injunctions liberalism is presumed to offer for or against regulation. The HP is evaluated as if it were a legal warrant, or an ideological mandate, regarding the precise delineation between self and other-regarding spheres of conduct. However, assessing the HP on these grounds again leaves aside Mill's own suspicion of such injunctions on social and political questions.

Mill, as the *Autobiography* indicates, does not resolve to think about social and political issues in absolute terms. Viewed through the lens of uncertainty, the HP should be reread as a deliberative trigger for critical reflection and experimentation with the boundaries between freedom and authority. The text of *On Liberty* bolsters this view of the HP as a stimulus for critical engagements, with its recurring attempts to tie perceptions of harm, discussion, and judgment together. Mill argues that the HP ought to be observed wherever one has attained the capacity to be guided by conviction or persuasion. The liberty afforded by the HP is for him inapplicable until "mankind have become capable of being improved by free and equal discussion."[94] In other words, the HP cannot be thought outside of, or apart from, the practice of deliberative engagements.

In line with his orientation toward uncertainty, the principle can be understood as a tool for examining the nature of harm in shifting conditions: Mill expects that particular notions of harm, and attendant questions about self and other-regarding acts, will be subject to contestation, so that considerations of harm will always be the products of special acts of inquiry. As acts of inquiry they cannot be terminated by categorical claims.[95] Instead, even once an agreement is reached that certain actions do constitute a harm, "whether the general welfare will or will not be promoted by interfering with it, becomes open to discussion."[96] The HP then necessitates successive stages of critical reflection: the first concerns whether or not something constitutes a harmful practice, the second stage then considers whether the harmful act outweighs the potential harm of limiting freedom in favor of regulation. And at all points, whatever decisions result will be subject to further contestation.[97]

Viewing the HP as a deliberative trigger can explain the wide and narrow ways in which it has been read. Though state intervention is only relevant in cases of other-regarding acts (the narrow reading), Mill is also willing to hold individuals responsible for taking up critical discussions about actions that appear to be voluntary or self-regarding in scope (the wider reading). Mill's own critique of marriage in nineteenth-century England offers a prime example of this. His analysis of gendered relations sought to shift perceptions of marital relationships from being strictly private to being issues relevant to the public interest. Thus, whether actions are self-regarding or other-regarding in nature, in all cases human beings "owe to each other help to distinguish the better from the worse, and encouragement to choose the former and avoid the latter."[98] His "very simple principle" does not therefore boil down to locating a hard line between liberty and interference. Reflecting his regard for uncertainty, Mill's HP instead calls for provisional determinations of where lines ought to be drawn or redrawn.

## Uncertainty as Politics

Mill's *Autobiography* makes evident that his lived experiences were important ingredients in his political thought. His education, family, personal and professional relationships all intertwine with Mill's account of his intellectual and political outlook. The connection between Mill's self-study and his thought is what makes his autobiographical account so essential to his overall corpus. It is in the story of his breakdown that we find Mill's intellectual orientation taking shape. Initiated by his fears of being preformed, a manufactured man robbed of the potential to think and act independently or creatively, Mill's crisis was both disorienting and generative. Even as his doubts about his early political foundations drew him into a depression, those doubts presented Mill with an opportunity to recognize that as much as we can be shaped by conditions and persons around us, we are also capable of reshaping ourselves.

Mill sought out that capacity for himself by entertaining new and contradictory perspectives and resolving to make room for a many-sided mode of living which could appreciate the unknowns of social and political action. Embracing uncertainty as a condition of political thought and action helped him to forge a path out of the crisis that afflicted him in his twenties and to actualize the critical modes of inquiry he was so taken with in his childhood. It was in the *not knowing* that Mill found space to reconfigure himself and to consider both the possibilities and risks of doing politics in a world that cannot guarantee the outcomes of our designs.

The question now is: how does uncertainty shape Mill's responses to conditions which might either help or harm individual and social development? Recovering Mill's uncertainty moves us to consider how this intellectual disposition (rather than the ideological tradition he's identified within) gets worked out in practice. I suggest it informs his politics in two ways. First, Mill's uncertainty generates different strategies for working out how reforms to relations of dependency or experiences with social and political exclusion might be undertaken. Second, his uncertain orientation creates tensions between *and* within his proposals for reform. This is primarily because Mill's uncertainty prohibits him from making absolute or universalizing claims about the path to alleviating restrictive dependencies. Rather, it necessitates a consideration of the *paths* that might be taken. Though Mill's commitment to individuality as an element of well-being remains steady, his very resistance to political certitude keeps him mindful of the influence of existing circumstances on persons—and of the unknown directions that changing those circumstances might take us.

Put another way—how does Mill's *politics of uncertainty* operate? I turn to this question in the subsequent chapters, with an examination of Mill's proposals regarding women, class identity and democratic character, and colonial despotism. Three core strategies repeat through Mill's work in these areas: (1) a radically oriented examination of political claims and of the effects of circumstance upon character; (2) a tendency toward gradually reworking those circumstances to alleviate conditions of dependency and in relation to this, (3) moments of paternalistic justifications for limiting freedom. That each of these strategies operates across Mill's work on gender, class, and empire illustrates the methodological consistency of his uncertain politics. Mill's repeated use of these critical strategies highlights both his rejection of absolutist claims about individual and social characters and the challenges of doing politics once illusions of certainty are abandoned.

My decision to look at Mill's proposals across gender, class, and empire is intentional. The affinities between his strategies on these questions have been concealed because a sustained comparative study of Mill's political proposals is often sidelined in order to focus on aspects of his purported liberalism. The degree to which scholars retain the presumptive divergence between Mill's domestic and colonial political proposals stems from a desire to view his work within that interpretive frame. But this divided view can lead to a silencing of those parts of Mill's corpus which do not "fit" the puzzle being worked out about the relative merits or demerits of liberal political thought.

Mill's political interventions on questions of gender equality, class, and colonial rule are thus taken to reflect differing, if not incompatible, aspects of his political thought—as concerns his domestic considerations of English society and his discussions of the British Empire. How, for example, can he offer a cogent critique of the despotic form of dependency that governs the relation between the sexes, while defending a government of the dependencies by British empire? Why did he advocate the social, legal, and political equality of women, while suggesting gradual suffrage, or forms of plural voting, to blunt the entry of the working classes into national politics?

While his proposals do evince such differences, I aim to show that Mill's political interventions have far more in common with each other than standing scholarship has allowed. A comparative study of Mill's interventions on these issues reveals not divisions that need resolution but a real sense of critical continuity. It is also a continuity of tensions. Mill's uncertainty gives rise to similar critiques of unjust social and political relations, while also producing hesitations about what to do about them. These are the complex effects of Mill's politics of uncertainty.

# 4
# The School of Virtues

## Emancipating Women, Wives, and Mothers

*Think of it: a few years ago, a few solitary voices like John Stuart Mill's exposed and denounced the "subjection of women," a few women like Mrs. Fawcett agitated for the suffrage. Then came the revolt, violent, vehement, and desperate, of a few more, and now the war has placed their cause in such a position that it can never be put back.*

Dr. Clifford, in Millicent Fawcett's *What I Remember*

Though Mill wrote on a wide range of social and political issues, his defense of women's equality surely counts among his most famous interventions. We can cite several reasons for that being the case, including the fact that, as a nineteenth-century white male, the position he took was unconventional. Mill's writings on gender inequality were unpopular, even with those he counted as friends and intellectual allies.[1] Dubbed a "very feminine philosopher" by *Vanity Fair*, Mill was ridiculed for his position by Tories and Liberals alike, and he became the recurring subject of mocking illustrations in the press.[2] He would later draw ire from men like Freud who, despite having sympathies with other aspects of Mill's thought, insisted that on the subject of women's equality, "That is altogether a point with Mill where one simply cannot find him human."[3] As the first Member of Parliament to introduce legislation extending the vote to women, Mill's efforts were also celebrated for their valuable contributions to the cause of equality. When the franchise was finally won in 1928, a wreath of remembrance was laid at his London statue by Millicent Fawcett, who was among the audience when he delivered his speech in support of women's suffrage some sixty years prior.[4]

Though *Subjection of Women* is the primary text we now associate with his feminism, Mill's work on the politics of gender ranges much wider. Together with Harriet Taylor, he published a series of op-eds concerning the marriage contract, issues of domestic violence, and family law.[5] He also spoke out extensively, and gave evidence before a Royal Commission, against the Contagious Diseases Acts, which sought to curb the spread of sexually transmitted diseases. The Acts Mill argued, policed women instead of men's sexual license over them, reflecting the greater problem of sex discrimination: "If women had had votes, we should not have had the 'Contagious Diseases Acts'; under which the wives and daughters of the poor are exposed to insufferable indignities on the suspicion of a police-officer."[6] It might even surprise some to learn that a philosopher described as staid and stodgy was arrested at age seventeen for distributing pamphlets about birth control. As one of his earliest and most enduring political commitments, Mill's feminism was never an auxiliary project, but a central pillar of his politics.

One of the unique aspects of Mill's feminism is that it was a position he took against his father's retrograde views on the sexes and despite the gendered household in which he was raised. Mill once described his mother, Harriet (née Barrow) as a "drudge" to her family, a woman whose marriage was decided by circumstance, and who was left to bear her husband's "asperities of temper."[7] Oddly though, and unlike his feminist writings, Mill's sparse references to his mother seem to capture the effect of her situation, but with little understanding for the causes of it. Of his mother's capacities, for instance, he said that for her family, what "she could do for them she did, and they liked her, because she was kind to them, but to make herself loved, looked up to, or even obeyed, required qualities which she unfortunately did not possess in service to both her husband and children."[8] His sister put a finer point on Mrs. Mill's experience asking, "how was a woman with a growing family and very small means . . . to be anything but a German Hausfrau? How could she 'intellectually' become a companion for such a mind as my father?"[9] Notably, following Harriet Taylor's edits on the early draft, Mill removed his unforgiving descriptions of his mother from the *Autobiography*.

But it is perhaps that gendered upbringing that triggered Mill's feminist politics. Once again, Mill's self-reflections shaped his philosophy. Having adopted the practice of interrogating the array of relationships, customs, and modes of living that work upon our development as social beings, Mill had reason to doubt the example set by his parents. And any doubts he had about the structure of their relationship were certainly reinforced by his long connection and eventual marriage to Taylor. With his mother and Taylor as examples, Mill was witness to the varied possibilities of individual development in the context of gendered social relations and customs. And the appreciation for uncertainty Mill developed in his youth fueled his study of the wide-ranging effects of the "legal subordination of one sex to the other."[10] It is worth examining, then, how Mill's intellectual disposition came to shape his critique of women's subjected status, as well as the proposals he made for addressing their subjection.

Beginning with his feminist politics in this chapter, I examine what Mill's appreciation for uncertainty as an intellectual disposition produced in practice. As a practitioner, Mill applied the view that though we *can* change the circumstances which shape our characters and those of others—such changes might not always produce the results we expect. The two central women in Mill's life, after all, represented critical instances of how outcomes can vary even given similar conditions. Both Mill's mother and Taylor were raised within the gendered confines of Victorian England. Both were formally uneducated, married young, and became mothers at an early age. But if his mother was held hostage by the restrictions upon her sex, in a household governed by a man who rejected women's suffrage "without inconvenience,"[11] Taylor found space to defy those restrictions and became an avowed political thinker and actor in her own right.[12] With their experiences in view, Mill's feminist politics aimed at divining how to advance women's freedom, while remaining acutely aware that the obstacles to doing so were diverse and not always easy to overcome.

This duality—of radical critique and cautionary awareness—is reflected in three overlapping strategies I identify across Mill's political proposals concerning first gender and later, in Chapters 5 and 6 respectively, class and empire. The first strategy disposes him toward rejecting absolutist arguments, which explain existing conditions or relations as a consequence of some natural or immutable quality of character. Because his critiques intervened against customary social expectations and beliefs, they constitute what I call his *radical strategy*. The second strategy pursues a more tempered assessment of how to proceed in addressing the inequities or failures of existing practices with regards to women, class, and democratic representation or colonial rule; this is his *gradualist strategy*. Finally, Mill's uncertainties about paths for reform produces a *paternalist strategy*, one which he employs both at home and abroad to control the unknown challenges that changes to existing conditions and relations might bring.

These strategies are among the nuances lost to our tradition of reading Mill, first and foremost, as a paradigmatic liberal thinker. That designation captures

Mill's identity and makes him perform to the very ideological rigidity he rejected in his youth. Moreover, to be described as paradigmatic, or as an exemplar, instills in the reader the sense that Mill represents some essential quality or aspect of the liberal label. Read as its founding father, he functions as a genetic link between liberalism's origins and its contemporary iterations. We then turn to Mill to sort out the tradition's birth and development and by extension, to give our descriptions and evaluations of the liberal idea genealogical weight. But this practice is damaging, both to Mill and to his readers. In occluding his uncertain disposition and the politics it produces, the liberal label alters *how* we read Mill. It also, as a result, controls what we might take from him to enrich our own political engagements with the questions of equality, liberty, and democratic society that he addressed himself to.

The chapter first illustrates how Mill's feminism has been trapped by different debates over liberalism's gender politics. It is inevitably a problem of liberalism that directs appropriations of Mill's thought in such studies, and which a priori conditions what scholars want from his texts. I then turn to contest such appropriations. I suggest that Mill's feminism highlights his multifaceted approach to politics: rather than pursuing any one method for diagnosing and correcting political ills, Mill blends several. This allows Mill to make critical interventions against the subjection of women while, at the same time, drawing back to consider the challenges of fundamental reform. As I conclude, Mill's radical challenges to the system of sex inequality is also inflicted by moments of caution—even reversal. On issues of divorce and women's employment beyond the household for instance, Mill's fears about the unintended consequences of women's social and political liberation take root.

Uncertainty thus generates a particular set of political anxieties for Mill, motivating a desire to expand the possibilities for individual and social progress while prohibiting him from taking a determinative approach toward obtaining such possibilities. In his radical, gradualist, and paternalist responses to the "woman question," Mill in fact rejects the deterministic, ideological attitudes he is often tapped to represent as a scion of liberalism.

## The Interpretive Orthodoxy: Mill for "Liberal" Feminism

In the tradition of western political thought, Mill remains a "rare exception to the rule that those who hold central positions in the tradition almost never question the justice of the subordination of women."[13] But that exceptionalism has been, and continues to be read, through the lens of his liberal status. Because the orthodoxy is to read Mill within the liberal canon, the attendant custom is to "interpret his feminism as liberal feminism."[14] The conflation of Mill's feminist writings with his canonical title has clear interpretive effects on the way his writings are studied and deployed in contemporary feminist analysis. Some, like Susan Moller Okin, Joan Scott, or Carole Pateman, see Mill as an important foil for the long line of western thinkers who actively suppressed women's political agency. For Okin in particular, Mill's attention to the relationship between justice and gender equality is unique even among contemporary liberal thinkers.

In his canonical role, however, Mill is more often taken up as a reflection of liberalism's promise or failings—sometimes both. And scholars have looked to Mill to organize the better from the worse elements of liberal feminisms. In this mode, Wendy Donner presents Mill as an example of how liberalism can balance individual freedom against the dangers of strong communities.[15] Donner aims at challenging "critiques which find fault with liberal feminism or its allegedly flawed values of individualism," with Mill as a representative of liberalism's better instincts.[16] Taking a different tack, Julia Annas sees in Mill's feminism weaknesses, as well as resources for critiquing them. She finds that though Mill begins his analysis with a far-reaching diagnosis of how women's natures are undermined by social control, he falls into a merely reformist argument for legal equality and inclusion. The inconsistency Annas identifies in Mill, argues Jennifer Ring, reflects the limits of a liberal feminist methodology.[17] Mill's liberalism in effect curtails the directions his feminist politics might go.

A more critical take comes in Janet Halley's evaluation of "feminism and the legal and political system—broadly speaking, liberalism—within which it attempts to secure its aims."[18] Mill's harm principle grounds what she calls the feminist "injury triad," a relationship that posits women as victims, men as perpetrators, and feminism as both defender (of women) and prosecutor (of men). The "machinelike formality of Mill's harm principle" she argues, attaches "distinct argumentative and justificatory advantages to the Injury Triad."[19] In Halley's reading, Mill's view of harm underwrites the extent to which contemporary liberal feminism has crowded out sexual agency and difference with political correctness and interventionist or carceral agendas.

Mill would likely cringe at the machinelike characterization of any aspect of his thought—particularly given what we know of his crisis and his fear of being his father's manufactured man. More interesting, however, is that

Halley's discussion of Mill does not involve his feminist writings. As noted in Chapter 3, those writings combined with Mill's broader views on deliberation and the contingencies of political judgments serve to challenge the kind of legalistic view Halley takes of his harm principle. Moreover, though Mill's explicit dealings with issues of marriage, sexual partnership, and prostitution are all issues Halley is invested in addressing, discussion of his work on these subjects is forgone in favor of an assessment of how the left/liberal/progressives make use of Mill's harm principle. Mill's name is invoked in this instance to give the critique of liberal feminism a genealogical footing. That invocation involves reading Mill around what one wants to say about liberalism and feminism, rather than through what Mill himself has to say about the politics of gender.

In an interesting departure from these deployments, Keith Burgess-Jackson suggests that Mill's status as a liberal theorist has actually prejudiced studies of his feminist writings. Identifying Mill with liberalism might be, he contends, unduly shaping what scholars find in his works. Contrary to Annas and Halley, Burgess-Jackson holds that Mill was indeed a radical—*not* a liberal—feminist. Because Mill premised his arguments (including those for legal equality) on a systematic understanding of power and its potentially corruptive influence on human development, Mill's account blends a defense of legal equality together with the broader social changes which must undergird it. But, he argues, that blended account is lost amid efforts to read liberalism into Mill's feminism.[20]

Burgess-Jackson's concern about how liberal readings of Mill might impinge upon his feminist politics is one I certainly share. Yet it is a testament to the power of that liberal label that even as he critiques liberalism's hold on Mill, Burgess-Jackson falls *back* upon it. In the course of questioning the "liberal" Mill, he states: "in social and political theory generally, Mill is a liberal—indeed, the paradigmatic liberal ... But it doesn't follow from this that Mill was a liberal feminist."[21] This is a statement worth unpacking. In the first place, how are we to maintain Mill's *paradigmatic* status as a liberal, while keeping separate from that identification the subject of one of Mill's essential political treatises, and a long-standing focus of his political activism? I would suggest, rather, that the *label* itself is problematic if and where we have to bracket out key texts and positions in the subject's corpus to validate its application. More broadly, this instinct to maintain liberalism's imprint on readings of Mill—even as we might question its utility—reflects the discursive power of our reliance upon the liberal idea: despite efforts to stretch our

THE SCHOOL OF VIRTUES    65

readings beyond it, our attachments to the idea snap back like an elastic band to hold our interpretive practices in place.

The preceding examples highlight the myriad ways in which preoccupations with liberalism, and in this case with liberal feminism, condition how and why we turn to Mill's writings (or just to his name alone). The practice of reading through and for debates about liberalism will inevitably detach Mill from his thought and politics. I focus on three illustrative cases to further outline the troubling interpretive politics of such appropriations: Saba Mahmood's postcolonial critique, Catharine MacKinnon's radical critique, and Wendy Brown's poststructuralist critique of liberal feminisms. Though they write from different political perspectives, all three authors use Mill to supplement frontal attacks on liberalism and the feminisms it might instantiate. Moreover, despite their efforts to critically distance themselves from the idea, each remains tethered to that unwanted order of desire Brown herself suggests attends contemporary political theory's relationship to liberalism. Each case illustrates how Mill and our readings of him become trapped by attachments to liberalism.

## Liberalism's Burdens: Mahmood

Saba Mahmood's work offers a formidable critique of the notions of freedom, agency, and autonomy she sees embedded in liberal feminisms, against which non-Western, and particularly Islamist cultural and political movements, have been judged. Her seminal book, *Politics of Piety*, rightfully called attention to the ways in which customary assumptions about freedom and autonomy in the west are culturally weighted, ignoring and obstructing alternative modes of individual agency and empowerment. Western liberal feminists, the book argues, ought to problematize the presumed universality of the desire to be *free from* relations of subordination, a desire she suggests is central "to feminism, as it is to liberalism, and critical scrutiny is applied to those who want to limit women's freedom rather than those who want to extend it."[22]

As I have argued elsewhere, Mahmood's focus on liberalism reflects a problematic practice in feminist debates about culture, which reinforces rather than addresses binary oppositions between west/non-west, liberal/nonliberal.[23] And Mill, in Mahmood's case, serves to cast those oppositions as the immutable consequences of western feminism's "liberal" lineage.

66　THE LIBERALISM TRAP

A footnote is all Mill is afforded in the text—but the interpretive labor it performs for Mahmood is significant.

Mill is identified as a thinker "central to liberal and feminist thought."[24] From Mill onward, Mahmood argues, liberalism and feminism in the west have required that only practices which limit women's freedom are questioned. Mahmood quotes the following lines from *Subjection* to push the point: "the burden of proof is supposed to be with those who are against liberty, who contend for any restriction or prohibition ... The *a priori* presumption is in favour of freedom." Mahmood cites this passage to argue that Mill, a founding liberal figure, places the burden of proof on anyone who argues in favor of limits to women's freedom.[25] This reading would seem to give evidence that liberal feminism, and the universalizing conceit Mahmood finds at its core, cannot comprehend how forms of subordination to religious authority might legitimately be viewed as a condition *of* freedom.

But these lines from *Subjection* offer a more complicated argument about the burdens of customary thinking than Mahmood allows. What Mill actually claims is that though he lives in an age where liberty is assumed to be desirable—that assumption is *not* applied to the status of women. Consider the full passage:

> In practical matters, the burthen of proof is supposed to be with those who are against liberty; who contend for any restriction or prohibition, either any limitation of the general freedom of human action, or any disqualification or disparity of privilege affecting one person or kind of persons, as compared with others. The *a priori* presumption is in favour of freedom and impartiality. It is held that there should be no restraint not required by the general good, and that the law should be no respecter of persons, but should treat all alike, save where dissimilarity of treatment is required for positive reasons, either of justice or of policy. *But of none of these rules of evidence will the benefit be allowed to those who maintain the opinion that I profess.* It is useless for me to say that those who maintain the doctrine that men have a right to command and women are under an obligation to obey, or that men are fit for governance and women unfit, are on the affirmative side of the question, and that they are bound to show positive evidence for the assertions, or to submit to their rejection.

Mill concludes: "a cause supported on one hand by universal usage, and on the other by so great a preponderance of popular sentiment, is supposed to have a presumption in its favour, superior to any conviction which an appeal to reason has power to produce in any intellects but those of a high class."[26] In essence, the perception that women's freedom ought to be *limited* was given the tenor of a universal truth in Mill's time. And against the customary opinion, Mill argues, the burden of proof will often fall to the counterargument. Mill is here making Mahmood's point about the difficulties of challenging doctrinaire assumptions.

Where for Mahmood it is the "trope of the autonomous individual" which dominates western liberal societies, in Mill's time it was the trope of women's subordinate natures that held sway. Consequently, on the subject of sex, Mill knew that critical scrutiny would be applied to those who wanted to *extend women's freedom*, and not to those who wanted to *limit* it. Mill's quarrel, as he says, was not with society "having too little faith in argument, but for having too much faith in custom and the general feeling" which fails to consider *why* restrictions on women's social and political freedoms are legitimate.[27] He did of course make the case for extending women's liberty—but he also knew the task of proving the case would fall to him. By drawing attention to the weight of customary thinking, and the ways in which it can overpower consideration of alternative views or experiences, Mill's argument bolsters Mahmood's insistence that we ought to draw our politics not from prefixed assumptions, but from careful attention to the "particular concepts that enable specific modes of being, responsibility and effectivity."[28] Though their aims differ, both can be said to share a critical investment in attending to the politics of case and context.

Mahmood could have turned to any number of contemporary feminists who make presumptions about the nature of freedom and agency she wants to dissect. Indeed, twentieth-century feminism is marked by continued controversy over what is meant by "freedom" in cross-cultural discourses. So why turn to Mill, even in a footnote (who, incidentally, appears nowhere else in the argument)? The answer to that question lies is in her description of Mill as a "figure central to liberal and feminist thought." Summoning Mill in this way provides canonical roots for a claim about the genetic makeup of liberal feminism. It is not *Mill's* arguments that matter in this case, but the fact that he can be called upon as a standard bearer of the tradition under review.

## Liberalism's Conceits: MacKinnon

Catharine MacKinnon's *Toward a Feminist Theory of the State* tackles issues of sexual politics and the law with characteristic argumentative force, and a compelling push for radical social change. But a critical moment in the book, which endeavors to distill the weak points of modern—liberal—feminism, echoes the same interpretive quandaries that Mahmood falls into. And it is, again, J.S. Mill who is sacrificed to the frame of the argument.

MacKinnon considers Mill's logic to be "embedded in the theoretical structure of liberalism which underlies much contemporary feminist theory."[29] Though she acknowledges that Mill's *Subjection* provides a "dazzling array of penetrating insights into women's situation," he nevertheless is used to mark the origin point of the conceits she finds endemic to the liberal tradition (and against which radical feminism is the solution): "from Mill to contemporary forms, liberal theory exhibits five interrelated dimensions that contrast with radical feminist theory, clarifying both. These are: individualism, naturalism, voluntarism, idealism, and moralism."[30] MacKinnon defines these "ism's" of liberalism as follows: (1) to be a person is to be an individual, defined against any group; (2) "nature is a fixed, certain and ultimately knowable reality"; (3) thinking is a transhistorical exercise, independent of "surroundings, advocacy or audience"; (4) rules are abstractly right or wrong; and (5) social life is "comprised of autonomous, intentional, and self-willed actions."[31] Taken together, these conceits ensure that liberalism "fails to grasp the group-based determinants of inequality" and remains blind "to organized power in diverse social forms."[32]

Mill in this reading is not only complicit with, but foundational to, the problematic elements she finds in liberalism. Yet Mill's own texts give us reason to question each of these dimensions in the ways MacKinnon wants us to—so much so that Don Herzog wonders if MacKinnon is *really* a liberal herself. For Herzog, Mill's *Subjection* proves that liberalism "is sociology" and "grounded in a lively apprehension of actual social life." Quoting at length from the text, Herzog points out that Mill presents a compelling "account of the social interactions that shape who we are, all for the worse," detailing not only the subservient status of women—but the ways in which that status negatively shapes the characters of men, of children, and of social relations at large.[33]

The simple line MacKinnon draws from Mill to contemporary liberal theory is puzzling, given what Mill writes about the social conditions of gender inequality. MacKinnon's argument that the fixed, certain, and knowable view of nature has roots in Mill (as a stand in for "liberal" theory) is also difficult to accept given what he actually says on the question of what our natures are. *Subjection* tells us that history proves "the extraordinary susceptibility of human nature to external influences, and the extreme variableness of those of its manifestations which are supposed to be most universal and uniform."[34] Mill further maintains, "we cannot isolate a human being from the circumstances of his condition, so as to ascertain experimentally what he would have been by nature."[35] Indeed—that inability to *know* what the natures of human beings are is a condition of uncertainty that Mill actively applies to his examinations of social and political relations. Mill remains dismissive of attempts to use human nature as a basis for policy precisely because he thinks that what constitutes our natures will always bear the effects of the shifting circumstances into which we are born and through which we develop.

For this reason, too, Mill never assumes that human thought and action can be transhistorical. Thinking critically for Mill requires being situated in the world and being in the world with others. An individual, he says, "is capable of rectifying his mistakes, by discussion and experience. Not by experience alone. There must be discussion to show how experience is to be interpreted."[36] The very exercise of good judgment bears a social component for him: "the only way in which a human being can make some approach to knowing the whole of a subject, is by hearing what can be said about it by persons of every variety of opinion, and studying all modes in which it can be looked at by every character of mind."[37] Indeed Mill fully understands that liberty and individuality must also be *cultivated* by society as a whole in order to make possible "well-developed human beings."[38] Mill's call for women's freedom is thus based on the recognition that freedom and individuality are tied to how people develop within social relationships.[39]

The roadblocks Mill throws up to MacKinnon's analysis leads Herzog to suggest that she might actually fall in line with Mill's feminist arguments. If so, her radical feminism rests "squarely within the liberal tradition" that both Herzog and MacKinnon situate Mill within.[40] Herzog is right about MacKinnon's misuse of Mill. But what purpose is served in calling MacKinnon a liberal *by way* of Mill? Indeed, MacKinnon contests Herzog's claims about her own liberal sympathies by pointing out that while she respects Mill's feminist analysis, she certainly cannot be said to align with the liberalism of, say, John Rawls. Their exchange draws down to an assessment of who qualifies as a liberal and circumvents a discussion of who or what might provide the resources needed for advancing the kind of feminist praxis MacKinnon and Herzog want to encourage.

Though Herzog correctly points to Mill as providing a grounded assessment of social relations, he might have pressed the critique differently.

Because, the curious thing is, MacKinnon *knows* all this about Mill. She admits that what Mill, together with Harriet Taylor, had to say about women's roles constituted a "stunningly insightful and prescient analysis" which "has more to offer women than many works that purport feminism today."[41] Yet turning to Mill to make her case about the liberal tradition, MacKinnon is forced to perform a "liberal" reading of him, even as she acknowledges that Mill does not really make the assumptions she thinks are central to the tradition. In effect, she admits that Mill operates in a supplementary role and does not actually *matter* to her analysis of *liberalism*. Consider the sticky interpretive terrain MacKinnon now has to navigate in her response to Herzog, with respect to Mill's and her own ostensible liberalism:

> That John Stuart Mill opposed many of the same things feminists oppose today does not make us liberals. That he was a liberal and capable of these insights does not redeem an entire tradition that, empowered, does not effectuate them. It does not make him not a liberal either, although his description of women's situation was arguably less so than anything he wrote ... That makes him an outlier in the liberal tradition in this respect.[42]

If this seems perplexing, it should be. Using "from Mill to contemporary forms" as an entrée to her earlier discussion cues the reader to think about the features she's about to challenge as *embryonic* to the liberal tradition, going all the way back to its paternal figure. Her shift in response to Herzog in the above passage, however, modifies that use by noting that Mill was "capable of insights" not otherwise found within his *own* tradition.

Deploying Mill under the liberal umbrella while also, at the same time, extracting those elements of his thought one likes against his liberal identity results in the kind of interpretive gymnastics we find in the above passage: Mill was a liberal, but his feminism was not; or Mill's feminism makes him an outlier in a tradition which ... he originates! MacKinnon at once seeks to use Mill's paradigmatic liberal status *and* to distance him from it when its deployment complicates the story she wants to tell about liberalism. Throughout, liberalism defines the terms of her analysis, even as her aim is to undercut the idea and its dominance in feminist political thought. MacKinnon may not *be* the liberal Herzog claims she is, but her interpretive practice is *wrapped up in the idea* of liberalism.

## Liberalism's Aversions: Brown

Little common ground lies between Catharine MacKinnon and Wendy Brown. Their views on sexual agency, state intervention, and what constitutes freedom are quite explicitly opposed.[43] It is therefore remarkable how parallel the structure of their arguments are when it comes to assessing liberalism through Mill. Like MacKinnon, Brown seems to recognize the complexities of Mill's works, while ultimately sidestepping those nuances in order to make claims about the systemic failings of the liberal tradition.

In *Regulating Aversion*, Brown critically examines what she calls "liberal tolerance talk" and its "retreat from stronger ideals of justice," because it is both inherently depoliticizing and non-emancipatory in its aims.[44] Embedded in liberal discourses on tolerance are uneven relations of power that delineate who tolerates (i.e., liberal cultures and societies) and who is tolerated (i.e., those external to, or on the margins of, liberal polities). It is a brilliant analysis on many fronts, not the least of which includes Brown's assessment of how and why nineteenth-century arguments for women's political inclusion were framed in terms of *rights*, while those concerning Jewish oppression were framed in terms of *tolerance*. What distinguishes the "Woman question" from the "Jewish question," Brown argues, is that the former's emancipation in public life would be mitigated by their continued "sexed" status in private life, where no such domestic check existed to manage Jewish identity in the body politic. The argument is a cogent one. But the way in which Brown frames the "Woman question" through liberalism is of particular importance here. Mill is called up in support of that frame.

The key maneuver made by liberal rights discourses concerning women's emancipation, in Brown's view, is to disassociate the androgynous character of the "liberal citizen," which women could adopt in their public actions, from the embodied, sexed characters of the private realm, in which women continued to be *women*. That disassociation has roots in two of liberal feminism's classic authors: Mary Wollstonecraft and J.S. Mill. Both, Brown says:

> can be seen to argue for a feminine subjectivity that is at once androgynous and different: androgynous in the rational, civic, and public order of things where mind alone matters, and saturated with its sex difference in the private realm where bodies, temperaments, emotional bearing, and "instinct" are thought to prevail.[45]

Brown's account pinpoints an important tension in Mill's work on gender, which calls for women's emancipation in social, political, and economic life while also, at times, assuming that such changes need not be "a ticket to gender integration in most of the substantive domains of life."[46] As I argue later in this chapter, these tensions have much to do with Mill's uncertain politics and the particular ways in which it navigates prospective social changes. How Brown understands these tensions, however, is shaped by her contentions with liberalism.

Brown jumps from the observation that Mill's feminism is strained by the kinds of roles he thinks women ought to occupy (particularly if they choose to marry) to the claim that his gender politics "privatizes the sexed female body—leaving it to individual men, as it were—*and* abstracts from women's embodied existence to make claims on behalf of women's capacity for public life." As a result, the liberal subject originating with Mill is "represented as free, equal, and solidaristic" in public discourse while in fact being "abstracted from its concrete existence where it is limited, socially stratified, atomized, and alienated."[47] This divided structure is the basis upon which theorists like Mill claim women's enfranchisement.

But the move from querying Mill's thinking about how women might *actually participate* in private and public life to the claim that he is a theorist of an atomized liberal individualism is textually unconvincing. The analysis would have to suspend the ways in which Mill intentionally upsets private/public boundaries in his critique of marriage. His critique also details the significance of embodied existence for the development of citizenship. As noted earlier in relation to MacKinnon, *The Subjection of Women* is a piercing exposé of the inequities hidden in the "private" realm of the household. It draws out the incompatibility of women's subordination in the family with the public belief that equality, justice, and democratic principles ruled nineteenth-century British society. Moreover, civic character for Mill is premised not on some atomized subject but on the relationships we develop: "Citizenship in free countries is partly a school of society in equality, but citizenship fills only a small place in modern life and does not come near the daily habits or inmost sentiments. The family, justly constituted, would be the real school of the virtues of freedom."[48] Mill here connects the private world of the family to the constitution of equality and liberty in public life. That he can make this case, while remaining (as we shall see) unclear about how far the domestic realm can be democratized and liberated from "sexed" occupations is a complication worth attending to, rather than relinquishing it to a focus on liberalism's subjectivity problem.

By ignoring that complication in Mill, Brown's ploy mirrors MacKinnon's and Mahmood's efforts to situate Mill in a genealogical story about liberalism's meaning. In this story, the dilemmas of liberal citizenship come about because "the methodological individualism of liberal theory produces the figure of an individuated subject by abstracting and isolating deliberative rationality from embodied locations or constitutive practices." And so, Brown can write:

> Across Lockean, Kantian, Millian, Rawlsian, and Habermasian perspectives, rationality transcends—or better, exceeds—embodiment and cultural location to permit a separation between rational thought on one side and the constitutive embodiment of certain beliefs and practices on the other.[49]

That such a range of thinkers, and with starkly different views on gender, can be so easily lined up in smooth succession ought to give readers pause. What is the goal of such a sequence, if not to put a liberal tradition on trial—a trial that must flatten the authors cited, and their texts, in order to achieve ideological clarity.

Whatever one makes of Brown's assertion as far as "liberal theory," it does not quite reach *Mill's politics*. The methodological preoccupation with liberalism that attends Brown's intervention gives short shrift to Mill's study of social relations and contexts for deliberative engagements. Where that preoccupation is dominant, Mill's writings are not as consequential as is his liberal title. Mill, across these cases, has been made and manufactured to suit the contemporary practice of reading through liberalism.

## An Unorthodox Approach: Recovering Mill's Feminist Politics

Whether in sympathetic or critical engagements with liberalism, Mill's name does a lot of work. It is sometimes shocking just how much he can be tasked to do, with how little of his actual arguments are involved. Striking too, is that scholars can be aware of the complexities of Mill's thought, while seemingly unable or unwilling to privilege those complexities above the labor

Mill performs as a liberal icon. And that practice is not a function of any one perspective: whether identified as liberal, radical, postcolonial, or poststructuralist, different political arguments get caught up in the *same interpretive method*. It is not merely a matter of "bad readings," but of the a priori interpretive conditions which attachments to liberalism are imposing on scholarship. This is the liberalism trap in action. In the context of feminist debates about liberal politics, Mill acts as a vessel for carrying forward this or that conclusion about the operation of liberal feminisms or the contradictions therein.

The remaining sections of this chapter set aside this interpretive trap to examine instead how Mill's appreciation for uncertainty becomes his political practice. Allowing Mill's uncertainty back into the reading also provides an explanatory guide for the array of differing interpretations scholars have made of Mill's analyses of gender, as well as of his class and imperial politics. With regard to the inclusion of women into legal and political life, as we have seen, readers have taken very different tacks on Mill's approach. Where some scholars laud elements of his radical feminism, others denounce him for not going far enough. Similarly, while some view his critique of property and class inequality as driven by an interest in freedom and democracy, others point to his proposals for graduated class suffrage and plural voting as inherently contrary to those interests.[50] And even as his willingness to defend the potential of British empire has made him a pillar in studies of the imperialist roots of liberalism, we see scholars attempt to retrieve a more complex understanding of Mill's imperialism and its tensions.[51]

But the varied resources we find in Mill's arguments—for a radical and a conservative feminist analysis or for a critique and defense of despotism—are products of the multiple strategies he employs in addressing political challenges. I suggest that Mill's proposals for women's equality demonstrate the material effects of his politics of uncertainty. His feminist practice is shaped by a radical orientation toward inequality; a gradualist approach to addressing it; and paternalist proposals aimed at guiding, or "readying," the social state for what might follow substantive changes to the organization of gender roles. That Mill employs these strategies is partly why his politics can be taken in the varied directions it has been. His uncertainty drives a prismatic rather than one-dimensional approach. Replacing Mill's canonical role with focus on his critically uncertain politics can give us something more than cannon fodder. It gives us a political actor, to whom I now turn.

## The Masquerade of "Nature"

Mill's political radicalism on the question of sex inequality stemmed from his attack on naturalist or naturalizing arguments about women's subordinate character. We know from his *Autobiography* that his suspicions about the use of "nature" as a basis for political claims developed during his crisis and were strengthened in its aftermath. However, where his work in "Nature," "Bentham," the *Logic*, and even *On Liberty* all offer a more philosophical account of the fallacy of such claims—Mill's work on gender provides an applied study of the consequences of rooting social analyses in arguments about what is, or is not, natural. His critique forces a sweeping examination of the social and institutional relations of power operating beneath the ruse of nature.

At the outset of *Subjection of Women*, Mill rejects the near universal presumption that the existing relation between the sexes is natural, and therefore absolute. His speaks in matter-of-fact terms, denying "that any one knows, or can know, the nature of the two sexes, as long as they have only been seen in their present relation to one another."[52] It is custom that maintains the belief that women's "ideal of character is the very opposite to that of men: not self-will, and government by self-control, but submission, and yielding to the control of others."[53] Under the weight of those customs "it would be a miracle if the object of being attractive to men had not become the polar star of feminine education and formation of character."[54]

The law gives further protection to this "feminine education" in two ways. First, it denies women the suffrage and a means to call for a "just and equal consideration" of their interests.[55] Second, a woman's legal identity is annexed to that of her husband through coverture, for the "purpose of inferring that whatever is hers is his, but the parallel inference is never drawn that whatever is his is hers."[56] So adamant was Mill in this critique that, before his marriage to Harriet Taylor, he fully renounced "all pretension to have acquired any *rights* whatever by virtue of such a marriage."[57] Though this carried no legal weight in England, Mill's intention was to make a public statement of respect and recognition of Taylor's autonomy and of the principles of justice they shared.

To those who might argue that the marriage contract was a voluntary association, Mill reminds them that most women (his mother perhaps coming to mind) "are so brought up, as not to be able to subsist in the mere physical sense, without a man to keep them . . . for all women who are educated for anything except to *get* married, are educated to *be* married."[58] Women, in other words, are bred into a position of abject dependency. The relation between husbands and wives reflects the "the primitive state of slavery lasting on."[59] And its duration even in a time of increasing antipathy toward any mode of government based on the law of force is, to Mill, a disturbingly brilliant example of the power of unexamined customs.[60]

But Mill does see the law of force operating in other contexts, particularly in the case of race. The perversion of political principles wrought by appeals to nature on the issue of race, is outlined in Mill's scathing repudiation of his former friend Thomas Carlyle. In "The Negro Question," Mill argues, "a doctrine more damnable . . . never was propounded by a professed moral reformer . . . that one kind of human beings are born servants to another."[61] Against Carlyle's justification of racial servitude on account of the "natural inferiority of blacks," Mill holds that "what the original differences are among human beings, I know no more than your contributor [Carlyle], and no less."[62] As in the case of women, it is historical circumstances and structural conditions that constructed the racial hierarchies in the colonies, and in the American states.

Drawing the parallel in *Subjection*, Mill notes that proponents of natural hierarchies wish us to believe that the "natural vocation of woman is that of a wife and mother," just as "negroes are born to serve."[63] Yet if it is nature that determines their subjection, the norms and laws regulating these groups are superfluous. In the case of gender equality, he points out, "what is contrary to women's nature to do, they never will be made to do by simply giving their nature free play."[64] The true doctrine behind claims of nature is compulsion: "it is necessary to society that women should marry and produce children. Therefore it is necessary to compel them." And in the case of racial servitude: "It is necessary that cotton and sugar should be grown. White men cannot produce them, Negroes will not, for any wages which we choose to give. *Ergo* they must be compelled."[65] Turning to nature to justify gendered and racial exclusions is a political strategy, which masks a *desire* for something to be so, as if it were a *certainty* that something is so.

Beyond unveiling political motivations behind using nature as a basis for policy, Mill also radically reorients how we ought to perceive human nature by accounting for "the extraordinary susceptibility of human nature to external influences, and the extreme variableness of those of its manifestations which are supposed to be most universal and uniform."[66] Because of its plasticity, human nature cannot be called upon as a fixed prepolitical boundary to determine which persons are fit for what. Claims about natural authority or inferiority, consequently, must first be subject to "conscientious comparison between different modes of constituting the government of society."[67] The subjection of women has, in contrast, been granted on the basis of theory alone, without being put to "deliberation, or forethought, or any social ideas, or any notion whatever of what conduced to the benefit of humanity or the good order of society."[68] Naturalizing claims work a series of illusions: they transform what has become habitual into what must be taken as fact, and they sustain that transformation by avoiding interrogation. In so doing, natural capacity arguments can ignore the conditions under which women's characters are *formed*. But for Mill, too, the customary laws and policies enforcing women's feigned "natural" subjection form not only the characters of the ruled but those of the rulers as well.

## The Shrew, the Sultan, and the School of Virtues

Mill understood that casting off the explanatory power of nature was necessary to direct individuals toward the influence of circumstances (historical, social, political, and economic) on the formation of character. Molded by gender norms and legalized relations of subordination, woman have little recourse in alleviating, much less escaping, the chains of their "education." That education, Mill argues, prunes women into "hot-house plants, shielded from the wholesome vicissitudes of air and temperature, and untrained in any of the occupations and exercises which give stimulus and development . . . ." This description of hothouse characters is presented to readers who would otherwise take cases of so-called hysteria in women to reveal a natural "disqualification for practice, in anything but domestic life," being "unequal and uncertain in the power of using their faculties."[69] But, once having noted the conditioning effects of women's social education, paired with the barriers to their legal and political independence, Mill asks if anything else can be expected but that "those of them who do not die of consumption, grow up with constitutions liable to derangement from slight causes . . . and without stamina to support any task, physical or mental, requiring continuity of effort."[70] Mill's portrait of the hothouse woman situates the perceived weaknesses of the "female character" in women's artificial education and exposes the contingent design of their subjection.

Mill does identify two exceptions to hothouse characters: those rare instances of women who manage to take hold of their own lives and prove themselves accomplished in politics, the arts, literature, etc. Given the overwhelming odds against them, such cases are damning proof of the fallacy of the existing system of subordination. In the other instance, Mill introduces the rather harsh portrait of the "shrew"—a woman who, having no ready course of resistance to marital despotism, retaliates instead: "she, too, can make the man's life extremely uncomfortable . . . But this instrument of self-protection—which may be called the power of the scold, or the shrewish sanction—has the fatal defect, that it avails most against the least tyrannical superiors."[71]

A shrew does no better than to establish "a counter-tyranny" and is thus an ineffective response to the hegemony of husbands. An additional, and I would argue more compelling, argument against the power of the shrew is implied in Mill's distinction between the power of *retaliation* and that of *resistance*. However gentle or susceptible to the demands of a shrewish wife he may be, a husband retains his despotic powers so long as he remains his wife's legal superior. In essence, the shrew can retaliate with the power of the scold, but she cannot truly resist the system of domination that gives her leave to do little but scold. Mill also observes that retaliation is the only avenue available when struggles for emancipation are in their infancy, such that challenges are made not to the relevant power but only to "its oppressive exercise."[72] In this stage, complaints against the despotism of husbands are localized rather than systemic, so that while women do not yet "complain of the general lot of women . . . each complains of her own husband, or of the husbands of her friends."[73]

A collective rebellion against the despotic power of husbands is further inhibited because "the case of women is now the only case in which to rebel against established rules is still looked upon with the same eyes as was formerly a subject's claim to the right of rebelling against his king."[74] Consequently, the practice of sex inequality not only generates weakened or shrewish characters but also establishes a social state in which challenges to the system are proscribed (by law and social sanction) and alternatives pre-empted.

Noting the effects of their subordination upon the characters of women, and the corollary obstacles to the collective rebellion of women against that status, Mill makes an important turn at the end of Chapter 3 of *Subjection*, to suggest that "women cannot be expected to devote themselves to the emancipation of women, until men in considerable number are prepared to join with them in the undertaking."[75] Mill knew that the passing of women's suffrage was dependent upon the support of British men in Parliament and that men would be among his readership. So, lest they think themselves unaffected by women's unequal status, he moves to describe the ways in which the existing relation between the sexes perverts the characters of *men*. From their youth into adulthood, argues Mill, men are every day impacted by having the most "universal and pervading of all human relations regulated" by injustice rather than justice.[76] Think, he asks, what is suggested to young boys when they come to recognize that woman are groomed to be the "bondservants" of men: "to grow up to manhood in the belief that without any merit or any exertion of his own . . . by the mere fact of being born a male he is by right the superior of all and every one of an entire half of the human race."[77] Twisting the point often made about women's natural gentleness and moral goodness, Mill argues that such "idle talk" is good "only as an admission by men, of the corrupting influence of power . . . and it *is* true that servitude, except where it actually brutalizes, though corrupting to both, is less so to the slaves than to the slave-masters."[78] The exercise of arbitrary power will always engender a corruption of moral character. Raised in a manner that breeds such power over women, a man grows up to either be a fool, assuming that no woman can ever be his equal in ability and judgment or worse, he recognizes an equal or superior talent in a woman of his acquaintance and nonetheless feels himself entitled to command and to expect her obedience.[79] How "sublime and sultan-like a sense of superiority" he must then obtain.[80]

If the system of subordination governing the sexes can so pervert the individual characters of adults and children, female and male alike, there must be corresponding repercussions for society. This is a broader target of Mill's argument for women's emancipation, and it highlights why attempts to situate him as a source of an abstracted "liberal subjectivity" are confounding. Being the first "example afforded, and the education given to the sentiments," the inequitable relationship between the sexes must have a "perverting influence of such magnitude."[81] Through the very constitution of the family, the relation of sex inequality is normalized and repeated. And though the practice of democratic citizenship "is partly a school of society in equality," that practice does not infiltrate the daily "habits or inmost sentiments" of persons in the way that familial relations do.[82] No matter how considerate children might be raised to be toward one another, they will inevitably encounter social facts as they really exist.[83] The notions and habits one develops in the family, and which are reinforced in society, will appear as "human nature itself; whatever varies from them is [seen] as an unaccountable aberration."[84]

A family founded upon a relation of inequality cannot school persons in the virtues of justice.[85] This is of paramount concern to Mill because he thinks that the family is the locus for the development of individuality and for the principles of justice that would protect it. In his defense of individuality, Mill insisted that to "give any fair play to the nature of each, it is essential that different persons should be allowed to lead different lives. In proportion as this latitude has been exercised in any age, has that age been noteworthy to posterity."[86] But his analysis of gender indicates that something else entirely occurs through the subjection of women. Rather than the cultivation of multiple and diverse characters, the family is directed toward conforming to gendered hierarchies. From birth onward, women and men alike are prefigured according to the characteristics denoted by the relation of slave to master, bondservant to despot. The dominion of husband over wife at home carries over into society. So long as the "first relation" of society is inequitable, attempts to defend and develop an appreciation for the virtues and qualities of democratic citizenship are frustrated from infancy.

## With All Deliberate Speed

Mill was a radical thinker in his time. Even in our own moment, as MacKinnon notes, Mill's arguments continue to present a dazzling takedown of gendered conventions which persist in different forms today. These are the qualities lauded by some scholars but ignored by others who look to Mill to see only the failings of liberalism on questions of gender. Still, my critique of how focus on liberalism can undermine understandings of Mill's feminism does not preclude his feminism from being duly critiqued. The difference lies in interpretive aims: reading through the lens of liberalism makes Mill incidental to what we need him to do as a liberal icon; reading through the arguments he makes himself, however, can offer critical purchase on the content of Mill's feminism and the tensions it harbors.

Those tensions speak to Mill's uncertainties about the effects that women's liberation from relations of subordination will produce. Even though Mill is, as we have seen, deeply committed to ending what he considers to be the legal and social enslavement of women, he is at the same time concerned with the potential ripple effects of major social change. And so, Mill adds provisos to his radical critique, conditions which do at times limit, and arguably undermine, the claims he otherwise makes about the emancipation of women. Such conditions were in fact a point on which he and Harriet Taylor disagreed. But Mill's political disposition, as much as it directed him toward challenging the inhibiting effects of sex inequality, also compels him to be cautious about how to move forward. To a thinker for whom no judgment is infallible, the responsibilities associated with advocating sweeping change were impossible to ignore. Mill's attempt to face those responsibilities, however, caused him to hesitate and to seek gradualist qualifications of his own radical critiques.

One instance of that gradualist strategy can be found in Mill's authorial decisions. He delayed publication of *Subjection of Women*. Written just shortly after *On Liberty* came out in 1859, his treatise on the sexes was held back till 1869. Mill tells readers the delay was an effort to improve "it from time to time if I was able, and to publish it at the time when it should seem likely to be most useful."[87] He feared too that "Ideas, unless outward circumstances conspire with them, have in general no very rapid or immediate efficacy in human affairs; and the most favourable outward circumstances may pass by, or remain inoperative, for want of ideas suitable to the conjuncture."[88] For Alan Ryan, Mill's caution in cases like this reflects his efforts "to convince those he could, not to outrage everyone."[89] Ryan's observation considers the contextual limitations of radical thinkers and the essential quality of timing. In the years he withheld publication of *Subjection*, Mill was elected to Parliament, observed the passing of the Reform Acts, proposed an amendment extending the vote to women, and became a prominent ally of the women's suffrage movement in England. He wrote to his friend Alexander Bain that the decision to postpone the release of *Subjection* in those years "was the right policy until the women's suffrage question had acquired such a footing in practical politics as to leave little danger of its being thrown back."[90]

But Mill's caution extended beyond questions of publication and audience to shape his political proposals regarding a future in which men's mastery over women was at an end. On the subject of divorce, for instance, he was curiously indeterminate. That is interesting given Mill's personal situation. After all, his involvement with Harriet Taylor prior to their marriage was one of the most infamous affairs of the nineteenth century. Their nearly two-decade relationship during her marriage to John Taylor constituted quite a scandal in Victorian England. And Mill's sullen letters to her during those years clearly show he was not always happy with their unusual arrangement.[91]

Harriet Taylor, notably, was vocally in favor of easing the requirements for divorce. Suppose, she wrote, that parties to the marriage contract were required instead to show proof of affection and where experience showed that proof to be lacking "would not the best plan be divorce which could be attained by any, without any reason assigned, and at small expence?"[92] In contrast, Mill focused on conditions of apparent harm as justifications for divorce. In cases involving the transmission of contagious diseases from husbands to wives, for example, he testified to a Royal Commission that there could be no stronger argument for the "remedy of divorce."[93] Outside of these circumstances, Mill encouraged only careful consideration of the question. In an 1834 review for the *Examiner*, he first rejects the equation of divorce with a license for "personal profligacy." Such arguments only reveal that "marriage as it now exists, is but a guarantee of exclusive property in an instrument of sensual gratification." But Mill does not then advocate for unlimited freedom to divorce, without any reason assigned (as Taylor wished). Instead, he writes:

> We think that divorce should be always pronounced by the Magistrate, in cases defined with more or less strictness according to circumstances, but in which the attempt should be to include all those instances, and no others, in which, after ample trial, the union had obviously and decidedly failed to attain the purposes for which it has been ordained.[94]

He maintained that position. Years later, writer and statesman John Morely recalled asking Mill why *Subjection* did not "speak plainly on the question of the limitations of divorce." To this, Mill replied that it would be imprudent to make such a determination "first without hearing much more fully than we could possibly do at present the ideas held by women in the matter; second, until the experiment of marriage with entire equality between man and wife had been properly tried."[95] Though Mill accepts that freedom to divorce ought to be available, the extent of that freedom, and processes by which it can be attained must be the subject of trial and error. In essence, redesigning social and political relations is time-consuming—both because change is difficult to bring about and because alterations must be tested in a deliberate fashion. The question of divorce would then depend upon the results of such tests over time.

Concerns with timing are a core feature of Mill's uncertain politics. In his earlier essay "On Marriage," Mill argues that women's legal and political enfranchisement is a goal that ought to follow preliminary changes in social education. Because the effect of women's education has rendered them artificially useless for anything but marriage the *"first and indispensable step . . . towards* the enfranchisement of woman, is that she be so educated, as not to be dependent either on her father or her husband for subsistence."[96] After generations of subservience, the move from the hothouse to the briskness of the outdoors could not, Mill might have imagined, be easy. Almost thirty years later, that expressly preparatory argument for emancipation is substituted with references to improved education, training, and exposure to equitable familial relations in *Subjection*. Any corrective to the artificially induced defects of women's characters would still require "access to the experience of the human race; general knowledge—exactly the thing which education can best supply."[97] These measures allow for experimentation with new modes of living, but they may also invite a slower pace of transformation.

Mill's positions will certainly frustrate contemporary readers. His inclination toward gradual shifts seems to run counter to his insistence that existing practices are both unjust and dangerous. Nevertheless, he advises stymying the current of change just a bit. Women's emancipation must be pursued with all deliberate speed—a call that is at once affirmative and imprecise. Indeed, Mill's references to questions of timing, experimentation, and educational readiness have led some readers to argue that it is difficult to follow exactly "what changes Mill thinks *are* appropriate,"[98] and at exactly what pace they ought to be pursued.

## Maintaining the Feminine

The imprecisions we find in Mill's defense of women's equality also give way to reversals with paternalist implications. Where he remains ambiguous on the issue of divorce and what preparatory education might be required for women to exercise their freedom, Mill's concerns about how their liberation could impact broader social practices lead him to narrow the scope of his reforms. Though he demands that experience, rather than a priori expectations, should determine what women are capable of, Mill holds to the notion that women will by and large choose marriage, and: "Like a man when he chooses a profession, so, when a woman marries, it may in general be understood that she makes choice of the management of a household, and the bringing up of a family, as the first call upon her exertions."[99] This statement would seem to reintroduce presumptions about gendered labor that he rejects through most of *Subjection*. To be sure, Mill never suggests that there be any law *requiring* that women marry or seek out motherhood. However, critics hold that even "if marriage became a freely negotiable contract, Mill expected that women would accept that they render domestic service."[100] That women should have the option of entering other occupations is not in question for Mill. On this point he keeps to his argument against limiting women's roles to the household. But he bends that assertion a little to allow that in "an otherwise just state of things, it is not therefore desirable that the wife should contribute by her labor to the income of the family."[101] In practice, men ought to remain the primary economic support for the family even when women's occupations are not legally restricted.[102] That Mill takes this position can be seen as damning to his overall argument. But his apparent concessions to the norm of a male breadwinner reflect a complex negotiation of concerns that is too often overlooked.

In the first place, the care a mother is "disabled from taking of the children and the household" by working outside the home "nobody else takes." Not only does she then absorb a larger share of labor (to the extent that she performs any household duties as well as work outside the home), but with her divided attentions the "the management of the household is likely to be so bad, as even in point of economy to be a great drawback from the value of the wife's earnings."[103] To avoid those dangers, Mill argues that in entering marriage a woman ought to make "the management of a household, and the bringing up of a family as the first call upon her exertions during as many years of her life as may be required for the purpose; and that she renounces, not all other objects and occupations, but all which are not consistent with the requirements of this."[104]

The quantity and quality of household management is not his only concern. Mill's assumptions about the "profession" of wives also operates in tandem with his worries about the labor market. "On Marriage" insists that "It does not follow that a woman should *actually* support herself because she should be capable of doing so . . . It is not desirable to burthen the labour market with a double number of competitors."[105] That concern surely informs Mill's position in *Subjection* as to the household labor married women ought to occupy themselves with "for as many years of her life as may be required." Even though we ought not to ordain that "any kind of persons shall not be physicians or shall not be advocates," we also need to plan for the potential economic fallout of fundamentally altering the supply of workers.[106]

Though it seems that Mill simply assumes women who marry are choosing to be wives and mothers alone, what comes across in his worries about the condition of household management and the market are the unexpected challenges their choosing *otherwise* might bring about—both for women themselves and for society at large. Those worries inadvertently allow for paternalist familial relations to remerge. Because he takes the gendered division of labor as a fair compromise (so long as it is not legally required), he stops short of suggesting that the labor of household management, including childcare, might be *distributed* between husbands and wives. Did he assume that such a distribution would be wholly rejected by his audience—anymore than his arguments against the "natural" division of the sexes? More, as a man who seemed to have little regard for his mother's capacities—who was raised instead under the watchful tutelage of his father and made responsible for the education of his younger siblings—surely, he might have drawn on personal experience to consider that household duties could be organized differently.

Even if not, Mill had available a ready critic of his views in Harriet Taylor. A wife and mother herself, Taylor argued in *Enfranchisement of Women* that "It is neither necessary nor just to make imperative on women that they shall be either mothers or nothing," just as no one "proposes to exclude the male sex from Parliament because a man may be a soldier or sailor in active service, or a merchant whose business requires all his time and energies."[107] She refutes Mill's willingness to concede, de facto, women's occupational possibilities to the politics of childcare. For the same reason, too, Taylor rejects Mill's emphasis on the stability of labor markets: "it is urged, that to give the same freedom of occupation to women as to men, would be an injurious addition to the crowd of competitors." More particularly, she addresses the question of whether an overcrowded labor market might depress earnings. In response she insists "how infinitely preferable is it that part of the income should be of the woman's earning, even if the aggregate sum were but little increased by it, rather than that she should be compelled to stand aside in order that men may be the sole earners, and the sole dispensers of what is earned."[108]

Mill of course did not require that women stand aside—but in framing the subject of their continued labor within the household in terms of desirability, practicality, and even efficacy, he gives the gendered division of labor intellectual as well as political cover. In so doing, Mill's uncertainties about the effects of women's emancipation steals ground from his more radical appeals for a revolution in the relationship between the sexes. As Taylor argues, conceding the norm of masculine breadwinners effectively reopens the door for masculine authority in the household.

Curiously, this is a point Mill seemed to have grasped in 1834, writing that so long as a woman depends upon a man for her subsistence, and a man "depends upon his wife for nothing but sitting at the head of his table, or looking after his servants, the ordinary relation between husband and wife can be no other than that of a helpless dependent towards, at best, an affectionate master, at worst, a cruel tyrant."[109] Though Mill certainly hopes that revolutionizing the way society views and treats women will curtail men's power to abuse, what he recognizes in this passage is that material mastery remains mastery. But when women's emancipation seemed to be gaining ground, in the era *Subjection* was written and published, the potential repercussions of success confronted Mill, and he curbed his radical arguments.

## Beyond Sex

Recentering Mill's politics of uncertainty can inform a more nuanced view of his feminist proposals—inflected, as they are, with tensions and challenges. Mill's politics builds on a tripartite political argument: (1) initiated through challenges to gender inequality, (2) tempered by appeals to time and preparation on matters relating to, for instance, divorce and education, and (3) undercut by reanimating appeals to women's roles *as* women in the case of household management and child rearing. Despite his radical critique of sex inequality across social, economic, and political spheres of life, his radicalism is also held in check by concerns with how *far* to press change when its consequences are not entirely visible. That question elicits his gradualist and paternalist responses alongside the radical critique that initiates his foray into the "woman question."

But is all this a result, as critics of liberal feminism might argue, of Mill's "abstract subjectivity"—his failure to give consequence to the embodied ways in which gender discrimination takes hold beyond strictly legal rules? I think not.

We cannot simply toss aside the fact that Mill makes a sociological rather than strictly legalistic argument about gender inequality and its effects on the characters of individuals and of citizens. But we must assess why, in the face of his own observations, he retreats into the space of customary expectations regarding gender roles when it comes to the marriage contract. And what we find in that assessment is uncertainty. Mill's beliefs about the inequity of women's subordination had still to contend with his worries about the direction and effects of making broad structural correctives to their condition. We find him managing several things at once. Recognized as part of a triad of radical, gradualist, and paternalistic tactics, Mill's reticence on the subject of how to restructure gendered institutions and relations are not simply the result of the inadequacies of liberal theory, they are instead reflections of his politics—a politics governed by the necessary uncertainties that attend the exercise of inquiry and judgment.

Behind his calls for what amounts to a revolution in the way society understands the politics of gender and his interdictions against the structural effects of such a revolution we see uncertainty as a political practice. But the case of women is far from an exception in the context of his broader political engagements. Mill, after all, did not view the question of women's emancipation as a niche issue but one centrally tethered to questions about political equality, liberty, and democratic governance. Indeed, scholars of politics would do well to attend to the subjects of gender in the same way. What Simone de Beauvoir observed over a century later, Mill also assumed in his writings: women are both a class in themselves and a class divided by matters of material and cultural experiences. Those experiences further complicate the arguments he makes for women's equality: the politics of gender are interspersed through Mill's discussions of political economy, representative institutions, and the civic requirements of democracy. A full reading of Mill's feminism, therefore, requires attention to his class politics as well.

# 5

# Earning Democracy

## Class Politics and the Public Trust

> *It wants to have a House of Commons which is not weighted with nominees of the landed class, but with representatives of the other interests. And as to contending for a reform short of that, it is like asking for a bit of an avalanche which has already begun to thunder.*
> — George Elliot, *Middlemarch*

For the protagonist of George Elliot's *Middlemarch*, speaking on the 1832 Reform Act in England, the effects of changes to the social and political organization of society cannot be easily bottled or bound; to expect that they can is to rest on an illusion. The wide and varied effects of fundamental reforms to the social state are something J.S. Mill understood with crisp clarity.[1] One year before the First Reform Act extended limited suffrage to the English middle class, Mill wrote that the demand for a new mode of government was not simply an institutional question, but a revolutionary one: the reforms in the air represented a change "in the human mind, and in the whole constitution of human society."[2] Yet his own reformist sympathies notwithstanding, his politics was always bracing for the avalanche on the horizon. For Mill, no change, however necessary, was without risk.

What scholars have missed in ascertaining or challenging the conceptual boundaries of liberalism through Mill's writings is the uncertainty that underpins his political thought and practice. As Chapter 4 discussed, though *Subjection of Women* pays detailed attention to the social and institutional conditions which maintain the division of the sexes, Mill's radical proposals on gender are inflected with concerns about the wider effects of women's liberation on the labor market and on the management of domestic life. Cautioning against reformist hubris, Mill insists "Before I compliment either a man or a generation upon having got rid of their prejudices,

I require to know what they have substituted in lieu of them."[3] And indeed, Mill's conflicted defense of women's emancipation flows from his critically cautious approach to reform. The gendered caveats he introduces into his proposals reflect an unwillingness to assume that changes to the status quo, in and of themselves, will bring about *only* fruitful transformations of either individual characters or broader social structures.

This chapter extends the previous discussion to consider the interactions between Mill's feminism and his approach to questions of class and economic organization. I show first how receptions of Mill's political economy have been unduly directed by preoccupations with liberalism before turning, in the balance of the chapter, to outline how Mill's radical, gradualist, and paternalist strategies draw his feminist and class politics together in critical ways. As with women, Mill's considerations of class inequity and reform reveal revolutionary interventions with moderated responses—all of which circle around his uncertain politics. The penultimate chapter will argue that the moderated radicalism which shapes his gender and class analyses crosses into Mill's writings on empire as well.

The comparative analysis presented in these chapters is a corrective to the dominant practice of treating Mill's politics on these issues separately, a treatment driven in part by Mill's conscription into various debates about liberalism. Traditionally, Mill's feminism has either been read apart from his writings on class and imperial policy or it has been used to offset arguments about how his liberalism performs (usually badly) in these other areas. In the first instance, the studies of Mill's "liberal feminism" outlined in Chapter 4 provide accounts of Mill's theories of progress, the ideal of improvement, and human development in the context of gender. But rarely if at all do they attend to the ways in which these theories interact with his writings on empire and the "development" of colonized subjects.[4] Similarly, studies of Mill's liberal imperialism have generally given "less attention to his treatment of women and the working classes, of whose rights he was a tireless champion."[5]

In the second instance, Mill's feminism is used to critique how his liberalism operates in other contexts. For example, C.L. Ten's analysis of Mill's class politics laments that Mill did not apply his radical arguments for extending the suffrage to women to other groups of citizens, namely those who were illiterate, who did not pay taxes, and who were recipients of parish relief—groups Mill argued should not yet be enfranchised.[6] In the case of empire, we are told that "Mill, for all his radicalism with regard to domestic politics, placed considerable faith in colonial government as a well-intentioned and legitimate despotism designed for the improvement of subjects."[7] Effectively, the relationship between Mill's work on gender, class, and empire is displaced in considerations of his liberalism, or deployed to establish boundaries between—rather than conversations across—his political engagements.

On the surface, Mill's interventions on questions of gender equality, class politics, and colonial rule might seem to reflect differing, even incompatible, conclusions. How can he offer a cogent critique of the despotic form of dependency that governs the relation between the sexes, while defending a government of colonial dependencies by the British Empire? Why would he advocate the legal and political equality of women, while placing caveats on extending the suffrage to all classes? The ostensible oppositions between Mill's proposals, I shall argue, are far less definitive than commonly thought. On a closer, comparative reading, Mill's concerns about the effects of women's emancipation, class, and imperial politics evince parallel uncertainties, as well as strategies for managing them. There are strong interactive elements to Mill's proposals across these subjects.

On issues of gender and class, it becomes clear that Mill limits his arguments for women's emancipation by way of his proposals regarding class reform and representation. Beyond his remarks on women's household labors, which have occupied feminist critics, lie the legal and institutional barriers to emancipation he establishes for men *and* women in particular classes. Women are subjects not only of gender inequity but also of class identity.[8] Recall his early essay *On Marriage* argued that the "first and indispensable step, therefore, towards the enfranchisement of woman, is that she be so educated, as not to be dependent."[9] Though that preparatory requirement of education to end women's dependency is conspicuously absent in his better-known *Subjection of Women*, it reappears through his class-based qualifications for the suffrage and for full citizenship.

Mill knew that removing sex and class-based distinctions would fundamentally alter the electoral body, drawing in new and diverse political interests and groups. This was the avalanche that had begun to thunder and for which Mill thought to prepare. His response is grounded in his uncertain mode of politics. The radical, gradualist, and paternalist strategies he employs in relation to divorce, or to women's employment inside and outside the home, gain traction and become further institutionalized in his policies regarding class and representative politics—from excluding the poor to advocating plural voting for enlightened citizens. Mill's insightful critiques of gender and class inequality are attended by efforts to slow, if not forestall, the potential risks of class-based representation in Parliament.

This and the remaining chapters show that Mill considered revolutionary acts—the emancipation of women, of classes, or of colonies—to be avalanches in social and political life. What he endeavored to ascertain was how to *navigate* and, wherever possible, to direct the flow of radical change. Mill attuned himself to the uncertainties of even those reforms he most strenuously advocated for, and in so doing introduced measures that flummoxed some of his fellow reformers, and certainly later readers. But we ought to assess these measures in terms of the political practice which generated them—the practice of a thinker who has little faith in political certitudes. If we are fallible enough to construct inequities in social and political life, we are fallible enough to make mistakes in improving upon them. Thus, "A legislator is bound not to think solely of the present effects of his measures; he must consider what influence the acts he does now, may have over those of his successors."[10] All changes to the present must prepare for the future.

## From Ideology to Politics: Receptions of Mill on Class

The same challenges facing efforts to read Mill's feminism ideologically rather than politically flow through receptions of his work on political economy: conflating Mill with liberalism has produced a range of peculiar interpretive compromises and occlusions in the literature. These include underplaying the more radical elements of Mill's critique of class inequality and outright cynicism about his professed socialist sympathies.

In the *Autobiography*, Mill remarks that by the mid-1840s, he and Harriet Taylor placed themselves "under the general designation of Socialists."[11] That remark has been the cause of much consternation among readers of the "liberal" Mill. One line of attack has been to suggest that Taylor made her husband "sound more socialist than he really was, through some sort of domination or sexual manipulation."[12] Such deeply sexist views are misguided to say the least, and they severely underestimate the seriousness of both Mill and Taylor's political engagements with socialist thought.[13] But why go to such extremes to posit Mill as a "socialist cuckold" at all? His canonical status within the liberal tradition gives us a clue. Marked as the "forerunner of contemporary liberal economic policy,"[14] Mill's analyses of class politics are read through debates about liberalism and capitalism. In an especially enlightening review of such receptions, Quentin Taylor notes that the literature has tended to "underscore his liberal credentials" at the expense of what Mill actually has to say about issues of property, class, and economic reform.[15] Against Mill's own claims about his socialist sympathies, efforts to "save Mill from himself" following "disastrous experiments with socialism" in the twentieth century insist that he was, truly, only a "reformed capitalist.'"[16] To maintain his place within the classical liberal pantheon, we are told that Mill simply does not "cross the borderline" between capitalism and socialism, but concludes definitively "in favor of property and competition."[17] Mill's status continues to give weight to arguments supporting capitalism in popular writings today, some even equating his theory of individual liberty with unfettered commerce and competition.[18]

Yet scholars also decry Mill for recognizing the negative effects of capitalist economics, without fundamentally questioning its institutions. Through this lens, he appears as a confused liberal, that somehow "argued for the moral legitimacy of the economic institutions whose results he deplored."[19] Notably, the insistence on Mill's intellectual discontinuities becomes a convenient foundation for building a broader case about the liberal tradition. Thus, J.E. Broadbent argues that Mill's inability to reject capitalism given his recognition of its damaging effects on laboring and poor classes is simply more evidence of the contradictions present in traditional liberal theory, dating back to John Locke.[20]

In these receptions, Mill's work becomes supplemental to the question of his liberal credentials and to what those credentials enable for scholarly appropriations. Reading Mill as *the* liberal has wrongly placed "his strictures against bureaucracy and conformity as being equitable with an attack upon socialism."[21] And concluding that Mill's analysis of capitalism and socialism is a confused product of liberalism mistakes intellectual complexity for ideological incompetence. But these errors are more likely to be made when ideological narratives take priority over examining a thinker's particular political practice. More troubling, too, is the fact that defending Mill's credentials as a market liberal against any socialist claims "forecloses serious attention to just the kind of synthesis between these traditions that Mill himself sought."[22] To Bruce Baum, Mill's "stipulations about who does and who does not merit" access to certain democratic goods—like suffrage—can be read as symptomatic of the inegalitarian features of contemporary liberalism. Baum is also careful to argue that contemporary approaches to inequality fail to entertain the democratic socialist correctives Mill advocated.[23] What we miss in reading Mill's politics through our preoccupations with liberalism are the ways in which *Mill* could negotiate the different views of political economy that some modern readers insist on marking as incompatible. His efforts to both call for radical change *and* to refute the lure of reformist certainties fall out of view. If we are to avoid this cost, we should heed Helen McCabe's warning that "Conscripting Mill for a specific political campaign ... is not the same as understanding Mill or explaining his position."[24]

Ideological receptions of Mill ought to be suspended in favor of Mill's own arguments about the nature of class inequality, the need for reform, and the caution reformists should take in working out alternatives. They should give way to Mill's politics and the insights it still holds out for us. The next section looks first at Mill's radical moments with respect to class and his critical disavowal of arguments regarding the natural infirmities of the working or poor classes, which (like women's natural inferiority) supposed them to be unfit for politics. Just as Mill outlined the social conditions that produce the subjected characters of women (from the hothouse flower to the shrew), he also targets the material inequities that produce deficiencies in the characters of workers and poor classes. Drawing on his public and parliamentary writings, Mill's observations about the inequities of the class system clearly inform his case for revolutionizing the representative system of government in England.

## Radical Parallels: Women and Workers

By the 1860s, Mill concluded that "The most important questions in practical politics are coming to be those in which the working classes as a body are arrayed on one side, and the employers as a body on the other."[25] That tension is one Mill takes seriously in his efforts to think through possibilities for reform. Unfortunately, Mill's attentions to the interests of workers have often been bypassed, in part because his concerns with individual conformity in *On Liberty* have been conflated with "an attack upon socialism."[26] Yet the radical dimensions of Mill's class politics—from his assessment of the enervating effects of material conditions upon the character of the working and poor classes to his propositions for reforming the gulf between workers and employers—not only cleave out space for a democratic socialist politics but also remain active challenges to market conditions in modern societies.[27]

Take, for instance, Mill's rhetorical strategies concerning understandings of individual character. An effective debater, Mill's arguments about reform frequently deploy public opinion about slavery for political effect. In an essay concerning US slavery, Mill remarks that "when it is wished to describe any portion of the human race as in the lowest state of debasement, and under the most cruel oppression... they are compared to slaves," and further that "when words are sought by which to stigmatize the most odious despotism... the despots are said to be like slave-masters or slave-drivers."[28] Writing at a time when justifications for slavery were losing ground in England, Mill noted that using the image of slavery in political argument could shake complacent readers into re-evaluating their presumptions regarding existing relations of power.[29] It is no coincidence that *Subjection of Women* uses the terms "slave" and "slavery" sixty-five times in its descriptions of the existing relations between the sexes. The text deftly reminds its audience that "the disabilities of women are the only case, save one, in which the laws and institutions take persons at their birth, and ordain that they shall never in all their lives be allowed to compete for certain things."[30]

Mill continues this rhetorical strategy in his analysis of class inequality. In his "Chapters on Socialism," for example, Mill points to the oppressive effects of poverty upon the English working classes. Though they are no "longer enslaved or made dependent by force of law, the great majority are so by force of poverty; they are still chained to a place, to an occupation, and to conformity with the will of an employer."[31] But as with women, the condition of their dependency has often been justified on the basis of capacity, and more prominently, as a consequence of nature. In "The Claims of Labor" Mill observes that "the poverty, bordering on destitution, of the great mass of mankind, being an universal fact, was (by one of those natural illusions from which human reason is still so incompletely emancipated) conceived to be inevitable;—a provision of nature and as some said, an ordinance of God."[32]

As we might expect, Mill rejected these determinist explanations for the condition of the laboring and poor classes. Instead, the lower classes are *structurally* "debarred by the accident of birth both from the enjoyments, and from the mental and moral advantages, which others inherit without exertion."[33] Where women are de jure blocked from the privileges and duties of citizenship on the basis of sex, the condition of poverty places de facto limits upon those born into it. Material inequalities ensure not "that those who are born poor do not obtain the great objects of human desire unearned, but that the circumstances of their birth *preclude* their earning them."[34] The rhetorical linking of sex and class inequality to the condition of slavery evokes a sense of discontinuity between English society's ostensible regard for principles of justice and the lived experiences of its women and workers.

The effect of those experiences on the social state was also a key object of his critique. Living under conditions of exclusion and poverty, the classes "which the system of society makes subordinate have little reason to put faith in any of the maxims which the same system of society may have established as principles."[35] For Mill, poverty does not simply limit opportunity, it obviates any claim society might otherwise make on the civic loyalty of subjected classes. Because the material conditions of the lower classes shape their political relation to state and society, what duties and responsibilities could such groups be asked to uphold, when their primary measure of life is rooted in exclusion and chronic suffering? As with women, whose dependent condition could not but result in their becoming little more than domestic playthings, Mill insisted that careful analysis "of the sources of faults of character and errors of conduct amongst the labouring and poor classes would establish far more conclusively the filiations which connects them with a defective organisation of society." No one could be surprised to learn that through "the connection between fortune and conduct," the evils of poverty generate instances of misconduct—crime, vice, folly, and "all the sufferings which follow in their train."[36]

Against the specter of natural capacity arguments justifying the existing social order, Mill maintains that deficiencies in the character of the working and poor classes are the products of unjust social arrangements. And he was not satisfied with the patchwork promise of *noblesse oblige*, for which "the lot of the poor, in all things which affect them collectively, should be regulated *for* them, not *by* them."[37] For Mill, neither the benevolence of a good husband nor that of a well-meaning upper class could render the facts of inequality in representation and opportunity inert—a point made all the more convincing as no examples "can be pointed out in which the higher classes of this or any other country performed a part even distantly resembling the one assigned to them in this theory. It is an idealization, grounded on the conduct and character of here and there an individual."[38]

Likening the moral imperative of class reform to that of ending slavery, Mill argues that a growing awareness of, and sympathy for, the poor in English society "has been awakened, which would soon be as influential in elections as the anti-slavery movement some years ago."[39] It is that awareness he calls the working classes and their allies to capitalize upon. As observable defects in the character and condition of workers "stem from contingent social, historical, and sociological circumstances,"[40] Mill insists that the subjected classes ought to demand "that the *whole field of social institutions* should be re-examined, and every question considered as if it now arose for the first time."[41] Of course, Mill himself engaged in precisely that kind of radical inquiry.

## Entertaining Alternative Systems

Reevaluation of the material circumstances produced by existing social institutions, in Mill's view, necessitated a serious discussion of alternative arrangements. His examinations produced several critical interventions into the current system, which included (1) a passionate but qualified defense of socialist reforms; (2) a turn toward cooperative worker's arrangements to bridge the realities of commercial life with the requirements of democratic practice; and (3) an argument for the representative and educative value of universal suffrage.

Mill's intervention on issues of economic reform entertained a careful consideration of existing and prospective challenges. He fluctuated, for instance, in his assessments "of the desirability of communism" on questions of human liberty and ingenuity, a variance that highlights his "uncertainty as to the efficacy of means."[42] And though his interest in socialism is more evident across his writings, we still find an unwillingness to throw his weight entirely for or against socialist politics.[43] These nuances are widely downplayed in the literature on his economic writings, which pivot around his status as a liberal and which treat "liberalism and socialism" as opposites.[44] However, Mill upsets efforts to imprison him within ideological boundaries. Thus, noting challenges to socialism which take property to be an inviolable "natural right," Mill maintains that "It would be necessary to settle, in the first instance, what this expression means . . . what is called natural right, would be more properly described as a first appearance of right."[45] Contrary to readings that maintain his dedicated commitment to property and competition, Mill recalls of his early encounters with St. Simonian thought that their "criticisms on the common doctrines of liberalism seemed to me full of important truth." They made him aware of the "limited and temporary value of the old political economy, which assumes private property and inheritance as indefeasible facts."[46] And Mill would insist that any honest examination of existing social institutions must account for the fact that the "idea of property is not some one thing, identical throughout history, but is variable like all other creatures of the human mind" and subject to interpretation.[47]

To contemporaries who claimed that the socialist argument failed prima facie to afford the freedoms enjoyed under the present system of private property, Mill retorts that under existing economic arrangements, "The generality of labourers in this and most other countries, have as little choice of occupation or freedom of locomotion, are practically as dependent on fixed rules and on the will of others, as they could be on any system short of actual slavery;" socialists, in contrast, "are the last who can be accused of undervaluing the right of those who work, as against those who take without working. Their quarrel with existing arrangements is precisely because that right is not, as they contend, respected sufficiently."[48]

Essentially, critics have failed to consider the shortcomings of the system they purport to defend against socialism—a consequence of hubris and custom: "However irrefutable the arguments in favor of the laws of property may appear to those to whom they have the double prestige of immemorial custom and of personal interest, nothing is more natural than that a working man who has begun to speculate on politics, should regard them in a very different light."[49] A proper consideration of the issue requires attention to existing circumstances as well as reflection upon their contingent (rather than natural) quality. Indeed, together with private property, Mill argues that the classification "laboring class" ought to be altogether interrogated as a designation specific to a particular set of social conditions. In the present state of things, it results from one part of society toiling for their survival, while another is exempt by the privileges of birth and circumstance from doing the same. But justice demands society move in a direction "when it should no longer either be, or be thought to be, impossible for human beings to exert themselves strenuously for benefits which were not to be exclusively their own, but to be shared with the society they belong to."[50]

Importantly too, socialists had the advantage of considering "the entire domestic subjection of one half the species," to argue that no system which does not include women as full citizens, is properly free. For Mill, "it is the signal honour of Owenism and most other forms of Socialism that they assign equal rights, in all respects, with those of the hitherto dominant sex."[51] Attending to these details, Mill held that it was simply not "acceptable to denounce the restriction on freedom under socialism while accepting the restrictions on freedom of the existing society."[52] All these observations make evident that efforts to pigeonhole Mill as a representative of "contemporary liberal economic policy,"[53] who never seriously entertained socialist ideas, are out of step with the arguments he actually offered.

## Competition and Cooperation

But Mill's socialist sympathies are not without caveats. His uncertainty ever operative, Mill tempers his support for socialist proposals about private property and distributive interests with his own concerns about the role of competition in any plans for reform. On this point, he moves to question the assumptions made by socialist critics, which assume that competition in its *existing* state negates its utility in principle: "while I agree and sympathize with Socialists in this practical portion of their aims, I utterly dissent from the most conspicuous and vehement part of their teaching, their declamations against competition." Mill argued that socialists erred by charging "upon competition all the economical evils which at present exist."[54] Instead—as with property—the principle of competition must be examined not as one thing but as a variable of history, subject to re-examination: "competition may not be the best conceivable stimulus, but it is at present a necessary one, and no one can foresee the time when it will not be indispensable to progress."[55] Under the current system, "there has been no alternative for those who lived by their labour, but that of labouring either each for himself alone, or for a master."[56] Competition under *these* conditions was untenable, driving wages down while doing little to improve either independence or ingenuity in production. And such circumstances are sure to lead the working classes to "think the interests of their employers not identical with their own, but opposite to them."[57]

Mill would later note that both he and Harriet Taylor came to consider the "social problem of the future ... to be, how to unite the greatest individual liberty of action with an equal ownership of all in the raw material of the globe and an equal participation of all in the benefits of combined labour."[58] But obtaining that union meant first addressing the fact that "the most serious danger to the future prospects of mankind is in the unbalanced influence of the commercial spirit."[59] The commercial spirit of capitalism is in tension with the collective spirit of democracy—a tension he took Tocqueville to task for mischaracterizing. One of the few criticisms Mill offers of *Democracy in America* is that it "bound up in one abstract idea the whole of the tendencies of modern commercial society, and given them one name—Democracy."[60]

Mediating between both his investments in, and criticisms of, socialist arguments, Mill turned to the possibilities of worker cooperatives as a way of addressing distributive inequality, without removing the utility of competition for liberty and creative endeavors. By the 1840s, he began to see "cooperative partnership as an ideal towards which society both might be tending and ought to aim."[61] There could be a balance between the individualizing interests of the commercial spirit and the collective aims of democracy in cooperative associations. They combined "the freedom and independence of the individual, with the moral, intellectual, and economical advantages of aggregate production; and which, without violence or spoilation . . . would realize, at least in the industrial department, the best aspirations of the democratic spirit." Cooperatives could end the custom of obtaining social distinctions by anything other than "personal services and exertions."[62] Such ventures solicited the collective buy-in of workers and managers precisely because they brought together interests that had so far been separated. In this way, cooperatives are "the economic means by which the majority could begin to share in the vision of the individual development and richly varied self-forming character" that guided Mill's hope for the improvement of mankind.[63] Cooperatives might direct the spirit of individual competition *toward* the interests of democracy.

Mill's economic analysis begins here to reflect a deeply educative aim. In Chris Barker's reading, Mill understood that cooperatives could enhance "the education of working men and women and the reformation of the characters and habits of the owners, managers, and privileged classes who rely on unearned wealth."[64] For all parties, the relational effects of cooperatives could arm democracies against the "unbalanced influence of the commercial spirit" by developing a kind of public spiritedness in and through economic relations.[65] Much like the family functioned as the first school of virtues within which citizens are raised, Mill looked at the practices of collective discussion and management granted in cooperative associations as another "great school of that public spirit, and the great source of that intelligence of public affairs, which are always regarded as the distinctive character of the public of free countries."[66]

All told, Mill's evaluations of socialism, its critics, and the relationship between competition and cooperation are at once radical and cautious. They operate with the aims of equity and justice in mind, while remaining characteristically attuned to the different sides of debates over reform. What becomes clear, however, is that his analyses of class politics and strategies for correcting the ills of economic inequality do not conform easily to ideological labels; they rather demonstrate a practice of negotiated reasoning in view of existing circumstances and hopes for bettering them. Mill can declare himself to be a socialist without abandoning his critical perspective on policies and arguments concerning, for instance, the utility of competition. And he can think more carefully about the measures that might mitigate the challenges of commercial society through collaborative economic relationships.

But even with their distributive and educative value, Mill knew that neither socialist critiques of private property in its current forms nor cooperative ventures involving workers and employers would be enough to fully restructure the condition of the working class or the nature of class relations more broadly. Such transformations required an additional measure of reform: direct political participation. As the poor "have come out of their leading-strings, and cannot any longer be governed or treated like children. To their own qualities must now be commended the care of their destiny."[67] But how are their capacities for self-determination to be developed? For Mill, beyond material improvements to everyday life, the subjected classes must have the ennobling benefits of citizenship.

## The Reform Acts and the Case for Suffrage

Considerations of the lowering impact of inequity on the working classes drove Mill to advocate for fundamental reforms to parliamentary representation in England—most notably in terms of extending the suffrage. Though Mill supported the first reform movement in the 1830s, his defense of the bill (finally passed in 1832 after two failed attempts) was decidedly lackluster, in part because he feared truly progressive change to parliamentary representation would be muted in the effort to get something passed. Writing for the *Examiner* in 1831, Mill noted that "No one has the least expectation that the Bill will pass, unless mutilated and made almost worthless."[68]

But he was consistent in his arguments in favor of delivering a more representative parliament to the people. The "subjection of any one individual or class to another, is always and necessarily disastrous in its effects on both," a condition requiring the remedy of "giving to everyone a vote."[69] If the bill were won, he wrote, "we shall gain all; and every nerve ought to be strained by every Reformer throughout the nation, for the success of the ministerial measure" and the "consternation which it has spread among the whole tribe of the people's enemies."[70]

Mill's defense persisted during his career as a Member of Parliament, which coincided with the debates over, and eventual passage of, the Second Reform Act in 1867. In a series of speeches delivered to the House of Commons the year prior, Mill gave his fellow parliamentarians lengthy lessons on the benefits of extending representation to the working classes. "Reflecting men" he insisted "are glad to associate themselves with others of different habits and positions which very fact peculiarly qualifies them to see the precise things which they themselves do not see."[71] Drawing on his characteristic interest in taking a many-sided view of things, Mill reminds his audience that good policy ought to take into consideration varied experiences and opinions: "Is there, I wonder, a single member of this House who thoroughly knows the working men's views of trade unions, or of strikes, and could bring these subjects before the House in a manner satisfactory to working men?"[72] Operating on the principle of imperfect information, Mill argues that "Every class knows some things not so well known to other people, and every class has interest more or less special to itself and for which no protection is so effectual as its own . . . I claim the benefit of these principles for the working classes."[73] A crafty public speaker, he presented the act as a reflection of both liberal and conservative principles. The conservative view of the constitution tells us that individuals "cannot complain of not being represented, so long as the class they belong to is represented." The Reform Act therefore merely applied the theory to practical matters, claiming "a large and liberal representation of the working classes, on the Conservative theory of the constitution."[74]

Using the same logic, Mill laid out a proposal to include women in the suffrage in 1866, with a petition brought by Emily Davies and Elizabeth Garrett.[75] During debates over the "woman question" the following year, Mill would introduce an amendment to the Second Reform Act, replacing the word "man" with "person." In an extraordinary speech, he distilled nearly the entirety of *Subjection of Women* to make the case that women, with workers, ought to be afforded the right of representation through the vote. Against insistence that women were adequately represented by their fathers, husbands, or male guardians, Mill pointed out that "this is exactly what is said of all unrepresented classes," yet he noted, "we do not live in Arcadia, but, as we were lately reminded, *in faece Romuli*: and in that region workmen need other protection than that of their employers, and women other protection than that of their men."[76] Though the amendment was defeated, 194 to 73, Mill later described his efforts to extend the suffrage to women as "perhaps the only really important public service I performed in the capacity of a Member of Parliament."[77]

Along with his discussion of economic cooperatives, Mill's defense of the Reform Act and the inclusion of women in its provisions for suffrage frequently touted the enriching effects of participation itself. Drawing women into the franchise would make their influence over husbands "a responsible power . . . I want her to feel that it is not given to her as a mere means of personal ascendency. I want to make her influence work by a manly interchange of opinion, and not by cajolery. I want to awaken in her the political point of honour."[78] Similarly, speaking of the laborer in *Considerations on Representative Government*, he argued:

> It is by political discussion that the manual labourer . . . is taught that remote causes, and events which take place far off, have a most sensible effect even on his personal interests; and it is from political discussion, and collective political action, that one whose daily occupations concentrate his interests in a small circle round himself, learns to feel for and with his fellow-citizens, and becomes consciously a member of a great community.[79]

In contrast, Mill argues that whomever is denied the vote and left with no prospect of obtaining it is denied a path to developing public feeling: "What he will know or care about them from this position, may partly be measured by what an average woman of the middle class knows and cares about politics, compared with her husband or brothers."[80] More bluntly, whoever is excluded from political business is not properly a citizen, as it is the very *practice* of citizenship that "elevates the mind to large interests and contemplations; the first step out of the narrow bounds of individual and family selfishness, the first opening in the contracted round of daily occupations."[81] Out of the hothouse of the household or the drudgery of the factory, women and workers could be drawn to the public interest only through their participation in political life.

Evidently, Mill's interventions into questions of class reform in England took a wide view of the social effects of class inequality, as well as of the measures that might be taken to correct them. Attaching the character of marginalized classes to the material conditions of English society thoroughly inverted standing defenses of the status quo, which purported to justify existing social relations as a provision of nature. Taking that approach gave

Mill's negotiated defense of socialist arguments and his support for extending the suffrage firm footing.

If what was required to address the present state of inequality was a fundamental rethinking of social institutions, then by necessity we ought to seek out reforms which would elevate the marginalized to the rights of citizenship. In bringing their voices more fully into the public realm, society could better consider the different habits and positions of those whose exclusions have been wrought by the existing state of things; by the same token, the elevating effects of democratic practice would attract those excluded classes into the work of collective political action, thereby advancing the improvement of mankind. These arguments show Mill at his radical best.

## Managing the Avalanche: Mill's Class Anxieties

Given Mill's cutting analysis of material inequality, and his progressive remedies for reform, some scholars have suggested that his class analysis, like his feminism, mark a radicalism in his domestic politics quite distinct from his approach to the colonies.[82] But this view holds only insofar as we fail to account for the uncertainty Mill carries into his political reasoning on class reform. Concerned especially with the threat of class-based legislation, which would reduce the vote to a matter of self-interest instead of, as Mill saw it, an exercise of public duty, Mill was unwilling to assume that even the electoral reforms he supported would by themselves trigger improvements in the characters of persons or the social structures shaped by existing inequities. Inclusion into participatory politics, though important, might not by itself guarantee either the competence or the public mindedness necessary for exercising the franchise *responsibly*. Thus, despite his critiques of existing class relations, his call for economic cooperatives, and his push for extending the suffrage, Mill's politics of uncertainty lead him to make gradualist and paternalist provisos for class-based electoral reform.

Those provisos include advocating for a graduated entry to suffrage, open ballots, and additional or plural votes for learned citizens. Each measure introduces a surprising note of educative elitism into Mill's otherwise egalitarian calls for electoral reforms. Mill ostensibly intends these caveats to slow the negative effects of self-interest and class legislation. They will, he insists, remind voters of their responsibility to act in accordance with the public trust, apart from their private interests as members of a particular class.

Focused on the "improvement of mankind" as he is, Mill tweaks institutional reforms, not to block the avalanche of change universal suffrage will trigger, but to manage and direct its effects.

With the Reform Bill in mind, Mill observes that the vices and weaknesses of men will not simply disappear "until mankind shall have attained a degree of civilization, to which parliamentary reform may remove some of the obstacles, but which of itself it gives not, nor ever can give."[83] Mill remains, as ever, cautious. However necessary social and institutional changes are, the pace, extent, and consequences of reform may not be readily visible. That caution leads to two gradualist provisos aimed at managing the extension of the suffrage: (1) a standard of education should temporarily bar certain groups from it; and (2) that ballots should be open to public scrutiny.

On the first point, though Mill maintained that no plan of permanent exclusion from the suffrage was legitimate, temporary exclusions could be reasonably applied without conflicting with the principle of participation he so elegantly defends in his critiques of gender and class inequality. And interestingly, he uses the same educative criteria that he applies *to justify the suffrage* (and its salutary effects on the mind) to then *circumnavigate* its full and immediate extension to all. Any persons who relied on parish relief and who could not "read, write, and, I will add, perform the common operations of arithmetic" ought to be kept from the ballot box.[84] These qualifications held that a minimal degree of competence ought to be required for the suffrage. To be sure, Mill also held that it was the duty of society to make these elementary abilities accessible to all through a basic, public education. The state, he argued, has the right to "insist on all children who are born into the community receiving education up to a certain point, and also to give facilities for educating them still higher."[85] By such efforts a higher standard of public ability might be attained. In *Considerations* he argues that where that duty was *neglected*, the "hardship [of exclusion] ought to be borne." As the more fundamental of the two, "universal teaching must precede universal enfranchisement." And those who contribute nothing in the way of taxes should not be allowed to vote for general or local assemblies: these groups, by "disposing by their votes of other people's money, have every motive to be lavish, and not to economize."[86] Inverting the expression of the American colonists, Mill called for no representation without taxation.

Despite the elevating effects of participation Mill promises in his arguments for cooperatives and for the vote, he is wary of how long these effects will take to materialize. We see here a direct application of the preparatory requirement for freedom which Mill implies in his essay "On Marriage" almost thirty years earlier: the "first and indispensable step, therefore, towards the enfranchisement of woman, is that she be so educated, as not to be dependent."[87] Read against his educative mandate for the suffrage, the gendered and classed implications of this indispensable step are on display. Women with limited education, particularly those counted among the workers and poor, are effectively excluded from the argument for women's suffrage he defends in Parliament and in *Subjection*. For this reason, C.L. Ten's lament that Mill does not apply his radical arguments for women's suffrage in the cases of the illiterate poor neglects the fact that Mill understands that there are women in that demographic. Mill assumed that women's suffrage would be *regulated by their class*.[88] And indeed, the preparatory reasoning that ties Mill's thoughts on the political inclusion of women and workers together extends through his anxieties about the broader effects of reforms on the efficacy of representative government. This becomes especially clear in his arguments against the secret ballot, where the educative standard he applies to voting is joined by his emphasis on public accountability. Political inclusion is vital for Mill; but in all cases it must be directed to the public trust.

## Shifting Priorities: From Protection to Accountability and the Secret Ballot

Mill understood political inclusion not solely in terms of *presence* in the political process, but in terms of *service* to a broader democratic good. Nadia Urbinati argues that Mill's caveats for voting do not reflect a "mistrust of democracy," but are calculated to hold the practice of democracy up to its promise.[89] Baum similarly argues that assertions as to Mill's "weak democratic egalitarian credentials" are mistaken when viewed against his "calls for universal education, and the larger democratic socialist arc of his thought."[90] Consequently, though one might disagree with his proposals, Mill's remarks on democratizing education and economic ventures *combined* with his arguments for graduated suffrage and the secret ballot reflect his efforts to evaluate how best to turn social and political life toward democratic ends.

Those efforts also speak to Mill's political rather than ideological mode of reasoning, reflecting his considered judgments of existing circumstances and his eye toward their amendment. In his early years as a Philosophic Radical, for example, Mill was a vocal supporter of the secret ballot, influenced in large part by the arguments of his father James Mill. Like the father, the son viewed the ballot as a hammer that could break the sinister power of landed interests.[91] In "Use and Abuse of the Ballot" (1830), Mill argued that the primary aim of the secret ballot was to "withdraw the voter from the influence of hopes and fears held out by other persons, and leave him free to act according to those interests and inclinations which are independent of the will of other people."[92] Kept out of the sight of those upon whom one might be dependent, a secret vote could be an honest one.[93] Writing to Tocqueville in 1837, he expressed the hope that when the ballot issue became a cabinet measure, "reform will have finally triumphed: the aristocratic principle will be completely annihilated, & we shall enter into a new era of government."[94]

In his initial defense of it, the secret ballot constituted an important protection for voters from landed elites and corrupt influences and thus a mechanism by which those influences might be wrenched out of government. But Mill's position changed a few years later to assert the potentially dangerous effects of the secret ballot.[95] What explains this about-face? In essence, it stemmed from Mill's response to the reforms that had taken place in the intervening years and to the changing power of constituencies in the political arena. Notably, even his defense of the ballot in the 1830s left open room for revision based on practical affairs. Citing his father, Mill accepted that there "are occasions on which the use of the ballot is advantageous; there are occasions on which it is hurtful."[96] By the 1840s, Mill's saw reason to focus on those latter instances.

Writing on parliamentary reform in 1859, he argues that it was once the coercion of landlords, employers, and customers that had to be checked with the ballot. But those influences were no longer the only, nor even the most pernicious, to be found among the electorate: A "base and mischievous vote is now, I am convinced, much oftener given from the voter's personal interest, or class interest, or some mean feeling in his own mind, than from any fear of consequences at the hands of others."[97] The necessary reforms Mill defended concerning suffrage and the representation of laboring classes generated new challenges. Namely, a new set of interests had entered the fray: that of the middle classes and of workers.

Looking at England, Mill became concerned with how to manage the growing tensions between the middle-class and working-class interests that had come to operate in public affairs. On one hand, the "men of thews and sinews" are not likely to have confidence in a party seen to represent the new "shopocracy" he argued; on the other, the press for universal suffrage by workers was likely to be read as little more than a Chartist threat to middle-class interests.[98] The effects of these class tensions on the quality of suffrage had to be addressed, as the "events of that quarter of a century have not only taught each class to know its own collective strength, but have put the individuals of a lower class in a condition to show a much bolder front to those of a higher."[99] No longer passive instruments of the old order, a growing middle class, with their awakened interests, were at risk of becoming a new oligarchy. In such conditions, Mill worried, "the interpretation likely to be put on it in the mind of an elector—is that the suffrage is given to him for himself; for his particular use and benefit."[100] In that context, the secret ballot could become a weapon of class interest for men of thews and sinews and of the shopocracy.

But Mill advises judicious statesmen to take account, first, of the rising middle class whose numbers "can give him a majority in parliament."[101] It is these emergent interests the reformer must address first if the dream of universal suffrage is to be achieved and achieved sensibly. "Let Universal Suffrage be ever so desirable, let it even be ever so practicable when the minds of the other classes have been for some time gradually prepared for it by intermediate measures."[102] Mill's point here is not that the middle class ought to dominate the reform agenda, but rather that the task of the reformer was to "carry them with him in all he does," and in doing so, to shape their view of the working class. Those classes, he noted, "are now the Parias of society" thus, the "motto of a Radical politician should be, Government by means of the middle for the working classes."[103]

That Mill turns in this direction is striking, given his insistence that any theory of a higher class acting *for* a lower is an "idealization, grounded on the conduct and character of here and there an individual."[104] Faced with the practical challenges he identified with the ballot, however, Mill was willing to compromise on the exact path to (if not the ultimate aim of) universal suffrage. And he did insist on some further mitigations to keep a middle-class government alert to working-class interests. Suffrage, he argued, should be extended to a sufficient number of "respectable working men" to "keep the middle classes in that salutary awe, without which, no doubt, those classes would be just like any other oligarchy."[105]

Governing through the middle class and inviting the mediating influence of respectable working men, with the added support of an open ballot, would focus public scrutiny on the interests *motivating* electoral decisions. In Mill's view, "To be under the eyes of others—to have to defend oneself to others—is never more important than to those who act in opposition to the opinion of others, for it obliges them to have sure ground of their own."[106] Mill's reliance on the power of public opinion as concerns the ballot might sound an odd note to those familiar with *On Liberty*'s careful deconstruction of the dangers mass opinion poses to individuality and free thought. But a closer reading suggests that Mill saw the ballot in a different light than he did the free expression of original thinkers and nonconformist characters. Drawing upon women as an example, Mill asks why all men should obtain the suffrage and be tasked with voting on issues respecting women, when their wives and daughters are not informed of the positions they take? These men are under an "absolute moral obligation to consider the interest of the public . . . the duty of voting, like any other public duty, should be performed under the eye and criticism of the public."[107] The ballot was not an exercise of individual expression but an execution of a public duty, and because "Mill's citizens are never alone . . . he uses this voting procedure to foster responsibility or responsible participation, rather than mere participation."[108] An open ballot could help illustrate the social impact of the vote, while making the voter accountable for it.

Of Mill's transforming views on the ballot question, Bruce Kinzer finds that he never held to "an abstract doctrinaire commitment to the principle of secret voting . . . Political developments both inside and outside parliament had in 1839 persuaded him that the ballot, as an issue, had lost much of its usefulness."[109] In other words, politics, and not ideological doctrine, drove Mill's shifting priorities. The changes brought about by electoral reform and the increased role of the middle and working classes in politics necessitated that some provisional measures be taken to ease these groups into the activity of citizenship. Read in this light, his gradualist proposals for educational standards and an open ballot speak to Mill's concern with the practical steps needed to obtain—in the long run—an effective representative system in which all could participate and from which all could benefit.

Mill's confidence in the utility of educative barriers to voting, and of open ballots, can certainly be challenged. In the first place, he assumes that voters who require public assistance, or fall below an arbitrary literacy standard, cannot therefore exercise a rational vote. But as *Subjection* points out, there is no prima facie reason to support their exclusion from participation on these grounds; in fact, Mill repeatedly tells us that the benefit of drawing the disenfranchised into these political activities can spark the very capacities he thinks necessary for effective civic engagement. That Mill considered the educative standard to be a temporary block to suffrage might offer a defense of his position. If it was meant to gradually ease the transition to full suffrage through proper "training," Mill's condition reveals a cautionary approach embedded *within* his radical vision of social and political equity. It is less clear that he intended the open ballot to be a temporary measure, however.

> The universal observation of mankind has been very fallacious, if the mere fact of being one of the community, and not being in a position of pronounced contrariety of interest to the public at large, is enough to ensure the performance of a public duty, without either the stimulus or the restraint derived from the opinion of our fellow-creatures.[110]

Though universal education might be achieved, there remains no guarantee that that anyone will perform their vote as a matter of public responsibility if cloaked in secrecy. But in order to maintain this view, evidence that the secret ballot's protections against intimidation and corruption were no longer needed ought to be ironclad—and it certainly was not in Mill's time. Writing in support of his election to Parliament, a *New York Times* editorial opined that, on the ballot question, Mill's "theory proceeds upon optimist principles far ahead of his time."[111] Contemporary concerns with the exclusionary effects of restrictive voter registration requirements, and with instances of voter intimidation even in established democracies, speak to ongoing electoral challenges to the principle of political equality.

## Shaping Citizens: Our Learned Guides and the Plural Vote

The problems with Mill's educative and ballot qualifications may appear muted against his third, and arguably more controversial, stricture on extending the suffrage: a system of plural voting. That system should "prevent the labouring class from becoming preponderant in Parliament," by awarding some persons two or more votes on the basis of education and occupation.[112] Mill hoped that giving more votes to those better educated and employed in professional occupations would help to mitigate the threat of class-based legislation. Adding influence to educated voices could secure a "balance preserved among personal interests, as may render any one of them dependent for its successes, on carrying with it at least a large proportion of those who act on higher motives, and more comprehensive and distant views."[113] Substantial enough to weigh against the threat of class legislation, but modest enough not to dictate the result by itself, the plurality vote could "stamp the opinions of persons of a more educated class" onto the public forum.[114]

Turning to France for justification, Mill argues that in the French custom of talking rhetorically about the rights of man, they have neglected "to say anything about the duties. The same error is now in the course of being repeated with respect to the rights of poverty."[115] In the case of the working and poor classes, Mill is primarily concerned that their circumstances have not tended toward building a sense of civic responsibility—particularly because the existing system has not given them much cause to develop one.[116] He remains uncertain that redistributive policies and institutional representation will be enough to alter the states and minds of these groups. Education, as he says, is "not the principal, but the sole remedy" such that "Whatever acts upon the minds of the labouring classes, is properly their education. But their minds, like those of other people, are acted upon by the whole of their social circumstance," which ought to be continually accounted for.[117]

Unlike his gradualist justifications for the educative standard for suffrage and open voting to enhance the efficacy of each vote/voter, Mill's interest in plural voting points to a more distinctly paternalist strategy. That he wanted the additional check of an educated elite—on top of his proposals for graduated suffrage and open ballots—highlights the extent of his uncertainty about the capacities of the average voter. Enhancing educated voices through plural votes, in light of those uncertainties, allows broad-thinking persons (presumably, like Mill himself) to stimulate deliberation between groups who might otherwise simply struggle to retain or recover power over each other. Of course, Mill sees the plurality system as a boon *to* the interests of the laboring and uneducated members of society. John Rawls explains Mill's justification of the measure in terms of the organization of a ship: "The passengers of a ship are willing to let the captain steer the course, since they believe he is more knowledgeable and wishes to arrive safely as much as they do." For Mill, "the ship of state" is somewhat "analogous to a ship at sea."[118] In Rawls's reading, the plurality system rests on the logic of shared interest. If all parties are properly invested in public ends that are to the benefit of all— those whose votes are weighted less ought to recognize the utility of having enlightened citizens navigate the joint enterprise. By directing the electorate toward the educative benefits of participation and away from the dangers of class legislation, the virtue of competence embedded in a plural voting system would justify the arrangement.[119]

The salutary effects Mill expected of this plural system ought to be weighed against their gendered implications, however. In an excellent analysis of how Mill's moral psychology operates at the intersection of his feminist and class politics, Linda Zerilli sees in Mill's proposals for class suffrage a deep-seated middle-class bias, which leads to "troubling, even illogical" calls for exclusion.[120] Zerilli's critique of his appeals to Victorian morality is convincing and draws in the possibilities of working without a liberal reading in view—a reading she herself notes may have misdirected scholars from the psychological complexities of Mill's work on sex-class. Instead, Zerilli's analysis looks closely at the kinds of moral anxieties Mill experienced in response to the "larger social forces of capitalism" and their impact upon the formation of the will.[121] Those anxieties douse Mill's ardent defense of women's political rights when they intersect with their class status. After all, Mill's graduated and paternalist proposals for the vote would have effectively denied the women "most in need of political rights" the protection he himself argued they required in *Subjection*.[122] But alongside Mill's powerful rendering of the ways in which the forces of dependency and poverty undermine individual character, his apprehension about how deeply rooted those forces might be inform his hesitancies about drawing the laboring and poor classes (and the women among them) into the fold of representative government.

Mill's position on the plural vote stands in curious contrast to his critique of other expert-driven theories of representation as well. His rejection of Comte, for instance, centers on the latter's investment in rule by an intellectual elite; the Comtian turn toward expertocracy, Mill insisted, "stands as a monumental warning to thinkers on society and politics, of what happens when once men lose sight ... of the value of Liberty and Individuality."[123] Of this, Barker notes that Mill simply "refuses to pay for enlightenment with the coin of individual agency."[124] Yet, on the subject of the suffrage—Mill was clearly happy to insure legislative enlightenment through limits to electoral equality.

Did he intend this measure to be temporary—a transitional mechanism in the move to perfect equality of suffrage? Here there is some scholarly disagreement. Many seem to think so, grouping Mill's interest in plural voting with his educative standard for voting.[125] But others have suggested that Mill's plans for plural voting were in fact intended to be a permanent feature of representative government. Mill, in this view, would not have assumed that once obtained, an educated society would be self-sustaining; rather "for each new generation, Mill would expect that the contribution that plural voting makes to this process [of education] would retain its value indefinitely."[126] Given Mill's insistence on the utility of the open ballot even where contrariety of interest was minor, the notion that he would prefer an ongoing plural system to advance the better argument in legislative debates has merit.[127] And it is the case that Mill never specifies how or when a society might be ready to transition from a system which, for all intents and purposes, privileges a designated "intellectual class" over the egalitarianism of one person, one vote.

## Democracy and the Challenges of Identity

Taken together, Mill's anxieties about the "base and mischievous vote" raised by the electoral changes of the previous thirty years reflect, first, his insistence that legislators keep an eye on the effects of reform for the good of the public interest. Second and relatedly, they speak to Mill's understanding of democratic citizenship as not merely a legal status but as a call to act as a representative of the public trust.

That trust could be easily undermined by an uneducated public. More dangerously, as his arguments concerning the ballot and plural voting indicate, it could be broken when and where the right to vote was understood to be a matter of individual or class interest rather than of public duty. This is a concern that Mill emphasizes across his considerations of radical reform. On the effects of the revolution in France, for example, Mill argued that while it brought about rapid conditions of equalization, "No institutions capable of fostering an interest in the details of public affairs were created by the Revolution."[128] Similarly, he warns that if calls for reforms in England induce the rich to repair the conditions of poverty, while allowing the poor to think that "they need not attend to the lesson . . . we may succeed in bursting society asunder by a Socialist revolution; but the poor, and their poverty, we shall leave worse than we found them."[129] Without mechanisms to safeguard public spiritedness, democratically oriented reforms would have little chance of flourishing. Though Mill's reticence about the dangers of class-based legislation rightly lead many to critique his overconfidence in systems like plural voting, not to mention his calls for education-based requirements for suffrage, it is important to relate these proposals to his comparatively radical assessments of class politics and its effects on the characters of individuals and groups.

That comparison suggests that Mill carries both a radical orientation to reform and a moderating approach to achieving it. From his observations of the material conditions of laborers and his defense of the suffrage as a mechanism not solely of inclusion but of improving the representative efficacy of the governing system as a whole, Mill did take a sweeping view of the sources, character, and impacts of inequality on the social state. But that sweeping view is marked by caution; progress and its risks are always at play in Mill's social and political assessments. These are the conditions and consequences of Mill's politics of uncertainty.

In many ways, too, Mill's reasoning regarding class suffrage is reflective of his concerns for something like a "politics of identity." He seems to think of class identity as being sticky, if not entirely intransigent: "In all countries there is a majority of poor, a minority who, in contradistinction may be called rich. Between these two classes, on many questions, there is complete opposition of apparent interest."[130] Class identity might explain why Mill assumed that the "majority of the women of any class are not likely to differ in political opinion from the majority of the men of the same class" on general or national issues.[131] The circumstances surrounding class status have a strong enough effect on character that a class-based standpoint will supersede a gender-based one.[132] Class for Mill, Katherine Smits argues, is "so fundamental a source of identity that numerical majorities must inevitably be class majorities." This inevitability stands as one of the "greatest dangers of democracy."[133] I would argue that Mill also views it as one of the greatest dangers *to* democracy, supervening the protection of the collective through emergent class oligarchies.

Mill's concerns about the stickiness of class identity may not justify his gradualist and paternalist proposals for suffrage. But we ought to note that his analysis reflects his attention to the profound and enduring effects of circumstance upon character and his hesitancies about how best to transform those circumstances. The result is the same tempered radicalism we find in his discussion of women's emancipation. Additionally (and perhaps unexpectedly given his usual label within the canon), Mill's concerns bear some affinities with arguments against identity-based politics offered in contemporary critiques of liberalism. Scholars like Judith Butler and Wendy Brown, for example, have questioned the use of identity in the construction of political claims. Brown points out that the politicization of racial, gendered, and sexual identities, in contrast to a Marxist vision of transformation, might require marginalized groups to maintain "a standard internal to existing society against which to pitch their claims."[134] By entering political deliberation *as* politicized identities, such groups maintain rather than challenge the structures and conditions that shape them. In Butler's account, if "identities were no longer fixed as the premises of a political syllogism, and politics no longer understood as a set of practices derived from the alleged interests that belong to a set of ready-made subjects, a new configuration of politics would surely emerge from the ruins of the old."[135]

Mill would seem to agree on both counts. From the "moment a man or a class of men, find themselves with power in their hands, the man's individual interest, or the class's separate interest, acquires an entirely new degree of importance in their eyes."[136] And a democracy, as any other form of government, is subject to the dangers of "class legislation; of government intended for (whether really effecting it or not) the immediate benefit of the dominant class."[137] Mill understands that the problem lies with how the inclusion of identity-based groups *as such* might entrench, rather than transform, the conditions which produce them.

Mill's politics therefore highlights the challenges with working out the terms upon which politicized identities can be uprooted in the first place. When Mill proposes plural voting, his argument is that it might encourage a collective dependence of interests, such that the terms of political claims would have to carry more comprehensive and distant views. The means by which Mill sought to break subjects out of their "ready-made" identities and interests certainly warrant scrutiny. Yet he gives an example of a historical thinker attempting to contend with the strictures of a politics of identity that contemporary theorists continue to struggle with. Mill's attempt involves both a radical orientation toward the inequities of class relations and conditional calls for change. He reveals that attention to the uncertainties of politics and reform can generate strategies that are at once liberating in their visions and imperfect in their applications. This is the political experiment Millian uncertainty embraces, and not without complications.

Importantly, the challenges of uncertainty are not limited to Mill's domestic political writings. Indeed, the educational criterion we find in Mill's domestic politics has long been a target in scholarly assessments of his writings on empire. We have seen that Mill clearly thinks the circumstances of gender and class inequality *must* be fundamentally altered, but is frankly unwilling to assume positive change will be the only predictable outcome of women's emancipation or of universal suffrage. His uncertainties in this regard spill across the ocean into his arguments for the British Empire. The gradualist and paternalist strategies Mill employs at home find a particularly fertile ground in his imperial policies toward places like India, where colonial mastery seemed to present him even greater opportunities to mold individual and social development. There, we find the educative and preparatory reasoning Mill applies to the cases of women and workers drawn through his hopes for the progressive benefits of colonial administration. But as with his domestic interventions, even his imperial proposals sit uneasily alongside Mill's more radical criticisms of the dangers and abuses of colonial government—criticisms which the now dominant "liberal imperialist" reading of Mill neglects.

# 6
# Governing Dependencies
## Between Authority and Self-Determination

> *The proceedings of the Committee may be said to have had three objects—to obtain a judicial inquiry into the conduct of Mr. Eyre and his subordinates; to settle the law in the interest of justice, liberty and humanity, and to arouse public morality against oppression generally, and particularly against the oppression of subject and dependent races.*
> Statement of the Jamaica Committee (1868)

Anyone with an interest in the politics of empire and imperialism will find an irresistible subject in John Stuart Mill. After all, what could be more appealing for such examinations than a public figure immersed in both the theory and practice of British colonialism? As an employee of the British East India Company (EIC) for over thirty years, Mill contributed to British imperial policies for much of his lifetime. But Mill's prominence in empire studies is surely made greater by his status in western political thought as *the* liberal. Mill's "talismanic position in the liberal canon,"[1] combined with his long employ with the EIC, positions him perfectly at the intersection of liberalism and empire, a connection that has captured the field's attention since its return to the imperial question in the twentieth century.

The revival of empire studies in political theory was partly a consequence of "the sense that global structural inequalities," particularly "American militarism and unilateralism since 2001, demanded a reinterrogation of the idea of empire."[2] Scholars rightly look to eighteenth- and nineteenth-century European thinkers like Burke, Bentham, James and John Stuart Mill, and Tocqueville—whose canonical works were occupied with questions of empire and imperialism—to see how the imperial project was variously defended or challenged. Unpacking their arguments and tracing their historical effects are important for considering the dynamics of power at play in the evolution of international law, global economic practices, and international relations generally.[3] If, as Sheldon Pollack argues, "it is only by looking at past empires that people have learned how to be imperial at all, since empire is a cultural practice and not some natural state,"[4] then the move to understand the theoretical grounds of empire and imperialism may well help us unearth resources for thinking about the nature of geopolitical power in the modern world. For all these reasons and more, Mary Dietz observes, "Empire is an idea whose time has come in political theory."[5]

Yet debates about empire and imperialism are routinely translated into a problem of liberalism or "liberal imperialism." For studies of empire:

> whether liberalism retains emancipatory possibilities in the current global order, or whether its persistent limitations—perhaps above all its potential blindness to the ways in which liberal languages and practices mask operations of power as well its obliviousness to the provinciality and partiality of liberal commitments—are questions that should continue to occupy these debates.[6]

And in fact, these questions about liberalism *are* the questions that dominate discussions of empire. Some of the most influential and compelling works on imperial politics are, at the same time, about liberalism. Uday Mehta's seminal *Liberalism and Empire* states: "This book studies British liberal thought in the late eighteenth and nineteenth centuries by viewing it through the mirror that reflects its association with the British Empire"; Thomas McCarthy meanwhile argues that "interrogating the tension in liberal thought between norms of equal respect and theories of sociocultural development is *critical* to understanding the relations of modern Europe to the rest of the world;" and for Shiraz Dossa, imperialism is simply "intrinsic to the articulation of liberal political theory, to its enabling concepts and ideas, to its claim to originality, which took shape in its zealous rejection of native cultures and values."[7] What we are seeing across studies of empire in political thought is a general consensus that liberalism and empire ought to be read together.

Though investigations of the imperial past and its architects are well warranted, the practice of examining empire in terms of its liberal roots is qualitatively different than doing so to discover empire's historical instantiations and to expand or deepen questions about its legacies. Seeking liberalism in empire, and vice versa, lays out a specific approach to the question of imperial politics, past and present. And as the previous chapters concerning Mill's gender and class politics gives evidence of, our preoccupation with liberalism as a core concern of the field has not only shaped scholarly debates in contemporary political thought, it has also transformed the texts and thinkers such debates turn to. As an icon of the liberal tradition, Mill's work is of course called in to represent liberalism for studies of empire. A survey of his reception in the field shows that he is generally read as "emblematic of the failure of liberal imperial thought."[8] Mill has become something of a canonical proxy in examinations of nineteenth-century liberal imperialism. I question that treatment in this chapter and evaluate the interpretive costs of reading Mill's imperial politics, and empire generally, through liberalism.

We ought to ask whether liberalism is what ties together imperial thinkers now situated within the liberal tradition—or if instead our pursuit of these authors through that idea can mask their variations, tensions, and contradictions? McCarthy, for instance, claims that "it is undeniable that the mainstream of liberal thought from Locke through Mill to contemporary neoliberalism, has continually flowed into and out of European-American imperialism, and that ideas of sociocultural development have been integral to that connection."[9] Leaving aside the undeviating line of descent suggested here between Locke, Mill, and neoliberalism, this claim also makes the conceptual history of western imperialism and the whole schema of development *indivisible from liberalism*. Making liberalism the focus of studies of empire and imperialism can, in this way, direct motivations for, as well as the object(s) of, inquiry and the range of political arguments which result. Mill is certainly not the only thinker caught by this interpretive practice. In a study of Edmund Burke, Daniel O'Neill finds that "the single-minded focus on liberalism and empire" in contemporary scholarship has "led interpreters to misread the imperial arguments of the greatest modern conservative and, thus, to overlook the very different mode of justifying empire evident in his thought."[10] Though recent work in empire studies has been invaluable, it "has also occluded as much as it has clarified."[11]

In the contemporary discourse, liberalism has become empire and empire has become liberalism. Focusing on Mill's politics of uncertainty will reveal the pitfalls of that transmutation, while uncovering a more capacious view of Mill's own imperial politics. Drawing my analysis of Mill's feminist and class politics into the question of empire, I begin by outlining the "liberal imperialist" construction of Mill in contemporary empire studies. I then offer an alternative account which takes seriously the critical connections between Mill's domestic proposals concerning gender and class and his colonial writings, including those which express radical critiques of empire. These critiques are too often muted, however, by the dichotomy the literature currently assumes between his "radicalism at home" and his "imperialism abroad." By outlining Mill's explicit concerns with empire and colonial practices, we can bring to light the strategic interests and lines of argument which cut across his proposals, from his respect for the diversity of experiences to his condemnation of inequities brokered on the basis of nature and, in the case of the colonies, racialized perceptions of difference.

As with the interactions between his feminist and class politics, the reading I give suggests that a clean divide between his domestic and imperial politics is neither possible nor fruitful once viewed in comparative perspective. This is not to suggest that Mill's interventions on gender, class, and colony are exactly identical. But I do contend that they are born of the same cautionary approach to altering social and political relations—even where Mill recognizes a desperate need to do exactly that.

What I am suggesting is that the full scope and nuance of Mill's arguments regarding women's emancipation, class reform, and even British imperial practice cannot be appreciated without attending to the uncertainty that conditions his politics. Beyond the convenient labels of liberal radical, liberal elitist, liberal imperialist, etc., which are differentially applied to him, what Mill's politics reveal are a complex and interactive set of strategies that recognize the necessity of fundamental political reforms, while remaining wary of their unknown consequences.

Tracing Mill's politics of uncertainty through his imperial work, this chapter closes the comparative account of Mill's proposals, which I have presented against the canonical liberal mantle he has long been forced to carry. Mill's politics speak more to the difficulties of engaging a critical orientation toward thought and action than he is given credit for. Freeing Mill (and ourselves) from the weight of that liberal mantle can open up different avenues of inquiry. But it will require, first, that we rethink our schematic readings of Mill through liberalism and, second, that we consider the effects of a critical approach such as Mill's. We might then begin to treat him not as an ideologue but as a political thinker and actor and to move our own political engagements beyond the liberalism trap.

## Constructing the Liberal Imperialist

In 1983, Eileen Sullivan wrote that "John Stuart Mill's justification of nineteenth-century English imperialism . . . has not been treated at any length by modern scholars."[12] In the decades since, Sullivan's foray into the subject has been joined by wide-ranging investigations of Mill's imperial politics. Indeed, her opening account of Mill as the author of "the first fully developed liberal defense of nineteenth-century English imperialism" has effectively become gospel. When we turn to Mill's imperial writings, we are primed with the knowledge that he is, simply, the foremost liberal imperialist of western political thought.

Mill's status within the liberal tradition has enabled this reading. It has also allowed scholars to insist that Mill, unlike eighteenth-century "anti-imperialists" like Burke or Bentham, gives a clear-sighted defense of the imperial project.[13] This argument has been advanced by Uday Mehta, who, along with Jennifer Pitts, offers among the most comprehensive and influential studies of the nineteenth-century British Empire. Mehta refutes the possibility that thinkers like Mill offer anything less than a coherent account of liberal imperialism. Focusing on Mill's conception of human nature and his exclusionary reworking of liberty, equality, and pluralism in the imperial context, Mill promotes a kind of "civilizational infantilism," limiting the exercise of such principles to those who "have become capable of being improved by free and equal discussion."[14]

As a result, the freedom and individual diversity celebrated in *On Liberty* are bracketed with the condition that they do not extend to "those backward states of societies in which the race itself may be considered as in its nonage" such that "Despotism is a legitimate mode of government in dealing with barbarians, provided the end be their improvement, and the means justified by actually effecting that end."[15] For Mehta, Mill's developmental view of human nature reflects and sustains the imperialist exclusion of the colonies that western liberalism engineered. An unqualified defender of empire, Mill's imperialism is built solidly *within* his "political and philosophic thought; any claim of discontinuity can be defended only by ascribing a deep self-delusion" in thinkers like Mill."[16] Rather, "the particular consistency Mill gives to his argument is one in which he leans heavily on a civilizational and historical index."[17]

Jennifer Pitts's *A Turn to Empire* delivers a captivating account of the imperial turn taken between the eighteenth and nineteenth centuries. Drawing widely on European thinkers from Adam Smith to Alexis de Tocqueville, the book tracks changes in the relationship between liberalism and empire through this varied cast of thinkers. It then carefully investigates the practices, contexts, and powers that shaped their writings on the French and British empires. Pitts is entirely right in observing that the "issue of empire draws out aspects of thinkers' theories in surprising and productive ways"; by investigating how these "thinkers' views about cultural diversity, progress and nationality affected their moral and political judgments regarding non-Europeans" we can gain a fuller account of their political thought and practice.[18] But the investigation is also motivated by understanding "what happens when liberalism encounters the world."[19] That interpretive premise has important implications. Following pedagogical practices in the field, Pitts collects Smith, Burke, Bentham, James and John Stuart Mill, and Tocqueville under a liberal umbrella by staking out the hallmarked concepts often presented to students as indicators of liberalism's lineage.[20] Thus, themes of "equal human dignity, freedom, the rule of law, and accountable, representative government," found among these theorists positions them all "as members of a liberal tradition, broadly conceived."[21] Their interactions with empire are then centered around the meaning of that shared liberal tradition, to address the question of liberalism's encounter with the world. If "liberalism can be said to rest on a commitment to human dignity and equality, then support for empire among so many nineteenth-century liberals poses a theoretical problem that requires explanation."[22]

That is the problem someone like Mill is brought in to address. And in contrast to thinkers like Tocqueville, who effects a "deep and unresolved ambivalence about European empires," Mill is read as having "achieved confidence in the benevolence of empire."[23] In Mill we find "theoretical rigor and parsimony" in a "logically coherent defense of the despotic rule of advanced societies over backward ones."[24] If the central tension to be worked out in studies of empire concerns liberalism's commitment to human dignity in one space and its support of colonial domination in another, then Mill shows us how that tension is resolved philosophically.

Some scholars of liberal imperialism have instead identified Mill as a key figure in liberalism's transition from "ethical frameworks," deploying the language of civilizational progress, "toward racial and cultural premises (as well as a revival of theories of rightful conquest)."[25] Departing from the coherence thesis, Karuna Mantena argues that Mill's works reveal a "deep theoretical tension between the commitment to liberal reform and improvement and the practical impediments for the realization of the progressive transformation of peoples."[26] Ergo, Mill represents the evolving and "fundamental inconsistencies" of nineteenth-century "liberalism."[27] Mill's account of imperial dominance was generative of discontinuities in the development of liberal thought on questions of progress and despotic rule. On this reading, "Mill's articulation of a liberal defense of empire was both the apotheosis and denouement of the project of liberal imperialism."[28]

Recent moves in the literature have begun to disrupt Mill's "liberal imperialist" identification, in ways that call for a more complex—though no less forgiving—account of his imperialist politics. These include Inder Marwah's excellent work on Mill's sociology of human development. Marwah notes that Mill's views on empire are too often conflated with James Mill's views on India, which were "infamously reprehensible."[29] He instead takes seriously J.S. Mill's attempts to assess the possibilities for, and impediments to, the formation of democratic characters—and crosses the "domestic" vs. "imperial" boundary to do so. From the "civilized poor" in England to the colonized in India, Marwah shows that Mill's justifications of empire take civilization and barbarism to be "less categorically distinctive states than unfixed and permeable ones."[30] In a similar vein, Barbara Arneil highlights Mill's permeable account of civilization and barbarism by looking closely at his support for "domestic colonies" in European contexts, drawing needed attention to the colonizing practices left unexamined by the dominant focus on liberal imperialism. In Britain and British settler societies like Canada, "domestic colonies for the irrational and/or idle European sought to 'improve' and transform those living within them."[31] Mill himself supported some of these practices, insofar as he assumed they could develop capacities for work and, ultimately, for citizenship.[32]

Mark Tunick advocates for reading Mill as a "tolerant imperialist." For Tunick, Mill's commitments to both liberty and moral development inflect his general discussions of the proper scope of government, and flow through Mill's imperial policies into his discussions of the "not so civilized peoples of the West."[33] Offering another compelling rereading, Nadia Urbinati's "The Many Heads of the Hydra" suggests that the question of how *all* forms of despotism (even those he defended) could come to an end is part of what motivates Mill's political thought.[34] Though I am not convinced that Mill assigns "liberalism a universalistic character," such that his approach to "nonliberal" contexts was entirely paternalistic,[35] Urbinati's study generally eschews the ideological Mill to capture his political engagements with the category of despotism and to "retrieve a critical tool of social and political analysis from oblivion."[36]

My intervention works both alongside and in tension with these studies of Mill and empire. I do not excuse the ethnocentric results of Mill's colonial policies. It is undoubtedly the case that Mill's defense of colonial rule is troubling and that it can be manipulated by perverse arguments about a racialized form of progressive inequality.[37] Still, there is more to unpack in Mill's imperial writings than what the liberal imperialist reading allows for. As with his work on gender and class, Mill's engagements with the British empire reveal his politics of uncertainty at work and the multiple strategies it generates. The cautionary moves he takes with respect to full liberty for women and workers are, I suggest, reimagined in his writings on empire as justification for colonial despotism. But uncertainty also leads him to make some radical observations about the wrongs of the imperial project. In essence, what ought to trouble us about Mill's defense of empire is not just that he gave one but that he did so even as *he was troubled* by its effects and implications. In bringing that tension forward, the chapter unveils a different angle from which to evaluate Mill's imperialism: we can, and should, attend to the injustice of it, but we can do so without sacrificing his intermediating radical critiques and gradualist proposals on issues of empire and colonial rule. In short, by suspending our preoccupations with liberalism and turning to Mill's political practice we can better examine the critical and analytical moves which generate his judgments.

Read comparatively, as I next argue, Mill's discussions of gender, class, and empire reflect a notable degree of continuity; but it is a continuity shaped by political uncertainties. He attempts to soften the revolution of reform, even where he himself calls for it. That is the ebb and flow of Mill's politics.

## Rethinking the Divide: Gender, Class, and Empire in Mill's Political Thought

Mill's imperial politics are often cordoned off from his work on women and workers by both scholars of empire and readers of his feminist and class politics.[38] But the interpretive costs of this segmented treatment are amplified where Mill's writings on empire and colonial rule are concerned. In a series of essays on Mill's "liberal" feminism, scholars provide accounts of Mill's theories of progress, the ideal of improvement, and human development in the context of gender, often without attending to the ways in which these theories interact with his writings on empire.[39] That omission speaks to a wider practice in evaluations of Mill's thought on other issues. In a discussion of Mill's theory of paternalism, C.L. Ten leaves aside any reference to Mill's defense of colonial paternalism, or empire generally.[40] From the perspective of Mill's interest in the study of ethology, scholars make persuasive cases for viewing Mill's thought through his interest in developing free and productive characters, without addressing his discussion of the characters involved in (and shaped by) colonial rule.[41] By staying within western borders, these omissions suggest that there is no space in which Mill's positions on national and imperial questions might interact.

And that imputation is bolstered by postcolonial scholarship on empire: "for all his radicalism with regard to domestic politics," we are told, Mill "placed considerable faith in colonial government as a well-intentioned and legitimate despotism designed for the improvement of subjects."[42] Treating his domestic and foreign politics separately, empire scholars thus contrast his calls for liberty, diversity, and equality at home with what they read as a coherent, single-minded notion of human nature and civilizational progressivism in his defense of the British Empire. And other readers have conceded this point. For Alan Ryan, though Mill is "aggressively anti-paternalistic" in general, those who were more favorable toward paternalistic policies frequently employed a "quasi-educational criterion, finding after all some support in Mill's views on India and medieval Europe."[43] To Bruce Baum, while Mill's understanding of freedom within relations of power is a strong counterweight to contemporary critiques of liberalism, Mill's "arguments about non-European societies typically betray the civilizing ethos that was common among nineteenth century European intellectuals."[44]

However, Mill's educational criterion and its relation to issues of dependency and reform are not peculiar to his colonial proposals. As Chapters 4 and 5 illustrate, his writings on women's emancipation and class representation reveal corresponding concerns about the readiness of subjected groups to ascend to the qualifications (and duties) of citizenship. The educative mandate that runs through Mill's defense of universal suffrage in England, for instance, persists, though with different properties, in the context of the colonies where the question of self-governance is continually raised and deferred in Mill's writings. His gradualist strategies offer parallels between his proposals for suffrage reform in England and his insistence that a colony like India had "not yet attained such a degree of civilization and improvement as to be ripe for anything like a representative system."[45] Those parallels do not make the conditions of English workers and colonized Indians identical; rather, in Mill's gradualist vision, the relative possibilities for self-governance—and essential to this was training persons in the qualifications of citizenship—were premised on the available institutional and social state.[46] For English workers and the poor, this transition involved the measured *expansion* of representation within the existing parliamentary system; but for colonized Indians, it involved the measured *replacement* of colonial administrators by native governors. To Mill, there were substantively different structural challenges to consider in the questions of parliamentary and colonial reform.

In the case of English suffrage, Mill thought necessary the introduction of educational standards, open ballots, and most controversially, plural votes for an educated elite to guide the English masses toward their civic duty. In the case of India, he testified to Parliament that colonial government ought to take "natives into its counsels much more than at present; but this I think would be better done by cultivating a greater degree of intercourse between intelligent natives and the members of the Government."[47] Were "intelligent natives" here to perform a parallel task to those plural voters Mill hoped to install among the English electoral body? Mill's conceit was that these Indian elites might work not simply to support the colonial administration but to act as transitional figures until such time as "when the natives shall be qualified to carry on the same system of Government without our assistance."[48] As Martin Moir argues, Mill seemed to believe that the path to Indian self-government involved drafting "'trustworthy' Indian bureaucrats [who] gradually prove themselves able to take over the system which their British superiors had in their wisdom installed."[49]

Where he hoped a group of educated plural voters could mitigate the worse aspects of class rule in English electoral politics, Mill's testimony on colonial administration suggests that recruiting elite Indians, too, could pave a path to Indian self-government. On the one hand, we have his insistence in *Subjection* that even if benevolent husbands were in the majority, they could not outweigh the systemic ills the marital institution enabled. On the other—for women, workers, and the colonized—Mill sought if not benevolent, then indifferent classes who could administer checks on the full political inclusion of these subordinate groups and facilitate their "readiness" for the higher callings of citizenship and self-determination. The preparatory note expressed in Mill's early work on women's equality, that the "first and indispensable step . . . towards the enfranchisement of woman, is that she be so educated, as not to be dependent"[50] is sounded again and again in his political proposals for progressive reforms. Mill called for a "revolution without a revolution," Urbinati says; he took the view that "liberation from despotic domination may require a *longue durée* perspective and synergistic transformations."[51]

Across these cases, we find Mill producing principles and policies which are at once rooted in his desire to achieve broad political inclusion and representation, alongside his unwillingness to unleash the storm, so to speak, of rapid, full-scale reforms. However much he rejects formal rule by an expertocracy of the sort Comte and others advocated, Mill repeatedly turns to some form of expert guides to secure a smoother transition from conditions of dependency and inequality to those of liberty, equality, and self-government. Frustratingly, Mill never specifies what conditions will signal proof that Indian bureaucrats are sufficiently prepared to assume control from colonial authorities.[52] Nor is it entirely clear that he thought the plural vote of a special educated class in England ought to be *only* a temporary feature of representative politics.[53] We are simply left with the conviction that preparation for self-government is essential.

Joint with these preparatory interests are the economic links between Mill's interventions into English class politics and his defense of colonial rule. Drawing heavily on the work of Edward Gibbon Wakefield, he argued that England's social and economic ills were rooted in problems of overpopulation and oversupply of laborers—a problem that settler colonialism offered a solution to.[54] In Mill's view, the Wakefield system of colonization, imperfectly undertaken in South Australia and New Zealand, served not just England, "but the collective economical interests of the human race."[55]

> The exportation of labourers and capital from old to new countries, from a place where their productive power is less, to a place where it is greater, increases by so much the aggregate produce of the labour and capital of the world. It adds to the joint wealth of the old and the new country, what amounts in a short period to many times the mere cost of effecting the transport. There needs be no hesitation in affirming that Colonization, in the present state of the world, is the best affair of business, in which the capital of an old and wealthy country can engage.[56]

Always concerned with the pressures placed on the English economy—a concern we see reflected in his worries about emancipated women flooding the labor supply, Mill saw colonization as a potential release valve for the market.[57]

These preparatory and economic considerations should highlight the significance of reading his work in comparative perspective. Together with his understanding of the relationship between class and colony, Mill's educational criterion for political enfranchisement points to the ways in which his gradualist proposals for reforming conditions of subjection and dependency operate at home *and* in the colonies. The shared logics he deploys in these cases are what get missed with the tidy designation of "liberal imperialist" he is given in the empire literature. And it is only with that designation in hand that we can place Mill's domestic and imperial politics on a "civilizational index."

A dichotomous view of Mill's domestic and imperial writings ignores the ways in which Mill applies consistent logics of critique and reform in situationally specific ways. Though his method of evaluating circumstances and reforms remains consistent, the uncertainty that drives it shapes his proposals to reflect the varying institutional mechanisms present in each case: for England the question concerned expanding a representative body already in place through the gradual inclusion of women and workers; for the colonies, it concerned replacing an entire administrative body with locally trained elites. Though Mill's gradualist strategy for reform entertains the same educative and preparatory logics then, the context in which potential reforms might unfold dictated the particular content of his proposals. Noting this connection between Mill's work at home and in colonial contexts does not reduce the harms of Mill's colonial advocacy—but it ought to reframe how we understand its roots and by extension, how we appropriate his writings to service contemporary arguments about empire or its liberal lineage.

And yet, even beyond these connections between Mill's gradualist and paternalist logics, the liberal imperialist framing misses another significant aspect of Mill's colonial writings, namely, the *radical* dimensions of his critiques of colonial practices. Indeed, the gulf that is now commonly assumed between his domestic and imperial politics trades on the view that Mill simply accepted the political agency and legitimate claims of English workers and women but ignored those of colonized peoples. Except, Mill did confront the dangers of colonial rule. That confrontation is uneasily balanced against his hopes for the broader imperial project, just as his calls for the freedom of women and workers are weighed against his fears about their readiness for citizenship and about the wider impact of their inclusion. Attention to Mill's doubts show that his belief in the productive potential of the British Empire is far more tenuous than the customary "liberal imperialist" designation suggests.

## Empire's Dangers: Mill on the Limits of "Benevolent Despotism"

A commonly acknowledged reading of thinkers like Tocqueville and Marx is that both understood empire's villainy perfectly. So, the aristocrat's defense of French empire is often regretfully explained by his nationalist concerns. The revolutionary's descriptions of empire as a necessary advance are taken to reflect his materialist analysis, rather than any normative commitments to empire itself.[58] Such nuance is rarely granted to Mill's writings on empire. And yet, this lifelong employee of the EIC, a defender of its political, economic, and even moral utility, voiced notable concerns about both the implementation and promise of British imperialism, even exhibiting a diminishing faith in empire's returns toward the end of his life. It is these qualified breaks from depictions of Mill's unqualified defense of empire that have too long been buried beneath the liberal sign his work is filed under.

Evidence of Mill's discontent with empire and its effects fall along three issues: (1) ensuring critical engagement with cultural knowledge and practices; (2) protecting the rights of the colonized; and (3) maintaining the accountability of the metropole, when confronted with its failures. Mill's analysis of each of these issues demonstrates not an absolute belief in empire's benevolence but an acute awareness of its normative fractures. As we move between his critiques of British empire on those three issues, into his continued defense of the imperial mandate, we find a political actor challenged by the failures of an enterprise he thought not simply to defend but to improve in the interest of humankind.

Rather than merely being grist for the liberal imperialist mill that has seized our contemporary focus then, Mill's imperialism ought to be read as the consequence of a complicated approach to political thought and action, one which demands considered judgments but offers no guarantee of their efficacy. This is the position of the cautionary radical. The same practice of uncertainty we find in his feminist and class politics operates in Mill's writings on empire and colonialism with hesitancies about whether, and how, a principled pursuit of the "improvement of mankind" might practically be achieved.

## On Character, Cultural Knowledge, and Local Practice

A chorus in the liberal imperialist opera finds Mill guilty of a stark "indifference to the array of social and political structures" of colonized nations, dismissing local values and practices in favor of applying European culture as the universal standard by which non-Europeans ought to be governed.[59] For Bhikhu Parekh, it simply "never occurred to John Stuart Mill that he only talked about *individual* diversity and difference, never about ethnic or group diversity or differences."[60] In essence, the coherence of Mill's liberal imperialism is in part grounded in his ability to ignore cultural difference. That charge might have surprised a man who instructed students to consider the views of "other people: and those of other nations" to mitigate the undue power of "preconceived notions."[61] But how well are assertions of his cultural universalism held up by Mill's colonial writings? Not very, if we look at his comments concerning the experiences of the colonized with colonialism. What we find instead is Mill both defending cultural diversity while, at the same time, *wielding it* to improve the quality of British colonial practices.

First compare his attendance to the role English rule plays in constructing both the character and conditions of subject populations. Mill's controversial pamphlet "England and Ireland" challenged English readers who considered the failures in Ireland to be an effect of *Irish* character, and not English missteps. Faced with the fact of Irish disaffection, he notes, there are always those "among us who liked to explain it by a special taint or infirmity in the Irish character," so that "Ireland or the nature of things was alone to blame."[62] Proponents will point to the nature of an Irish laborer as "idle" in justification of British land policies in Ireland.[63] But he cautions that such claims make the error "of imputing every difference which he finds among human beings to an original difference of nature."[64] To characterize the Irish laborer as naturally idle is to miss the practical effect that being "deeply in arrears to his landlord" has on the capacity of "a cottier" to work effectively.[65] In the case of Irish animosity toward England, "Our rulers are helpless to deal with this new outburst of enmity because they are unable to see that anything on their part has given cause for it."[66] Echoing his response to defenders of women's inferior characters, or the natural deficiencies of the lower classes, Mill points out that in making such claims English authorities abdicate their responsibility for improving the conditions in Ireland by falsely attributing the effects of policy to some inherent peculiarity of character.

In fact, in both Ireland and India, Mill argued that English policy regarding land tenure had done more to harm the local population than to improve local conditions. By blindly introducing "the English idea of absolute property in land"[67] in India, for instance, he thought the British had reduced the ryot or peasant class "into the miserable condition of Irish cottiers—rack-rented tenants-at-will. What little respect was anywhere paid to their rights or interests resulted solely from the still partially surviving influence of custom on the minds of persons whom the law had exempted from any necessity of observing it."[68] In this instance, Mill argues, local traditions corrected imperial harms. Mill pushed for the creation of "a nation of peasant proprietors" in Ireland and India as a means both of protecting cultivators who were dependent on the land and of cultivating their moral improvement through economic responsibility and opportunity. Notably, Abram Harris shows that Mill's proposals in both cases were "akin to his proposals for English land tenure reform," which sought to encourage cooperative agricultural ventures and associations.[69]

If economic policies were one way in which English rule could shape (or misshape) the character and conditions of subject populations, so too could interference with local religious practice and indigenous forms of education. In his "Memorandum of the Improvements in the Administration of India," Mill cites legislative amendments of 1840 which prohibited the interference of British functionaries in India with "all matters relating to their temples, their worship, their festivals, their religious practices, and their ceremonial observances."[70] Missionary proselytism, or other acts "intentionally or unintentionally offensive to the religious feelings of the people" raised Mill's ire as evidence of the destructive ways in which the English were "every now and then interfering, and almost always in the wrong place," particularly by forcing "English ideas down the throats of the natives."[71]

On matters of education and local knowledge, Lynn Zastoupil finds that Mill's dispatches on Indian education show his "participation in a discourse fashioned together by rulers and ruled," wherein the popular sentiments of Indians on the subcontinent concerning issues of education financing and curricula are attended to.[72] Mill called for the revival of classical Indian learning and literature alongside an introduction of Western education.[73] But for Shefali Misra, we should remember that "Mill is no supporter of guarding cultural boundaries *for their own* sake."[74] Rather his proposals for integrative education in India call to mind his position in *On Liberty*, that "it would be absurd to pretend that people ought to live as if nothing whatever had been known in the world before they came into it," such that the utility of particular customs, knowledge, and practices ought to be evaluated rather than assumed.[75]

Mill remained attentive to the diverse array of social and political conditions in India and to the possibilities for a pluralist, rather than absolutist, mode of cultural integration. That aim is most visible in his response to efforts by Lord Bentinck and Lord Macaulay in 1835 at redirecting all colonial funds to teaching only English literature and science in the English language and to cancel funding for the teaching of native languages and texts.[76] Macaulay's justification, presented in a speech to Parliament, was that he had yet to find "Orientalists" who "could deny that a single shelf of a good European library was worth the whole native literature of India and Arabia."[77]

Mill disagreed with that thesis and endeavored to show that its impact, if adopted, would be counter to the very aims Bentinck and Macaulay professed: to enlarge the number of qualified Indian employees for government work. In rejected dispatches he authored on Indian education, Mill argued that adopting their policy would effectively disparage the value of Indian cultural and religious knowledge in its entirety—a move that he was already critical of in connection to missionary proselytism and other forms of religious interference. More strategically, however, Mill noted that it was "altogether chimerical to expect that the main portion of the mental cultivation of a people can take place through the medium of a foreign language." The goal of the Bentinck-Macaulay proposal—to promote a class of Indian elite who could introduce the native population to European literature and ideas—required that they be able do so by translating those ideas into Sanskrit or Arabic "words and terms of expression."[78]

The necessity of protecting local knowledge and practices against total assimilation blends into Mill's expectations concerning the training of colonial officials in India. Indian administration, he says, cannot allow the "appointment of persons to situations of trust from motives of convenience, already so criminal in England" but must instead "be calculated to form [the best candidate]."[79] Unlike those convenient appointments to favored persons in the metropole, Mill held that colonial administrative officers should be "sent out in youth, as candidates only, to begin at the bottom of the ladder, and ascend higher or not, as . . . they are proved qualified."[80] For an employee of the EIC who had never been to India, his insight here is interesting. Of his own experiences, Mill acknowledges that "public business transacted on paper, to take effect on the other side of the globe" was not "calculated to give much practical knowledge of life."[81] Perhaps with his own deficits in mind, Mill maintained that for colonial officers on the ground, only by taking up "a more profound study of Indian experience and of the conditions of Indian government" than any English politician had engaged in could administrators properly act with "no duties to perform except to the governed . . . no interests to consider except theirs."[82]

Mill's comparative assessment of the particular forms and consequences of British policies posits that British India before becoming a Crown affair had the benefit of not being subject to English party politics—unlike Ireland.[83] When he condemns British policy in the latter case, he points out that "by a fortunate accident, the business of ruling India in the name of England did not rest with the Houses of Parliament . . . it devolved on men who passed their lives in India, and made Indian interests their professional occupation."[84] Indirect rule in India allowed colonial administrators to reconcile themselves to the "idea that their business was not to sweep away the rights they found established, or wrench and compress them into the similitude of something English, but to ascertain what they were; having ascertained them, to abolish those only which were absolutely mischievous."[85]

British India as a result was something of an example for those debating the Irish question. Those who are familiar with British rule in India "are even now those who understand Ireland best."[86] Mill's colonial observations here reveal his experimental sensibilities. Though in 1861 he thought it likely that colonies that were ethnically and linguistically similar to the metropole were more easily governable in line with the ruling nation, and thus more adaptable to representative institutions, by 1868, looking at the Irish famine and rising Fenian activism, the history of British India appeared to offer a better model of British colonial policy. That favorable comparison aside, Mill's views of British rule in India and other non-European colonies were not rosy. As evidence of colonial violence and abuse mounted, so too did his critical engagement with the failures of the imperial project.

## The Rights of the Colonized

In a damning account of Mill's "civilizational racism," Jimmy Casas Klausen argues that Mill simply failed to recognize the political subjectivity of the colonized and thus, in the case of the 1857 Sepoy uprising in India, which saw Indian soldiers (sepoys) and sympathetic civilians take up arms against local British authorities, Mill was blind to "the *political* significance of Indians' actions and British reactions during the revolt."[87] Instead, violent resistance was for him the ad hoc expression of barbaric characters. Mill's failure in this regard is taken to represent the patterns of epistemic violence normalized within liberal thought itself.[88]

The role of epistemic violence in imperialist theories cannot be discounted. Yet, while Mill may participate in its production, his contributions to it are not quite as straightforward or as blind as Klausen suggests. Even as Mill's defense of British India is a fact of history, we can attend to that fact without blinding ourselves to those moments in which he publicly and privately called the British Empire into question. And those moments do exist. In coming to terms with them, we need not negate the harms of Mill's colonial defense but can instead assemble its full content and character to consider what it suggests about his approach to broader questions of authority, liberty, and progress.

As to whether or not, for example, Mill recognized the political subjectivity of Indians, consider his discussion of the rights of the colonized. In his statements on the Black Act (1836), which subjected British residents of India to local EIC courts following native legal codes, Mill spoke on the "interests and rights of the natives" against the presumed entitlement of the English to be, always, under English law: an Englishman in India has no right to "say to the natives, I will regulate my transactions with you by the laws of my own country, and if you think I have injured you, you shall not have the redress your own laws would give you."[89] He understood that protections are *owed* to Indian subjects as individuals vulnerable to the power and abuses of English rule. There is, here, the seed of what Mill will compellingly argue in *Considerations*, some twenty-five years later: that nothing could be worse to the moral and political development of persons than to be forced to plead for their interests "outside the door to the arbiters of their destiny."[90] Establishing English law in toto would result in exactly that. Consequently, though Mill certainly critiqued certain local laws and practices (for instance, he condemned *sati* or widow burning which, despite colonial depictions, was unevenly practiced in India),[91] he did not view local legal practices to be inherently "barbaric" in comparison to English law.

Indeed, Mill's writings together with Harriet Taylor offer sound evidence of his willingness to challenge the rightness, even the civilizational "superiority," of English law where, for instance, the abuse of women was concerned. In a series of articles, Mill and Taylor argued that English laws left little to no protection for victims of domestic abuse precisely because the legal apparatus works in the interest of men; accordingly, victims of abuse "die in protracted torture ... without ever, except in the fewest and rarest instances, claiming the protection of law."[92] For English women under the despotic rule of husbands, and Indians seeking remedy in cases involving Englishmen in India, laws devised in the interests of the stronger party were prima facie unjust. In the case of the colonies, Mill could thus call for the preservation of local laws where civil injury or contracts between English and Indian parties were at issue. That he did so indicates recognition of the political interests of Indians and further pushes back against assertions about how benevolent he viewed the colonial system to be. As with English wives, Mill saw reason to expect abuses if safeguards were not in place and held that the first and greatest principle to be proclaimed is that "the Natives of India need protection against the English, and that to afford them that protection is one of the first duties of the British government in India."[93]

More striking are Mill's predictions about the state and status of British rule should such protections be eroded or eradicated. He warns that British misconduct in India *would* trigger events like the 1857 uprising. In his brief on the Black Act years prior, he says "our empire in India, consisting of a few Europeans holding 100 millions of natives in obedience by an army composed of those very natives, will not exist for a day after we shall lose the character of being more just and disinterested than the native rulers and of being united among ourselves." If the conduct of the English in India is not well managed, he warned, Britain would lose both its "moral supports—and physical support, independent of those, it has none."[94] The relationship between the quality of administrative rule, the justice of English conduct, and the due rights of natives were on Mill's mind well before the 1857 uprising.

Mill's anger over official responses to that event remains palpable in *On Liberty* (written during the uprising and published the same year England officially declared the conflict over). Citing the speech of state official William Massey, who argued that toleration of "local religions in India had had the effect of retarding the ascendancy of the British name, and preventing the salutary growth of Christianity," Mill spoke bitterly about the fact that

> a man who has been deemed fit to fill a high office in the government of this country, under a liberal Ministry, maintains the doctrine that all who do not believe in the divinity of Christ are beyond the pale of toleration. Who, after this imbecile display, can indulge the illusion that religious persecution has passed away, never to return?[95]

Mill in turn attributes support for Massey's imbecility to the "strong permanent leaven of intolerance in the feelings of a people, which at all times abides in the middle classes of this country."[96] Both official and public responses to the 1857 Sepoy uprising, in his observation, reflected a condition of prejudice among the British people, and it was a condition he recognized as having clear political ramifications.

Furthermore, Mill's censure of the British response to indigenous protest and violence against colonial authority in India amassed over time into a general pessimism about the attitudes of Englishmen on matters concerning the rights of the colonized. Criticizing arguments for direct rule, he wrote:

> Among a people like that of India, the utmost efforts of the public authorities are not enough for the effectual protection of the weak against the strong: and of all the strong, the European settlers are the strongest . . . they think the people of the country mere dirt under their feet: it seems to them monstrous that any rights of the natives should stand in the way of their smallest pretensions: the simplest act of protection to the inhabitants against any act of power on their part which they may consider useful to their commercial objects, they denounce, and sincerely regard, as an injury.[97]

The sense of entitlement attached to the ruling people was powerful enough that the Government could not always "keep it down in the young and raw even of its own civil and military officers." This was a concern that grew over time as Mill read colonial reports of indigenous abuse at the hands of English settlers and officials. In 1866, he wrote to an acquaintance about the untenable position of the Maori in New Zealand, who were increasingly at the mercy of a growing English settler population. "Knowing what the English are, when they are left alone with what they think an inferior race, I cannot reconcile myself to this." With evidence of colonial violence, Mill states the obstacle to achieving any kind of "colonial justice" when he asks how it might be "possible for England to maintain an authority there for the purpose of preventing unjust treatment of the Maoris, and at the same time allow self government to the British colonists in every other respect?"[98]

David Williams convincingly argues that Mill's attempts to bridge what he perceived to be the collective economic benefits of colonization with a broader educative and developmental mandate generated a paradox at the heart of his imperial defense. Williams shows on one hand, that the "economic development of India and the expansion of its trade . . . both encouraged and were encouraged by European settlers and traders," yet on the other, it was these very groups that Mill worried would trample the rights of Indians and undermine "the legitimacy of British rule."[99] Mill had to confront the fact that in India, New Zealand, and elsewhere, his assertion that "Colonization, in the present state of the world, is the best affair of business" was also expanding opportunities for the colonial violence he condemned.[100]

In raising fundamental questions about the efficacy of colonial policies, Mill directly challenges the current consensus that his politics were "devoid of any doubt that colonial government by a corps of administrators might itself be vulnerable to systemic problems, abuses, or injustices."[101] With these moments of comparatively radical critique in play—radical for an agent of empire to hold much less voice publicly—scholars have to confront Mill's negotiation of empire's dangers. Did he support Britain in its imperial missions? Yes. But not without questions, caveats, and concerns. And those concerns were far from trivial.

## The Accountability of the Metropole

Mill's claims about the rights of the colonized and the character of colonial rule play into one of his most radical public acts as an agent of the British Empire: his campaign against Governor Edward Eyre for the 1865 Morant Bay massacre in Jamaica. Reacting with increasing violence to anti-colonial protests led by Jamaican Baptist deacon Paul Bogle, Eyre declared martial law and authorized the indiscriminate execution and torture of hundreds under sham trials, and many without trial at all.[102] Now a Member of Parliament, Mill utilized his position to forcefully condemn the Morant Bay atrocities.

Appointed to chair the Jamaica Committee in 1866, he led the campaign to prosecute Eyre and members of the military who carried out the massacre. The committee was unsuccessful in its cause, a failure that affected Mill long afterward.

Mill's work with the committee has been read as further evidence of his inability to grasp the brutality of colonialism and representing in turn the "exclusionary imperial edge typical of liberal thought."[103] His arguments against Eyre are seen as reductive, framing the affair in terms of criminal liability, rather than taking account of the "colonial and racial context" in which the crimes were permitted.[104] While Mill could condemn individual behaviors and events, the argument goes, he could never understand them as *symptoms* of the disease of colonial despotism. And, we are told, his work for the Jamaica Committee means very little given that Mill "merely alluded in passing to the threats that some British persons sometimes pose to natives" in all the years prior.[105] Mill's campaign is also read as an effort to preserve the liberal conceit of operating on a ranked scale of sociological advancement. The effort to prosecute Eyre weakly represents "the most ambitious posture liberalism could muster."[106] The real danger of Eyre being excused for his crimes was that it might "leave no room for Mill's liberal model of benevolent despotism."[107] In essence, Mill's campaign against Eyre was in service to the interests of the British Empire—and to the civilizing mission of liberalism which underwrote it.

There is an alternative reading: the Eyre affair drew together Mill's worries about the abusive power of colonial authority and sets into relief the uneasiness of his colonial defense. Even as an employee of the EIC, he was not blind to the dangers of colonial administration. In his dispatches concerning education, religious tolerance, and cultural pluralism, through to his discussion of the rights of those under colonial rule—we have seen Mill document his worries about the various mechanisms by which colonial administration, settlement, and jurisprudence can damage the lives of native populations. And we know from his comments on the Black Act, alongside his reactions to English perceptions of the 1857 Sepoy uprising, that Mill acknowledged those damages. Mill in fact admits that he was *first awakened* to the poor moral condition of English society "by the atrocities perpetrated in the Indian Mutiny & the feelings which supported them at home."[108] Writing of the English in India a few years before the events in Jamaica, Mill cautions that being "Armed with the prestige and filled with the scornful overbearingness of the conquering nation, they have the feelings inspired by absolute power, without its sense of responsibility.[109] His experiences with the Eyre affair in England gave weight to this concern.

Taking his considerations of colonial abuse into account indicates that Mill was acutely aware of the colonial and racial context in which the Jamaica atrocities were committed and that his efforts to prosecute Eyre reflect an understanding of the systemic harms of colonial administration. But Mill retains his support of colonial rule alongside this understanding. His misgivings about the imperial project lived alongside his defense of it. Mill's position on the British Empire, consequently, is not one of unqualified confidence. It is terribly, and tragically, uncertain.

Mill's committee work publicly signals that rebellion against colonial authority should *not* be dismissed as a consequence of individual mismanagement and misconduct but interrogated for what it might suggest about the institutional and moral fragility of colonial rule. Failing to bring the perpetrators to account would signal to the world that the massacre was a consequence of ill-conceived severity and not, as Mill saw it, "an infraction of public rights and principles of justice sacred in all cases alike."[110] He thus sought to convince the public that the cause of the Jamaica Committee, "besides upholding the obligation of justice and humanity towards all races beneath the Queen's sway, is to vindicate, by an appeal to judicial authority, the great legal and constitutional principles which have been violated in the late proceedings, and deserted by the Government."[111]

Two points should be centered here. The first is that the committee identifies the victims of the Eyre massacre as British subjects. The second is that the very character of English rule depends on the outcome of the campaign. On the first point, Pitts is right to suggest that Mill is playing strategy with race. Though he recognizes the racial context of the Jamaica atrocities he did not want to center English racism in the trial. Doing so might elicit sympathy for the "white planter class," and play "into the hands of Eyre's defenders."[112] The *Autobiography* recounts his impression that the "perpetrators of these deeds were defended and applauded in England by the same kind of people who had so long upheld negro slavery."[113] Alert to English prejudices, Mill's description of the Jamaican victims of the Morant Bay massacre as "British subjects" and his insistence that *all* races subject to the Crown deserve the considerations of justice and humanity can be read as efforts to blunt the reactionary racism of English observers at home.

Does that rhetorical strategy mean that Mill "ignored the colonial and racial context of the official violence that Eyre oversaw?"[114] In fact, he directly *links* these subjects in his correspondence. Writing to U.S. abolitionist Rowland Hazard, Mill suggested that "What has just taken place in Jamaica might be used as a very strong argument against leaving the freedmen to be legislated for by their former masters." Reading the aftermath of the American Civil War against the backdrop of the Jamaica massacre shows why "America should refrain from giving back to the rebel states the rights already forfeited by them, except on such conditions as will secure equal laws and an impartial administration of justice between colour and colour." In contrast, what happened as a consequence of the colonial administration in Jamaica requires first, that "England will have to make a clean sweep of the institutions of Jamaica, and suspend the power of local legislation altogether, until the necessary internal reforms have been effected by the authority of the mother country."[115] Why do the Jamaica atrocities give support to the full enfranchisement of formerly enslaved Black Americans but not the self-determination of colonized Jamaicans?

Once again, attention needs to be paid to Mill's uncertain practice, and the situational considerations it imposes on his political reasoning. Remember that Mill argued for the eventual transition of Indian elites into the offices established by the colonial administration "to carry on *the same system of Government* without our assistance."[116] Once qualified, Mill's "intelligent natives" were to be tasked with replacing their English counterparts in the governing institutions established by British rule. He sees a parallel situation in the U.S. context, wherein the task of post-war reconstruction was to bring the governing principles and practices of the southern states into unison with the northern states. Emancipation, in Mill's view, afforded the republic the chance to finally correct the evils of slavery, by granting Black Americans full representation *within* U.S. democracy. The successful readmission of the southern states hinged on guaranteeing the suffrage to freedman and in turn changing "the structure of Southern society as will render such a relation between them and the Free States rational and safe.[117]

In Jamaica, however, Mill seems to think that the atrocities committed left a permanent stain on the colonial institutions in place, which only a "clean sweep" and suspension of local legislation could redress. Unlike in India, or the United States, the institutions established in Jamaica could neither be preserved (at some future point) by a native elite, nor extended to enfranchise a subjected class. Eyre's abuses revealed that there was nothing to salvage. Yet Mill could not support, it seems, the idea that the legitimate response to colonial failure in Jamaica was a retraction of colonial rule. His unwillingness to tear down colonial authority altogether is especially fraught because he *understood* that the massacre threatened to indict the imperial project itself. And indeed, the second move the Jamaica Committee made in calling for Eyre's prosecution was to read what happened in Morant Bay as putting the character of English rule on trial. In a letter declaring his "open war" with the *Daily Telegraph*, which supported Eyre, Mill states that the very "honour and character of England for generations to come, are at stake in the condign punishment of the atrocities of which ... the Jamaica authorities have been guilty."[118] Mill's comments do not speak to English pride or reputation as a matter of patriotic concern. Rather, his reflections here are characteristic of his study of conditions of subjection in general. Wherever he seeks to trouble conditions of deep power imbalances, Mill calls into view the effects of unchecked power on those who abuse it. This is certainly so in his discussions of the working and poor classes in England, and it is forcefully articulated in his writings on the family. There, Mill shows that women's subjection enables young boys "to grow up to manhood in the belief that without any merit or any exertion of his own ... by the mere fact of being born a male he is by right the superior of all and every one of an entire half of the human race."[119] Power without accountability is consistently a target of his analyses.

The massacre in Jamaica and its aftermath, in this sense, was not a "one-off" event, but a critical moment of accountability and reflective evaluation. The relations of power brokered by colonial rule inspire feelings of "absolute power, without its sense of responsibility."[120] And Mill sees this as a problem embedded in the project of empire itself: "As it is with the English in India, so, according to trustworthy testimony, it is with the French in Algiers; so too with the Americans, in the countries conquered from Mexico, so it seems to be with the Europeans in China, and already even in Japan."[121]

Mill's work with the Jamaica Committee shows that the central problem was not simply Eyre's criminal responsibility but the system of power within which he acted, and which ultimately acquitted him. Writing to a barrister in 1868, Mill points out that the prosecution of Eyre is not "like a contest for *some* political improvement, in which the only question is whether it shall be obtained a little sooner or a little later."[122] The issue, he insists, is much broader: "Ours is morally, a protest against a series of atrocious crimes, & politically an assertion of the authority of the criminal law over public delinquents."[123] The question was "whether the British dependencies and eventually perhaps Great Britain itself, were to be under the government of law, or of military license."[124] The legitimacy of English rule was at stake. To fellow committee member Henry Fawcett, Mill insisted that the two greatest questions of 1866 would be "Jamaica and Reform, and there will be an immensity to be said and done on both subjects."[125] Aligning domestic legislative issues and colonial affairs, the Morant Bay massacre and the Second Reform Act represented significant challenges for England. The legitimacy of its domestic and colonial political institutions was being held to account. And in the latter case, if the metropole proved unwilling to subject its rule to the demands of law and justice, the project could not be redeemed.

Rebuking criticisms of his position, Mill wrote: "I cannot say that it is possible to me as a man to regard Mr. Eyre's conduct in Jamaica without the deepest indignation, or as an Englishman without a sentiment of humiliation."[126] It called Mill to speak

> against acts of violence committed by Englishmen in authority, calculated to lower the character of England in the eyes of all foreign lovers of liberty; against a precedent that could justly inflame against us the people of our dependencies; & against an example calculated to brutalize our own fellow countrymen.[127]

His intent in prosecuting Eyre was not to adjudicate between the better or worse relationships among the colonial authorities, but to think about the broader conditions and effects of power within which these relations and events unfolded.

Two months following the Jamaica atrocities, Mill said that if "England lets off the perpetrators with an inadequate punishment, no Englishman hereafter will be entitled to reproach Russia or the French Revolutionists with any massacres, without at the same time confessing that his own country has done worse."[128] For Duncan Bell, the failure of the committee's aims, along with Mill's remarks on the abuses of colonial rule, mark his transition to a "melancholic colonialism," a condition of "anxiety, even despondency, about the direction of (colonial) history."[129] I have suggested that Mill's melancholia was always on the horizon; what captured him in his later years was that the troubling effects of the colonial project he observed throughout his career had only grown more evident. Mill's hopes for the moral promise of empire to improve the world dimmed; it was a promise that could not be delivered.

## Uncertainty's Perils

A telling effect of the liberalism trap is how little room it leaves for consideration of the parallel strategies Mill employs across his work on domestic and imperial politics. It renders void the tensions, nuances, and political qualifications Mill embeds in his justifications of empire and colonial rule. The trap effectively uncomplicates by decontextualizing. But it is us, as contemporary readers, that suffer as a result. Under the interpretive grip of liberalism, we are kept from the resources offered by Mill's own work to both deconstruct and challenge his imperialist defenses as sites, not of blind confidence but of discomfited commitments—to justice and the rule of law, and to despotism.

Though critics of his "liberal imperialism" rightly confront Mill's willingness to defend British colonialism against its rejection by colonized subjects, focus on what this means *for liberalism* has concealed a more complex view of the "epistemic violence" scholars see Mill committing. More particularly, my reading suggests that Mill *did* recognize the political subjectivity of Indians and other colonial subjects—but he defended their subordination to English rule anyway. He thus suspends the political capacities of colonial subjects *even as he questions* the political capacities of their British rulers. This is the aporia that Mill's uncertainty enables in his approach to the question of colonial rule, as he moves between both a radical critique of inequities inherent to the colonial project and his own efforts to sustain that project in the context of the British Empire.

Alongside critics like Mehta, I do not regard that negotiation as a symptom of "inconsistency"; but nor is it a consequence of liberalism's ideological consistency with regard to empire. Rather, Mill's fraught imperialism is the material result of *his* political practice. Uncertainty drives his radical challenges and gradualist and paternalist proposals concerning gender and class and so too does it generate his uneasy position between questioning and supporting British rule. This will rightfully not sit well with contemporary readers; but recognizing Mill's uncertain practice (as distinct from our investments in his standing as a liberal) affords a much different view of the character and content of Mill's colonial politics.

Against the tidy designation of liberal imperialist that now overwhelms Mill's writings, his policies on colonial governance reveal a more complicated set of normative and political investments. Mill's politics of uncertainty enables a kind of dual positionality: he can place himself on the border of radical critique and a cautionary, even regressive, politics. In the case of the colonies, Mill's uncertainty sways him toward utilizing and "improving" an established system of rule through surveillance of abuses and measured reforms to correct them. The choice for Mill is not one of maintaining colonial authority *or* granting the colonies immediate self-rule. It is rather a question of managing the space Mill sees *between* authority and self-determination and of minimizing the adverse effects of the former in efforts to realize the latter. This in-between perspective is manifest in the fact that Mill can so clearly point to the ineptitudes and injustices of British colonial policy, while retaining (an albeit diminishing) hope that such policies could be corrected to serve the interests of subject populations. That such measures proved ineffective in so many instances took their toll on Mill's imperial hopes—and we see that in his struggles to come to terms with the dangers of empire.

What is troubling about Mill's proposals, therefore, is not that he was a blind representative of liberalism's imperialism writ large; rather, what ought to concern us is that his uncertain politics, and its ostensibly productive refusal to accept existing conditions of inequality and injustice "as inevitable;—a provision of nature and as some said, an ordinance of God,"[130] nevertheless led him to problematic conclusions respecting the maintenance of colonial rule and to the interruption of his own defense of the rights and interests of the colonized. Put in comparative perspective, this tension becomes even more significant. Colonial despotism, graduated class suffrage, the exclusion of the poor, and his position on sex-class all reflect Mill's impulse to be critical but cautious in restructuring conditions of dependency. The colonial system must be oriented toward preparing colonial subjects, just as education must prepare women and workers, while graduated voting ought to temper their entry into representative politics.

Yet Mill gives us no clarity as to when these preconditions will be met in the colonies, nor is he forthcoming about the moment at which improvements in national education might finally make graduated suffrage or plural voting unnecessary. His otherwise radical interventions into the abject conditions of subject populations are shot through with efforts to forestall the kinds of reforms that such conditions would seem to call for. Across these cases, then, the gradualist and paternalist moments of Mill's political arguments repeatedly leverage the unanticipated effects of breaking individuals and societies out of despotic systems, against his calls to do exactly that.

Viewed in line with those examples of domestic gradualism and paternalism, Mill's defense of empire cannot easily be reduced to the imperial conceits of liberalism. We ought to consider his interventions, as a whole, as being the product of his uncertainty, and of the plural political tactics it generates. Mill's references to "backward" or "uncivilized" states may well have fed into culturalist and racialist sentiments about the "other" in international politics, however much he did abhor such positions. But recall too Mill's use of that language to describe his own youthful character: "I was so accustomed to being told what to do . . . that I acquired a habit of leaving my responsibility as a moral agent to rest on my father. I thus acquired a habit of backwardness, of waiting to follow the lead of others."[131] This self-reflection bears consideration alongside his description of women under the power of husbands, the laborer under the will of an employer, and those states for which a "stout despotism" is most appropriate. His own painful crisis of reform against his moral and intellectual "backwardness" might have tempered Mill's perception of how liberation might be achieved.

At no time does Mill operate as if with a tabula rasa; his appreciation for the invidious impact that existing social and political conditions have on the formation of characters and societies requires that he examine prospects for change within, alongside, and against those very conditions. "Backwardness" for Mill functions as a description of moral agency lost (or stolen)—a threat all individuals and societies are subject to. That Mill could both seek mechanisms for restoring that agency to various groups and introduce obstacles to achieving this goal reflects the varied effects of his uncertain political practice.

# 7
# Politics, Possibility, and Risk

## Beyond the Liberalism Trap

*The best guide is not he who, when people are in the right path, merely praises it, but he who shows them the pitfalls and the precipices by which it is endangered.*

J.S. Mill, "The Spirit of the Age" (1831)

Though there was no shortage of scholarly works on the life and death of liberalism over the past century, studies of the idea have ramped up in recent years. If, for some, the liberal idea is obsolete and in need of abandonment, for others it is under siege and in need of reinforcement.[1] Those two poles seem to have marked the discursive horizon of contemporary politics. Calls to interrogate liberalism often outline the parameters of investigation and debate: pressing discussions of material inequalities, racial and gender-based violence, the normalization of nationalist rhetoric and its consequent impact on policies concerning refugees and immigrants—as well as evaluations of human rights abuses writ large—are interpolated into questions about *liberalism*'s credibility and future.[2]

So normalized is the practice of reading politics through liberalism that it now constitutes a shared methodological premise of debate across the left and right of the political spectrum. And the strange bedfellows this debate creates are quite remarkable. Heralded as a champion for Catholic conservatism, Patrick Deneen's *Why Liberalism Failed* has captivated readers with its tales of modernity's collapse in the wake of liberalism's inadequacies. It calls for a return to a simpler time when "cultures of community, care, self-sacrifice and small-scale democracy" can take root (and where, notably, women's "emancipation from their biology" might be corrected).[3] The directions Deneen's critique goes are in no way in line with the arguments of scholarly icons of the left like Catharine MacKinnon or Wendy Brown (who themselves have widely different approaches to left politics). And yet, Deneen's interpretive investment in centering liberalism to address the challenges of contemporary democratic politics is the same investment we find in MacKinnon and Brown. Each makes interrogation of liberalism's failings the standard for discussing the challenges of modernity, whether that be in relation to culture and community, feminist praxis, or issues of democratic politics.[4] As the label under which contemporary crises are registered—from the specifics of Trumpism to a growing sense of democratic malaise—liberalism is now the sine qua non of modern political analysis.

This practice is a trap. Preoccupation with liberalism shifts the political questions that motivate scholarly investigations—into issues like inequality, violence, or withering civic engagement—out of view and instead redirects inquiry to ideological genealogies, divides, and debates about the liberal idea. Within the narrow confines of reading the world through liberalism, our interpretive practices as scholars, as well as the political insights and possibilities these practices must inform, are held hostage to the idea that we are, all of us, bound to a conceptual investment in liberalism.

This book has endeavored to identify that practice as not only unnecessary but also politically unproductive. The liberalism trap poses critical challenges for contemporary political theory: it can restrict how we receive texts identified with the liberal canon or apply them to issues of political import. As such, it constructs a method of inquiry that places concerns with the liberal idea at the heart of political analysis.

The need to move beyond the trap is why J.S. Mill is an important figure for this project. Read as the paradigmatic liberal, the way in which Mill has become a proxy for treatments of liberalism is revelatory. Mill's reception as a political thinker identified with liberalism shows us the costs of our contemporary preoccupations with this idea. His politics have been substituted with his status as a liberal icon. That substitution disables the innovations and challenges of Mill's political practice, one Chapter 3 locates in the appreciation for uncertainty Mill adopts following his crisis. Moreover, focus on his status has ignored the important ways in which Mill's interventions into questions of equality, freedom, and human development on policies concerning gender, class, and empire *intersect*. Put into practice, Mill's uncertainty generates political strategies that at once overlap and conflict, from radical critiques of the inequitable conditions that women, workers, and colonized subjects endure, to the gradualist and paternalist limits he himself places on efforts to resolve those conditions. But these strategies operate within and across his political proposals—a comparative view that has been largely undertheorized. That is a consequence of the fact that Mill's liberal status lays claim to how he is read and appropriated in ways that bifurcate his "domestic" and "imperial" writings.

At the project's close, I offer a few implications for drawing Mill's politics of uncertainty into contemporary interpretive practices—of reading beyond the liberalism trap. I do this in three ways: first, I consider how a Mill unbound from liberalism can speak to issues of gender and cross-cultural politics absent a liberal frame. Second, I outline some reasons why uprooting the liberal anchor in empire studies (and Mill's deployment therein) might be productive. Third, I conclude with a discussion of what Mill's complex and undoubtedly fraught practice of uncertainty might suggest to contemporary readers about the promise and challenge of critique itself. These implications are by no means exhaustive; I note them only to give some indication of where and how a recovery of Millian uncertainty might inform, and hopefully entice, scholarly thinking away from the confines of liberalism.

## Mill Untethered: Gender, Culture, and Empire

Moving our readings of Mill beyond liberalism creates new opportunities for engaging with him on matters of contemporary concern. One might, for example, see a surprising degree of congruence between Mill's thought and aspects of Saba Mahmood's discussion of the women's mosque movement in Egypt, discussed in Chapter 4. That congruence, however, opens up only once the requirements of reading Mill through his liberal status fall away.

According to Mahmood, the movement's participants are concerned with the "process by which practices that are supposed to be part of a larger program for shaping ethical capacities lose this function and become little more than markers of identity: such as when people fast because they have learned that this is simply what Muslims do."[5] Through a revival of the study and interpretation of religious principles, women in the mosque movement contested "what they considered to be an increasingly prevalent form of religiosity in Egypt, one that accords Islam the status of an abstract system of beliefs that has no direct bearing on how one lives, on what one actually does in the course of a day."[6] In these aims, Mahmood sees a form of embodied autonomy that seeks to reclaim one's religious identity as a lived experience, and which "regards conventions (socially prescribed performances) as necessary to the self's realization."[7] She positions this form of autonomy as a counter to the Western "liberal" model for which agency "is understood as the capacity to realize one's own interests against the weight of custom, tradition, transcendental will, or other obstacles (individual or collective)."[8] Mahmood locates Mill as one of the primary authors of that liberal position, so he then appears as an adversary to the reconfiguration of autonomy she pursues.[9]

And yet we know that Mill was deeply concerned with the degeneration of customs into lifeless dogmas. That concern is identified not only in *On Liberty* but also in Mill's *Autobiography*, where he details his fears of having become a made and manufactured man. Mill is intent to disrupt the extent to which "propositions are believed and repeated from habit," because he sees in his own time "so many doctrines of religion, ethics and even politics, so full of meaning and reality to first converts" decaying into abstract systems of belief.[10] What is significant here, in relation to Mahmood's study, is that Mill does not abandon tradition or customary knowledge, but rather understands that their continued value requires that they remain *active* subjects of everyday debate and practice. His primary concern is that conformity *for conformity's sake* not be the motive for belief or conduct. Akin to the mosque movement leaders Mahmood observes, Mill wants persons to think about and follow customs and practices that actively connect to the way they live—and in so doing, to exercise their responsibility as moral agents in the world.[11]

Of course, this does not mean that Mill's political thought can simply be overlaid with that of the women Mahmood writes of. The utility of this comparison lies not in making their projects the same, but rather in making room for points of dialogue between them. To put these perspectives into conversation, rather than assuming their opposition within a liberal frame, might be regarded as a process of cultural translation: an opening to develop shared idioms premised upon broader concerns about the meaning and value of customary knowledge.[12] Such idioms are developed through a set of translations between rhetorical and cultural contexts, which gives the claims that result a broader base of support. As these claims are worked out politically, they remain open to investigation.[13] But it is precisely that translative potential which gets evacuated by forcing Mill into a liberal frame, and for the primary purpose of positing a fundamental divide between liberal, western, and nonliberal, non-western approaches to autonomy. Instead of rejecting, a priori, Mill's thought on account of its associations with western "liberal feminism," why not consider the ways in which his concerns with dogma might speak to the motivations of the mosque movement participants? Given this possibility for a more cross-cultural assessment, we might also direct Mill's own practice of interrogating foundationalist claims toward (western) feminist understandings of gender, autonomy, and Islam that Mahmood identifies as limited. To move in this direction would, I think, place the onus on normative work concerning the culturally weighted relations of power that help to structure transnational gender politics. It would give us more material with which to actively disturb and reconfigure the inequalities we seek to address.

## Empires Past, Imperial Futures

In a similar vein, we can consider how recognizing Millian uncertainty in the context of empire might inform or reform contemporary approaches to the study of empire itself, as well as its intellectual and material legacies. By drawing attention to the ways in which western thinkers are implicated in projects of empire and imperialism, empire studies not only recover the western canon's encounters with the "other" but also allow us to consider how those encounters continue to inflect contemporary challenges to democracy, international law, and cross-cultural politics. And yet, as Chapter 6 argued, these discussions are often directed through and toward concerns about liberalism such that the current custom has collapsed liberalism into empire and vice versa. Indeed, even as imperial histories are widely understood to inform contemporary relations, a now-standard theme in studies of those histories is that "the evolution of liberal thought coincided and deeply intersected with the rise of European empires."[14] In search of the coherence and structure of that evolution, canonized liberal thinkers from "Locke through Mill to contemporary neoliberalism" are investigated as the basis of "European-American imperialism."[15]

The conflation of liberalism and empire will impact how scholars turn those seminal texts and thinkers toward the politics of empire and its contemporary effects or iterations. This is an interpretive practice with political ramifications. In the first place, it positions thinkers like Mill within narrow ideological and geographical boundaries. Though Mill's thought is clearly relevant to theories about imperial legacies and neo-imperial strategies, where that relevance is committed to assessments of liberal imperialism—and not to Mill's own complicated imperial advocacy—he would seem to offer few resources for discussions of empire that exceed the conceptual boundaries of liberal imperialism. Second, and following, focus on liberal imperialism might limit our perceptions of an era where globalized economic networks create structures of "weaponized interdependence"[16] and enable the use of economic, cultural, and military coercion by strategic actors like the United States, China, and Russia.[17] Evaluating the global strategies of these different actors would entail a comparative historical approach to empire and imperialism, a study not well-served by the "east/west" dichotomy implied by the liberal imperialist rubric.

How much more might we discover about the questionable logics and the dangers that accompany national and international actions which rely on forms of domination, whether they emerge as cultural production, material control, or military flexing, if our examinations are not bound to a practice of ideology tracing? What resources can we pull from Mill and past imperial thinkers now managed under the liberal imperialist sign for examining the evolution of those forms of domination today, not only in the "liberal west" but also in the policies and practices of competing actors on the world's stage? In the contemporary era, widespread focus on "liberal imperialisms," and the entrapment of past thinkers within that focus, may conceal the range of cases to which our assessments of empire, and its complex legacies, might be directed.

## Search and Search with Much Travail

A recovery of Millian uncertainty can also shed light on the challenges of critical inquiries which eschew the comfort of (presumed) certainties. Judith Butler suggests that the task of the contemporary critic is to interrogate moves which establish foundations that lay "beyond power or force . . . through tropes of normative universality." The aim is to question what exactly a particular claim "*authorizes*, and what precisely it excludes or forecloses."[18] In many ways, Mill's embrace of uncertainty foreshadows the task Butler lays out for the critic. Confronting his own Benthamite foundations, Mill found himself taking up no system in its place, but rather a practice of working in view of the complex and many-sided quality of political thought and action.

Against tropes of universality, Mill's uncertain approach connects inquiries into the dominant norms of social and political life with the specific circumstances in which they unfold. Whether it be gender, class, or colony, what Mill's political engagements repeatedly consider are what might be authorized, foreclosed, or excluded not only by established social and political relations, but also by the pursuit of alternatives. Thus, while Mill did not shy away from making judgments, as is clearly evident by his proposals, those judgments are invariably tempered by his sense that the only certainty we can be assured of possessing is the certainty that we are fallible beings. Mill's politics of uncertainty, in other words, approaches critique in the way Butler argues we should: it relieves particular practices or claims of their "foundationalist weight in order to render [them] as a site of permanent political contest."[19]

But it is also the case that the overlapping strategies Mill employs in place of those foundationalist claims, which oftentimes sieve his radical interests through his cautionary concerns, bear risks. What Mill's politics of uncertainty affirms is that critical interrogation has "no *necessary* political consequences ... only a possible political deployment."[20] It is precisely that openness, and the tensions it produces around Mill's complex set of strategies, which explains why he has been "claimed, and continues to be claimed, by pretty much everyone, from the ethical socialist left, to the laissez-faire, libertarian right—and at various points by every major political party."[21] Mill shows us the ways in which an uncertain politics puts the critic in a tenuous position: without recourse to the conceit of ideological guarantees for political judgments, they must confront the effects of those judgments, and the varied ways they might be manipulated in different contexts.

We should question Mill's policies on women's roles, class identity, and colonial despotism. We should also attend to the fact that Mill performed his role as critic in its fullest form—without being beholden to doctrinaire or ideological identities, or to presumptions as to where criticism must lead him. To not "dogmatically anticipate the future," and to be unafraid of any conflict with the powers that be, seems an apt description of Mill's critical disposition.[22] Finding value in that disposition, however, while contending with the problematic directions it sometimes took him, is a difficult equation to balance. It calls into question just what it is that we expect of a critical project, especially if we are uncomfortable with its results. The strategies and perspectives we have seen Mill employ in his role as a social critic reveal his willingness to work within that uncomfortable space.

As John Morely once said, following the posthumous publication of the *Autobiography*, "Search, and search with much travail, strikes us as the chief intellectual ensign and device of that eminent man whose record of his own mental nurture and growth we have all been reading."[23] With Morely, we ought to understand Mill not as the staid representative of an ideological tradition, but as a practitioner of a critical politics that can appeal to no knowledge beyond that given by a considered examination of the world and which can, therefore, never fully be at rest with its own conclusions. Mill's politics of uncertainty takes seriously the notion that doing is always subject to peril, such that we might be hit by the ricochet of our own ideas. His reformist and cautionary approach to matters of social and political justice are the ricochet effects of his own critical practice.

We might say that, with Marx, Mill knew it would be insufficient to investigate who is to emancipate, or who is to be emancipated, unless the critic pursues a necessary third question: "*What kind of emancipation* is in question? What conditions follow from the very nature of the emancipation that is demanded?"[24] Mill understood that the identification of oppressive conditions, and of the persons shaped by them, does not by itself offer a political solution; one must also cultivate general awareness of those experiences alongside consideration of the conditions which might follow from the nature of any remedy proposed. This is what occurs when he attempts to negotiate the best means of addressing the inequities of gender, class, and colony.

Mill's uncertain politics then, while radical in its assessment of relations of power and their effects on the characters and quality of persons and institutions alike, is not necessarily revolutionary in its approach to change. The tensions between his multiple political strategies reflect the dilemmas of taking up a politics unanchored by ideological certainties or conceits, a politics of radical critique and normative risk. That Mill's resultant judgments leave us with challenging questions about what it means to adopt an uncertain disposition in the operation of political thought and practice is something contemporary readers ought to examine, rather than subsume beneath the heady cloud of our infatuation with liberalism.

## Different Colored Glasses

I turned to J.S. Mill for this project because his own politics contest the liberalism trap within which he has been caught. But Mill, as it turns out, also offers an example of struggling against the frames we are accustomed to working within. His is a story of a mind that was once held captive by a rigid intellectual framework, and which managed in spite of that to break free and to look at the world through different colored glasses.[25] What Mill sought was not a blueprint for social and political decisions, but an intellectual practice that orients us to think creatively and critically about given circumstances and about the futures we envision to be possible. From his unique education, through his crisis and experiences, into his political interventions on gender, class, and empire, we see Mill tuning into a political perspective that is experimental and vigilant in its resistance to certitude. That every question has many sides; that politics thrives, not in universals or absolutes, but in the creative exercise of the imagination; and that a measure of uncertainty in the face of the familiar is the real spring of progress—these were the principles he followed. And it is this eclectic orientation to politics that still gives his readers a diverse array of material to delve into, well over a century after his death.

This book calls for a reconsideration of the liberal preoccupations we are accustomed to viewing our politics through. Following Mill, we might instead start from the premise that politics exists in the space between the known and the unknown, and the challenge of that space is that it demands our interpretations and judgments, but grants us no assurance that the outcomes will be entirely what we predict.

In many ways, however, we have saved ourselves from the disquiet of an uncertain politics by committing ourselves to working within the confines of liberalism. Our relationship to liberalism constitutes a kind of identity for the field, giving us a sense of certainty not only about what political inquiries we pursue but also *how* we ought to pursue them. That certainty undermines the work of political theorizing by failing to question the interpretive authority now granted to this idea. What political horizons are left unseen by theoretical work conceived under that authority? And what might we find if we let ourselves out of it?

Breaking out of the liberalism trap will certainly entail some disciplinary anxiety, but it will also make us aware of the political costs of entrapment. And thinking differently about the interpretive bulwarks we are accustomed to working within, alongside, or against may expand the resources we have to make considered interventions into the questions and concerns of political life.

At the very least, I hope to have shown how our theoretical and political orientations can be unduly influenced by liberalism. And to suggest that, if our preoccupations with this idea are in fact foreclosing ways of thinking about politics, it might be time to for us to initiate our own crisis of certainty—to flex against confinement within this much mined frame of study. With liberalism as neither the proverbial savior nor the boogeyman of contemporary political analysis, we will find ourselves disoriented, unmoored from the interpretive customs we have long been tied to. But in that position of uncertainty, we might also find more freedom to navigate the promise and the perils of doing politics.

# Notes

## Preface

1. Lionel Barber, Alex Barker, and Henry Foy, "Vladimir Putin Says Liberalism Has 'Become Obsolete,'" *Financial Times*, June 27, 2019, https://www.ft.com/content/67003 9ec-98f3-11e9-9573-ee5cbb98ed36.
2. Jonathan Chait, "Trump Thinks Putin's Attack on 'Western-Style Liberalism' Was About California," *New York Magazine*, June 29, 2019, http://nymag.com/intelligen cer/2019/06/trump-thinks-western-style-liberalism-is-about-california.html.
3. Though most identify liberalism with nineteenth-century political developments, scholars often note that liberalism's core ideas can be traced as far back as "curiosity will take you." E. Fawcett, *Liberalism: The Life of an Idea* (Princeton: Princeton University Press, 2018), 1.
4. John Lloyd, "The New Illiberal International," *New Statesman*, July 18, 2018, https://www.newstatesman.com/world/2018/07/new-illiberal-international.
5. Robert J. Samuelson, "Opinion | Does Vladimir Putin Have a Point?," *Washington Post*, July 8, 2019, sec. Opinions, https://www.washingtonpost.com/opinions/putin-decla red-that-liberalism-is-obsolete-is-he-right/2019/07/08/a6f13070-a1a3-11e9-b732-41a79c2551bf_story.html; Helier Cheung, "Is Putin Right? Is Liberalism Really Dead?," June 28, 2019, sec. Europe, https://www.bbc.com/news/world-europe-48798875.
6. "Putin Derides Liberalism as 'Obsolete' before G20 Summit," *Al Jazeera*, June 28, 2019, https://www.aljazeera.com/news/2019/06/putin-derides-liberalism-obsolete-g20-summit-190628052108100.html.
7. Martin Wolf, "Liberalism Will Endure but Must Be Renewed," *Financial Times*, July 2, 2019, https://www.ft.com/content/52dc93d2-9c1f-11e9-9c06-a4640c9feebb; Editorial Board, "No, Mr. Putin, Western Liberalism Is Not Obsolete.," *Financial Times*, June 28, 2019, sec. Opinion, https://www.ft.com/content/34f3edc0-9990-11e9-9573-ee5cb b98ed36.
8. Raymond Geuss, "A Republic of Discussion: Habermas at Ninety," *The Point Magazine*, June 18, 2019, https://thepointmag.com/2019/politics/republic-of-discussion-haber mas-at-ninety; Seyla Benhabib, "Jürgen Habermas's 90th Birthday," *Medium*, July 2, 2019, https://medium.com/@arendt_center/j%C3%BCrgen-habermass-90th-birth day-2c2a720a4f5b; Martin Jay, "'The Liberal Idea Has Become Obsolete': Putin, Geuss and Habermas," *The Point Magazine*, July 5, 2019, https://thepointmag.com/2019/criticism/the-liberal-idea-has-become-obsolete-putin-geuss-and-habermas.
9. Wendy Brown, *Edgework: Critical Essays on Knowledge and Politics* (Princeton: Princeton University Press, 2005), 53.

10. Quoted in R. Adcock, *Liberalism and the Emergence of American Political Science: A Transatlantic Tale* (New York: Oxford University Press, 2014), 280.
11. Francis Fukuyama, "The End of History?," *The National Interest*, no. 16 (1989): 4; "Against Identity Politics: The New Tribalism and the Crisis of Democracy," *Foreign Affairs* 97, no. 5 (October 9, 2018): 91; see also: Louis Menand, "Francis Fukuyama Postpones the End of History," *The New Yorker*, August 27, 2018, https://www.newyorker.com/magazine/2018/09/03/francis-fukuyama-postpones-the-end-of-history; Nathan Gardels, "Opinion | Francis Fukuyama: Identity Politics Is Undermining Democracy," *Washington Post*, September 18, 2018, https://www.washingtonpost.com/news/theworldpost/wp/2018/09/18/identity-politics/; Francis Fukuyama, "Francis Fukuyama On Why Liberal Democracy Is In Trouble," NPR, April 4, 2017, https://www.npr.org/2017/04/04/522554630/francis-fukuyama-on-why-liberal-democracy-is-in-trouble.
12. Fukuyama, "Against Identity Politics," 91.
13. Francis Fukuyama, *Liberalism and Its Discontents* (New York: Farrar, Straus and Giroux, 2022); Barber, Barker, and Foy, "Vladimir Putin Says Liberalism Has 'Become Obsolete'"; Lawrence B. Glickman, "Forgotten Men," *Boston Review*, December 12, 2017, http://bostonreview.net/politics/lawrence-b-glickman-forgotten-men-the-long-road-from-fdr-to-trump; Roger Cohen, "Opinion | The Death of Liberalism," *The New York Times*, April 14, 2016, sec. Opinion, https://www.nytimes.com/2016/04/14/opinion/the-death-of-liberalism.html.
14. Michael Freeden, *Liberalism: A Very Short Introduction*, vol. 434, *Very Short Introductions* (Oxford: Oxford University Press, 2015), 4.
15. Timothy Stanley and Lee Alexander, "It's Still Not the End of History," *The Atlantic*, September 1, 2014, https://www.theatlantic.com/politics/archive/2014/09/its-still-not-the-end-of-history-francis-fukuyama/379394/; Francis Fukuyama, "Francis Fukuyama: Putin's War on the Liberal Order," *Financial Times*, March 3, 2022, https://www.ft.com/content/d0331b51-5d0e-4132-9f97-c3f41c7d75b3.
16. Stanley and Alexander, "It's Still Not the End of History."
17. Elaine Kurtenbach and Klug Foster, "G-20 Leaders Clash over Values, Face Calls to Protect Growth," AP News, June 28, 2019, https://www.apnews.com/6d4457a0692e44b29e3793e7cc7e0ecb; Samuelson, "Opinion | Does Vladimir Putin Have a Point?"; Madeline Roache, "Russian President Putin Calls Liberalism 'Obsolete' Amid G20" *Time*, June 28, 2019, https://time.com/5616982/putin-liberalism-g20/; Wolf, "Liberalism Will Endure but Must Be Renewed"; Lloyd, "The New Illiberal International."

# Chapter 1

1. Raymond Geuss, *Not Thinking Like a Liberal:* (Cambridge: Belknap Press of Harvard University Press, 2022); Fred Dallmayr, *Post-Liberalism: Recovering a Shared World* (Oxford; New York: Oxford University Press, 2019); Patrick

J. Deneen, *Why Liberalism Failed* (New Haven: Yale University Press, 2018); Katrina Forrester, *In the Shadow of Justice: Postwar Liberalism and the Remaking of Political Philosophy* (Princeton: Princeton University Press, 2019); Duncan Bell, *Reordering the World: Essays on Liberalism and Empire* (Princeton: Princeton University Press, 2016); W. Brown, *Undoing the Demos: Neoliberalism's Stealth Revolution* (New York: Zone Books, 2015); Joseph Massad, *Islam in Liberalism* (Chicago: University of Chicago Press, 2015); A. Sartori, *Liberalism in Empire: An Alternative History* (California: University of California Press, 2014); Larry Siedentop, *Inventing the Individual: The Origins of Western Liberalism* (Cambridge: Belknap Press, 2014).

2. John Gray, "Why Liberalism Is in Crisis," *New Statesman* (blog), January 26, 2022, https://www.newstatesman.com/ideas/2022/01/the-light-that-failed-why-liberalism-is-in-crisis; James Traub, "Liberalism Isn't Dead—but It's Very Sick," *Foreign Policy*, May 10, 2022, https://foreignpolicy.com/2022/05/10/liberalism-democracy-decline-autocracy-mounk-fukuyama-books/; Ross Douthat, "Is There Life After Liberalism?," *The New York Times*, January 13, 2018, sec. Opinion, https://www.nytimes.com/2018/01/13/opinion/sunday/life-after-liberalism.html; Roger Cohen, "Opinion | The Death of Liberalism," *The New York Times*, April 14, 2016, sec. Opinion, https://www.nytimes.com/2016/04/14/opinion/the-death-of-liberalism.html; Katrina Forrester, "The Crisis of Liberalism: Why Centrist Politics Can No Longer Explain the World," *The Guardian*, November 18, 2019, sec. Books, https://www.theguardian.com/books/2019/nov/18/crisis-in-liberalism-katrina-forrester; Theodore Lowi, *The End of Liberalism: The Second Republic of the United States* (New York: W.W. Norton & Company, 1969); Herbert Hoover, *The Challenge to Liberty* (New York: Scribner's and Sons, 1934); Winston Churchill, *Liberalism and the Social Problem* (London: Hodder & Stoughton, 1909).

3. Daniel B. Klein, "The Origin of 'Liberalism,'" *The Atlantic*, February 13, 2014, https://www.theatlantic.com/politics/archive/2014/02/the-origin-of-liberalism/283780/; Jonathan David Gross, *Byron: The Erotic Liberal* (Lanham, MD: Rowman & Littlefield Publishers, 2000); Andrew Heywood, *Political Ideologies: An Introduction* (New York: St. Martin's Press, 1992), 15.

4. Heywood, *Political Ideologies: An Introduction*, 15; Duncan Bell, "What Is Liberalism?," *Political Theory* 42, no. 6 (2014): 693; Terence Ball and Richard Dagger, "The 'L-Word': A Short History of Liberalism," *Political Science Teacher* 3, no. 1 (1990): 1–6.

5. Bell, "What Is Liberalism?," 693; Emil Kirchner, *Liberal Parties in Western Europe* (Cambridge: Cambridge University Press, 1988), 2–3.

6. Thomas Nagel, "Rawls and Liberalism," in *The Cambridge Companion to Rawls*, ed. Samuel Freeman (Cambridge: Cambridge University Press, 2002), 62.

7. Uday Mehta, *Liberalism and Empire* (Chicago: University of Chicago Press, 1999); S. Hopgood, *The Endtimes of Human Rights* (Ithaca: Cornell University Press, 2013); Massad, *Islam in Liberalism*; Menaka Philips, "Feminist Preoccupations: Liberalism as Method in Debates Concerning Gender and Culture," *Signs: Journal of Women in Culture and Society* 44, no. 4 (May 21, 2019): 955–77.

8. Harold Laski, *The Rise of European Liberalism: An Essay in Interpretation* (London: George Allen & Unwin, 1947), 12.
9. John Dewey, *Liberalism and Social Action*, Great Books in Philosophy (Amherst, NY: Prometheus Books, 1999), 15; Judith N. Shklar, *Political Thought and Political Thinkers* (Chicago: University of Chicago Press, 1998), 3.
10. Henry Barnes, "Cannes Faces Backlash after Women Reportedly Barred from Film Screening for Not Wearing High Heels," *The Guardian*, May 19, 2015, sec. Film; Bryan Wright, "I'm a Democrat but There's Something Great about Trump's Travel Ban," *Fox News*, January 31, 2017; John Cassidy, "Liberalism Will Survive Obamacare," *The New Yorker*, November 27, 2013; Julian Zelizer, "Opinion: Obamacare and the Failure of Half-Baked Liberalism," CNN—Opinion, November 11, 2013.
11. Rachel Sylvester, "Jeremy Browne: 'Many Lib Dems Support the Opposite of True Liberalism,'" *The Times*, 2014, https://www.thetimes.co.uk/article/jeremy-browne-many-lib-dems-support-the-opposite-of-true-liberalism-86zckcvnl20; Don Herzog, "Is(n't) Catharine Mackinnon a Liberal?," *Newsletter on Philosophy and Law—The American Philosophical Association* 12, no. 2 (2014): 11–16.
12. Bell, "What Is Liberalism?," 689.
13. Jay, for instance, links his discussion of Putin and Geuss's comments on liberalism as follows: "Since guilt by association may not be a fair tactic—although in this case, it is hard to resist—let's look at Geuss's argument on its own terms." Martin Jay, "'The Liberal Idea Has Become Obsolete': Putin, Geuss and Habermas," *The Point Magazine*, July 5, 2019, https://thepointmag.com/2019/criticism/the-liberal-idea-has-become-obsolete-putin-geuss-and-habermas.
14. Wendy Brown, *Edgework: Critical Essays on Knowledge and Politics* (Princeton: Princeton University Press, 2005), 53.
15. Raymond Seidelman, "Political Scientists, Disenchanted Realists, and Disappearing Democrats," in *Discipline and History: Political Science in the United States*, ed. James Farr and Raymond Seidelman (Ann Arbor: The University of Michigan Press, 1993), 311.
16. Dorothy Ross, "Robert Adcock. Liberalism and the Emergence of American Political Science: A Transatlantic Tale. Oxford: Oxford University Press, 2014," *American Political Thought* 4, no. 4 (September 2015): 4; R. Adcock, *Liberalism and the Emergence of American Political Science: A Transatlantic Tale* (New York: Oxford University Press, 2014), 19; John G. Gunnell, "Pluralism and the Fate of Perestroika: A Historical Reflection," *Perspectives on Politics* 13, no. 02 (2015): 408–15.
17. Adcock, *Liberalism and the Emergence of American Political Science*, 3–4.
18. John G. Gunnell, "American Political Science, Liberalism, and the Invention of Political Theory," *American Political Science Review* 82, no. 1 (1988): 80; John G. Gunnell, "The Founding of the American Political Science Association: Discipline, Profession, Political Theory, and Politics," *American Political Science Review* 100, no. 4 (November 2006): 479–86.
19. Mark Hulliung, *The American Liberal Tradition Reconsidered: The Contested Legacy of Louis Hartz*, American Political Thought (Lawrence: University Press of Kansas, 2010); Louis Hartz, *The Liberal Tradition in America* (New York: Harcourt Brace

Jovanovich Publishers, 1955); Irving Louis Horowitz, "Louis Hartz and the Liberal Tradition: From Consensus to Crack-Up," *Modern Age* 47, no. 3 (2005): 201–9; Rogers Smith, "Beyond Tocqueville, Myrdal and Hartz: The Multiple Traditions in America," *American Political Science Review* 87, no. 3 (1993): 549–66; David Greenstone, "Political Culture and American Political Development: Liberty, Union and the Liberal Bipolarity," *Studies in American Political Development* 1 (1986): 1–49.

20. Stephen Skowronek, "The Reassociation of Ideas and Purposes: Racism, Liberalism, and the American Political Tradition," *American Political Science Review* 100, no. 3 (2006): 384–401; John G. Gunnell, "Louis Hartz and the Liberal Metaphor: A Half-Century Later," *Studies in American Political Development* 19, no. 2 (October 2005): 196–205.

21. Gunnell, "American Political Science, Liberalism, and the Invention of Political Theory," 84.

22. Bell, "What Is Liberalism?"

23. John Rawls, *A Theory of Justice* (Cambridge: Harvard University Press, 2003); Robert Nozick, "Distributive Justice," in *Communitarianism and Individualism*, ed. Shlomo Avineri and Avner de-Shalit (Oxford: Oxford University Press, 1992), 137–50; Martha Nussbaum, *Women and Human Development: The Capabilities Approach* (Cambridge: Cambridge University Press, 2000); Joshua Cohen, Matthew Howard, and Martha Nussbaum, eds., *Is Multiculturalism Bad for Women* (Princeton: Princeton University Press, 1999); Seyla Benhabib, *Situating the Self* (New York: Routledge, 1992); Michael Sandel, *Liberalism and the Limits of Justice* (Cambridge: Cambridge University Press, 1998); Kevin McDonough and Walter Feinberg, eds., *Citizenship and Education in Liberal-Democratic Societies: Teaching for Cosmopolitan Values and Collective Identities* (Oxford: Oxford University Press, 2003),; Jennifer Pitts, *A Turn to Empire* (Princeton: Princeton University Press, 2005); Uday Mehta, "Liberal Strategies of Exclusion," in *Tensions of Empire*, ed. Fredrick Cooper and Ann Laura Stoler (Berkeley: University of California Press, 1997), 59–86; Glen Sean Coulthard, *Red Skin, White Masks: Rejecting the Colonial Politics of Recognition* (Minneapolis: University of Minnesota Press, 2014); Iris Marion Young, *Inclusion and Democracy* (New York: Oxford University Press, 2000); Wendy Brown, *States of Injury* (Princeton: Princeton University Press, 1995); Will Kymlicka, ed., *The Rights of Minority Cultures* (Oxford: Oxford University Press, 1995).

24. Based on Google tracking applications.

25. John Lawrence Hill, *The Prophet of Modern Constitutional Liberalism: John Stuart Mill and the Supreme Court* (Cambridge: Cambridge University Press, 2020); "Against the Tyranny of the Majority," *The Economist*, August 4, 2018, https://www.economist.com/schools-brief/2018/08/04/against-the-tyranny-of-the-majority. ; Nadia Urbinati and Alex Zakaras, eds., *J.S. Mill's Political Thought* (New York: Cambridge University Press, 2007); Jonathan Riley, "Mill's Neo-Athenian Model of Liberal Democracy," in *J.S. Mill's Political Thought*, ed. Nadia Urbinati and Alex Zakaras (New York: Cambridge University Press, 2007), 221–49; Introduction, J.S. Mill, *On Liberty and Other Writings*, ed. Stefan Collini (Cambridge: Cambridge University Press, 1989).

26. Richard Ashcraft, "John Stuart Mill and the Theoretical Foundations of Democratic Socialism," in *Mill and the Moral Character of Liberalism*, ed. Eldon J Eisenach (Pennsylvania: Pennsylvania State University Press, 1998), 169–90.
27. J.S. Mill, *Autobiography*, in *Autobiography and Literary Essays*, vol. 1, *The Collected Works of John Stuart Mill*, ed. John Robson and Jack Stillinger (Toronto: University of Toronto Press, 1981), 5.
28. Leslie Stephen, *The English Utilitarians: John Stuart Mill*, vol. 3 (London: Duckworth & Co., 1900); Nadia Urbinati, *Mill on Democracy: From the Athenian Polis to Representative Government* (Chicago: University of Chicago Press, 2002); Helen McCabe, *John Stuart Mill, Socialist* (Montreal: McGill-Queen's University Press, 2021).
29. Richard Reeves, *John Stuart Mill: Victorian Firebrand* (London: Atlantic Books, 2007), 8.
30. Urbinati and Zakaras, *J.S. Mill's Political Thought*.
31. Isaiah Berlin, *Four Essays on Liberty* (London: Oxford University Press, 1969); Cass Sunstein, "It's For Your Own Good!," *The New York Review of Books*, March 7, 2013; Barbara Arneil, "Liberal Colonialism, Domestic Colonies and Citizenship," *History of Political Thought* 33, no. 3 (2012): 491–523; Alan Ryan, "Mill in a Liberal Landscape," in *The Cambridge Companion to Mill*, ed. John Skorupski (Cambridge: Cambridge University Press, 1998), 497–540; John Gray, *Liberalism* (Minneapolis: University of Minnesota Press, 1995); Stefan Collini, "Liberalism and the Legacy of Mill," *The Historical Journal* 20, no. 1 (1977): 237–54; Gertrude Himmelfarb, *On Liberty and Liberalism: The Case of John Stuart Mill* (New York: Alfred A. Knopf, 1974).
32. Thomas Hueglin, *Classical Debates for the 21st Century: Rethinking Political Thought* (Toronto: Broadview Press, 2008).
33. Dorothy Ross, "Against Canons: Liberating the Social Sciences," *Society* 29, no. 1 (1991): 10.
34. Leigh K. Jenco, "Histories of Thought and Comparative Political Theory: The Curious Thesis of 'Chinese Origins for Western Knowledge,' 1860–1895," *Political Theory* 42, no. 6 (December 1, 2014): 658–81; Ross, "Against Canons."
35. Penny A. Weiss, *Canon Fodder: Historical Women Political Thinkers* (Pennsylvania: The Pennsylvania State University Press, 2009), xv.
36. Weiss, *Canon Fodder*; Jennifer Forestal and Menaka Philips, eds., *The Wives of Western Philosophy: Gender Politics in Intellectual Labor*, 1st edition (New York, NY: Routledge, 2020).
37. bell hooks, "Theory as Liberatory Practice," *Yale Journal of Law & Feminism* 4, no. 1 (1991): 1–12; Michael Hanchard, "Contours of Black Political Thought: An Introduction and Perspective," *Political Theory* 38, no. 4 (August 1, 2010): 510–36; Mary Hawkesworth, "From Constitutive Outside to the Politics of Extinction: Critical Race Theory, Feminist Theory, and Political Theory," *Political Research Quarterly* 63, no. 3 (2010): 686–96.
38. Melissa S. Williams, "Deparochializing Democratic Theory," in *Deparochializing Political Theory*, ed. Melissa S. Williams (Cambridge: Cambridge University Press, 2020), 201–29, ; Loubna El Amine, "Beyond East and West: Reorienting Political

Theory through the Prism of Modernity," *Perspectives on Politics* 14, no. 1 (2016): 102–29; Navid Hassanzadeh, "The Canon and Comparative Political Thought," *Journal of International Political Theory* 11, no. 2 (June 1, 2015): 184–202.
39. Ross, "Against Canons," 13. See also: Hueglin, *Classical Debates for the 21st Century*.
40. Roxanne L. Euben, *Enemy in the Mirror: Islamic Fundamentalism and the Limits of Modern Rationalism: A Work of Comparative Political Theory* (Princeton: Princeton University Press, 1999), 9.
41. J.S. Mill, *On Liberty*, in *Essays on Politics and Society*, vol. 18, *The Collected Works of John Stuart Mill*, ed. John Robson (Toronto: University of Toronto Press, 1977), 224.
42. Margaret Kohn and Kavita Reddy, "Colonialism," in *The Stanford Encyclopedia of Philosophy*, Fall 2017, ed. Edward N. Zalta, https://plato.stanford.edu/archives/fall2017/entries/colonialism/; Bell, *Reordering the World*; Pratap Bhanu Mehta, "Liberalism, Nation, and Empire: The Case of John Stuart Mill," in *Empire and Modern Political Thought*, ed. Sankar Muthu (New York: Cambridge University Press, 2012), 232–60; Pitts, *A Turn to Empire*.
43. Don Herzog, "Review: The Enlightenment, Republicanism, and Other Ghostly Afflictions," *Political Theory* 31, no. 2 (2003): 297.
44. Quentin Skinner, "Meaning and Understanding in the History of Ideas," in *Meaning and Context: Quentin Skinner and His Critics*, ed. James Tully (Princeton: Princeton University Press, 1998), 31.

# Chapter 2

1. Damon Linker, "An Ominous Prophecy for Liberalism," *The Week*, January 22, 2018, https://theweek.com/articles/749378/ominous-prophecy-liberalism.
2. For Fawcett, notably, "definitional puzzles are less worrisome than the blunt matter of liberalism's survival." Fawcett, *Liberalism: The Life of an Idea* (Princeton: Princeton University Press, 2018), xii.
3. Inder S. Marwah, *Liberalism, Diversity and Domination: Kant, Mill and the Government of Difference* (Cambridge: Cambridge University Press, 2019), 15.
4. Bhikhu Parekh, "A Varied Moral World," in *Is Multiculturalism Bad for Women?* ed. Joshua Cohen, Matthew Howard, and Martha Nussbaum (Princeton: Princeton University Press, 1999), 71.
5. Duncan Bell, *Reordering the World: Essays on Liberalism and Empire* (Princeton: Princeton University Press, 2016), 2.
6. Jennifer Pitts, *A Turn to Empire* (Princeton: Princeton University Press, 2005), 3.
7. Duncan Bell, "What Is Liberalism?," *Political Theory* 42, no. 6 (2014): 682–715.
8. Erkki Berndston, "The Development of Political Science: Methodological Problems of Comparative Research," in *The Development of Political Science: A Comparative Survey*, ed. David Easton, John G. Gunnell, and Luigi Graziano (New York: Routledge, 1991), 39.
9. David Easton, John G. Gunnell, and Luigi Graziano, *The Development of Political Science: A Comparative Survey* (London; New York: Routledge, 1991), 1.

10. Bernard Crick, *The American Science of Politics: Its Origins and Conditions* (Berkeley: University of California Press, 1959).
11. Dorothy Ross, "Robert Adcock. Liberalism and the Emergence of American Political Science: A Transatlantic Tale. Oxford: Oxford University Press, 2014," *American Political Thought* 4, no. 4 (September 2015): 670; Robert Adcock, Mark Bevir, and Shannon C. Stimson, *Modern Political Science: Anglo-American Exchanges since 1880*, Princeton Paperbacks (Princeton: University Press, 2007).
12. Jean Blondel, *The Discipline of Politics* (Boston: Butterworth-Heinemann, 1981).
13. James Farr, "Remembering the Revolution: Behavioralism in American Political Science," in *Political Science in History*, ed. James Farr, John S Dryzek, and Stephen T Leonard (Cambridge: Cambridge University Press, 1995), 198.
14. R. Adcock, *Liberalism and the Emergence of American Political Science: A Transatlantic Tale* (New York: Oxford University Press, 2014).
15. Adcock, *Liberalism and the Emergence of American Political Science*, 3–4.
16. Adcock, 19, 20, 275.
17. Ross, "Robert Adcock. Liberalism and the Emergence of American Political Science"; Dorothy Ross, *The Origins of American Social Science* (Cambridge: Cambridge University Press, 1991); John G. Gunnell, "American Political Science, Liberalism, and the Invention of Political Theory," *American Political Science Review* 82, no. 1 (1988): 71–87.
18. David M. Ricci, "Contradictions of a Political Discipline," in *Discipline and History: Political Science in the United States*, ed. James Farr and Raymond Seidelman (Ann Arbor: The University of Michigan Press, 1993), 165–78.
19. Raymond Seidelman, "Political Scientists, Disenchanted Realists, and Disappearing Democrats," in *Discipline and History: Political Science in the United States*, ed. James Farr and Raymond Seidelman (Ann Arbor: The University of Michigan Press, 1993), 311.
20. Ricci, "Contradictions of a Political Discipline," 175.
21. Sheldon S. Wolin, "Political Theory as a Vocation," *American Political Science Review* 63, no. 4 (1969): 1062–82; John G. Gunnell, "Behavioralism," in *The Encyclopedia of Political Thought*, ed. Michael Gibbons, Diana Coole, Elisabeth Ellis, and Kennan Ferguson (Malden: Wiley-Blackwell, 2014), 272–77; Terence Ball, "From Paradigms to Research Programs: Towards a Post-Kuhnian Political Science," *American Journal of Political Science* 20, no. 1 (February 1976): 151–77; See also: Josh Berkenpas, "'The Behavioural Revolution'? A Genealogy of a Concept," *European Political Science* 15, no. 2 (June 2016): 233–50.
22. Farr, "Remembering the Revolution: Behavioralism in American Political Science," 202.
23. Farr, 206.
24. John Gunnell, "Political Science, History of," in *The Encyclopedia of Political Science*, ed. George Thomas Kurian (Washington: CQ Press, 2013), 1276–89, 1283.
25. Gunnell, "American Political Science, Liberalism, and the Invention of Political Theory," 80.
26. Gunnell, 79; See also: Wolin, "Political Theory as a Vocation."

27. Farr, "Remembering the Revolution: Behavioralism in American Political Science," 205.
28. Leo Strauss, *Liberalism Ancient and Modern*, 1st edition (Chicago: University of Chicago Press, 1968), 223.
29. Herbert J. Storing, ed., *Essays on the Scientific Study of Politics* (New York: Holt, Rinehart, & Winston, 1962), 326–27.
30. John G. Gunnell, "Pluralism and the Fate of Perestroika: A Historical Reflection," *Perspectives on Politics* 13, no. 2 (2015): 408–15; John S. Dryzek, "Revolutions without Enemies: Key Transformations in Political Science," *American Political Science Review* 100, no. 4 (2006): 487–92.
31. Timothy W. Luke and Patrick J. McGovern, "The Rebels' Yell: Mr. Perestroika and the Causes of This Rebellion in Context," *PS: Political Science & Politics* 43, no. 4 (October 2010): 729.
32. Dryzek, "Revolutions without Enemies," 490.
33. Judith N. Shklar, "Redeeming American Political Theory," *American Political Science Review* 85, no. 1 (March 1991): 3.
34. Ira Katznelson, "APSA Presidential Address: At the Court of Chaos: Political Science in an Age of Perpetual Fear," *Perspectives on Politics* 5, no. 1 (2007): 3.
35. Peter Laslett, *Philosophy Politics and Society*, 1st edition (Oxford: Blackwell Publishers, 1956), 1.
36. Jurgen Habermas, "Reconciliation through the Public Use of Reason: Remarks on John Rawls's Political Liberalism," *The Journal of Philosophy* 92, no. 3 (1995): 109–31; Seyla Benhabib, *Situating the Self* (New York: Routledge, 1992); Susan Moller Okin, *Justice, Gender, and The Family*, 2008 edition (New York: Basic Books, 1989); Michael Sandel, "The Procedural Republic and the Unencumbered Self," *Political Theory* 12, no. 1 (1984): 81–96.
37. William Galston, "Defending Liberalism," *American Political Science Review* 76, no. 3 (1982): 621–29.
38. Lila Abu-Lughod, *Do Muslim Women Need Saving?* (Cambridge: Harvard University Press, 2013); Saba Mahmood, *Politics of Piety: The Islamic Revival and the Feminist Subject* (Princeton: Princeton University Press, 2005); Alison M. Jaggar, "'Saving Amina': Global Justice for Women and Intercultural Dialogue," *Ethics & International Affairs* 19, no. 3 (2005): 55–75; Susan Moller Okin, "Feminism and Multiculturalism: Some Tensions," *Ethics* 108, no. 4 (1998): 661–84; Denise Schaeffer, "Feminism and Liberalism Reconsidered: The Case of Catharine MacKinnon," *American Political Science Review* 95, no. 3 (September 2001): 699–708; Marwah, *Liberalism, Diversity and Domination*; Bell, *Reordering the World*; Karuna Mantena, *Alibis of Empire* (Princeton: Princeton University Press, 2010); Jennifer Pitts, "Political Theory of Empire and Imperialism," *Annual Review of Political Science* 13 (2010): 211–35; Seyla Benhabib, "The Liberal Imagination and the Four Dogmas of Multiculturalism," *Yale Journal of Criticism* 12, no. 2 (1999): 401–13; Will Kymlicka, "Liberal Multiculturalism as a Political Theory of State-Minority Relations," *Political Theory* 46, no. 1 (February 1, 2018): 81–91; Anne Philips, *Multiculturalism without Culture* (Princeton: Princeton University Press, 2009); Joan Wallach Scott,

*Sex and Secularism* (Princeton University Press, 2017); W. Brown, *Undoing the Demos: Neoliberalism's Stealth Revolution* (New York: Zone Books, 2015).
39. Bell, "What Is Liberalism?," 689.
40. Bell, 698.
41. David Armitage, "John Locke: Theorist of Empire?," in *Empire and Modern Political Thought*, ed. Sankar Muthu (New York: Cambridge University Press, 2012), 84.
42. Bell, "What Is Liberalism?," 689–90.
43. Pitts, "Political Theory of Empire and Imperialism," 216.
44. Helena Rosenblatt, *The Lost History of Liberalism: From Ancient Rome to the Twenty-First Century* (Princeton: Princeton University Press, 2018).
45. Don Herzog, "Review: The Enlightenment, Republicanism, and Other Ghostly Afflictions," *Political Theory* 31, no. 2 (2003): 296.
46. Terence Ball and Richard Dagger, eds., *Political Ideologies and the Democratic Ideal*, 8th edition (New York: Pearson/Longman, 2011), 47.
47. Ball and Dagger, *Political Ideologies and the Democratic Ideal*, 82.
48. Michael Freeden, *Liberalism: A Very Short Introduction*, vol. 434, *Very Short Introductions* (Oxford: Oxford University Press, 2015), 9.
49. Fawcett, *Liberalism: The Life of an Idea*.
50. Freeden, *Liberalism*, 20.
51. Michael Hörnqvist, "Machiavelli's Three Desires," in *Empire and Modern Political Thought*, ed. Sankar Muthu (New York: Cambridge University Press, 2012), 8; Freeden, *Liberalism*, 20, 22; See also: Rosenblatt, *The Lost History of Liberalism*.
52. Fawcett, *Liberalism: The Life of an Idea*, 1.
53. Ball and Dagger, *Political Ideologies and the Democratic Ideal*, 45–47.
54. Ball and Dagger, 52, 45–91.
55. Ball and Dagger, 54.
56. Lawrence Berns, "Thomas Hobbes," in *History of Political Philosophy*, ed. Leo Strauss and Joseph Cropsey (Chicago: University of Chicago Press, 2012), 401.
57. Ball and Dagger refer to distinctions between "welfare liberals," "libertarians," and "neoclassical liberals" as a way of capturing some of the different approaches to issues of politics and governance that exist *within* "liberalism as a single ideology." Ball and Dagger, *Political Ideologies and the Democratic Ideal*, 82.
58. Nadia Urbinati and Alex Zakaras, eds., *J.S. Mill's Political Thought* (New York: Cambridge University Press, 2007), 2.
59. W. Whewell, "Comte and Positivism, MacMillan's Magazine" (1866), Mill-Taylor Collection/45, London School of Economics.
60. New York Times. "OBITUARY, John Stuart Mill," May 10, 1873. https://www.nytimes.com/1873/05/10/archives/obituary-john-stuart-mill.html.
61. Ball and Dagger, *Political Ideologies and the Democratic Ideal*, 67.
62. Steven Wall, *The Cambridge Companion to Liberalism* (Cambridge: Cambridge University Press, 2015), 8.
63. Isaiah Berlin, *Four Essays on Liberty* (London: Oxford University Press, 1969), 173.
64. Freeden, *Liberalism*, 72.

65. "The Literature of Liberalism—Open Future, *The Economist*, August 29 2018, https://www.economist.com/open-future/2018/08/29/the-literature-of-liberalism.
66. J.S. Mill, *On Liberty*, in *Essays on Politics and Society*, vol. 18, *The Collected Works of John Stuart Mill*, ed. John M. Robson (Toronto: University of Toronto Press, 1977), 218.
67. Mill, *On Liberty*, 18:241.
68. Mill, 18:230, 246.
69. It is particularly striking, for example, that while Mill served as a member of the Liberal Party in Parliament for a short period, he made efforts to distance himself from such labels noting that he ought not to be thought of as "an organ of their opinions." J.S. Mill, *Autobiography*, in *Autobiography and Literary Essays*, vol. 1, *The Collected Works of John Stuart Mill*, ed. John M. Robson and Jack Stillinger (Toronto: University of Toronto, 1981), 289.
70. Richard Reeves, *John Stuart Mill: Victorian Firebrand* (London: Atlantic Books, 2007), 8.
71. Mill was himself a proponent of taking into account the "many-sidedness" of social and political questions, as he details in his *Autobiography*.
72. Reeves, *John Stuart Mill: Victorian Firebrand*, 9, 465.
73. Reeves, 9.
74. Reeves, 8.
75. C. L. Ten, *Mill on Liberty* (New York: Oxford University Press, 1980), 173.
76. Alan Ryan, "Mill in a Liberal Landscape," in *The Cambridge Companion to Mill*, ed. John Skorupski (Cambridge: Cambridge University Press, 1998), 497.
77. Urbinati and Zakaras, *J.S. Mill's Political Thought*, 2.
78. Nicholas Capaldi, *John Stuart Mill: A Biography* (Cambridge: Cambridge University Press, 2004); Reeves, *John Stuart Mill: Victorian Firebrand*; Joseph Hamburger, *Intellectuals in Politics: John Stuart Mill and the Philosophic Radicals* (New Haven: Yale University Press, 1965); Maurice Cowling, *Mill and Liberalism* (Cambridge: Cambridge University Press, 1963); Ludwig von Mises, *Liberalism in the Classical Tradition*, 3rd edition (New York: Cobden Press, 1985); Gertrude Himmelfarb, *On Liberty and Liberalism: The Case of John Stuart Mill* (New York: Alfred A. Knopf, 1974); Berlin, *Four Essays on Liberty*; Wendy Brown, *Regulating Aversion: Tolerance in the Age of Identity and Empire* (Princeton: Princeton University Press, 2006); Nadia Urbinati, *Mill on Democracy: From the Athenian Polis to Representative Government* (Chicago: University of Chicago Press, 2002); Ryan, "Mill in a Liberal Landscape"; Uday Mehta, *Liberalism and Empire* (Chicago: University of Chicago Press, 1999).
79. Capaldi, *John Stuart Mill: A Biography*, 266.
80. Ten, *Mill on Liberty*, 1.
81. von Mises, *Liberalism in the Classical Tradition*, 194–95.
82. In his review of her work, Collini suggests that "most of what Professor Himmelfarb does not like about the modern world (which amounts to a great deal of it) is, in some not very clear way, derived from Mill's essay." Stefan Collini, "Liberalism and the Legacy of Mill," *The Historical Journal* 20, no. 1 (1977): 242.

83. Himmelfarb, *On Liberty and Liberalism: The Case of John Stuart Mill*, 336.
84. Murray N. Rothbard, *An Austrian Perspective on the History of Economic Thought*, vol. 2, Ludwig von Mises Institute (Alabama: Edward Elgar Publishing Ltd., 1995), 277, 287.
85. Cowling, *Mill and Liberalism*, 93, 41.
86. John Gray, *Liberalisms: Essays in Political Philosophy* (London: Routledge, 1989), 1, 224.
87. Gray, *Liberalisms: Essays in Political Philosophy*, 226.
88. Allan Bloom, *The Closing of the American Mind* (New York: Simon and Schuster, 1987), 29–30.
89. Reeves, *John Stuart Mill: Victorian Firebrand*, 485.
90. John Rawls, *Justice as Fairness* (Cambridge: Belknap Press of Harvard University Press, 2003), 156–57; Sandel, "The Procedural Republic and the Unencumbered Self," 189.
91. Urbinati, *Mill on Democracy: From the Athenian Polis to Representative Government*; Bruce Baum, *Rereading Power and Freedom in J.S. Mill* (Toronto: University of Toronto Press, 2000).
92. Will Kymlicka, *Liberalism, Community, and Culture* (Oxford: Clarendon Press, 1989), 11, 10–13.
93. Baum, *Rereading Power and Freedom in J.S. Mill*, 15.
94. Catharine MacKinnon, *Toward a Feminist Theory of the State* (Cambridge: Harvard University Press, 1989); Maria Morales, *Perfect Equality: John Stuart Mill on Well-Constituted Communities* (Boulder & New York: Rowman & Littlefield Publishers, Inc., 1996), 1.
95. Maria Morales, "Rational Freedom in John Stuart Mill," in *J.S. Mill's Political Thought*, ed. Nadia Urbinati and Alex Zakaras (New York: Cambridge University Press, 2007), 46.
96. Quentin Taylor, "John Stuart Mill, Political Economist: A Reassessment," *The Independent Review* 21, no. 1 (2016): 91.
97. Helen McCabe, *John Stuart Mill, Socialist* (Montreal: McGill-Queen's University Press, 2021).
98. Shiraz Dossa, "Liberal Imperialism?: Natives, Muslims, and Others," *Political Theory* 30, no. 5 (October 1, 2002): 739.
99. Pitts, *A Turn to Empire*; Uday Mehta, "Liberal Strategies of Exclusion," in *Tensions of Empire*, ed. Fredrick Cooper and Ann Laura Stoler (Berkeley: University of California Press, 1997), 59–86; Brown, *Regulating Aversion: Tolerance in the Age of Identity and Empire*; Eddy Souffrant, *Formal Transgressions: John Stuart Mill's Philosophy of International Affairs* (Oxford: Rowman & Littlefield, 2000); Karuna Mantena, "Mill and the Imperial Predicament," in *J.S. Mill's Political Thought*, ed. Nadia Urbinati and Alex Zakaras (New York: Cambridge University Press, 2007), 298–318; Talal Asad, *On Suicide Bombing* (New York: Columbia University Press, 2007).
100. Baum, *Rereading Power and Freedom in J.S. Mill*, 5.

101. Baum, 4-5, 10-12 For this reason, Baum sees Mill aligned in striking ways with thinkers like Foucault.
102. Urbinati, *Mill on Democracy: From the Athenian Polis to Representative Government*; Paul Kelly, *Liberalism* (Cambridge: Polity, 2004).
103. Dennis Thompson, "Mill in Parliament," in *J.S. Mill's Political Thought*, ed. Nadia Urbinati and Alex Zakaras (New York: Cambridge University Press, 2007), 167.
104. Jeremy Waldron, "Mill on Liberty and on the Contagious Diseases Acts," in *J.S. Mill's Political Thought*, ed. Nadia Urbinati and Alex Zakaras (New York: Cambridge University Press, 2007), 11–42.
105. Mill, *Autobiography*, 1:289. Emphasis added.
106. Mill, 1:227. Mill's reasoning for writing the essays echoes his arguments for considering different facets of an argument in *On Liberty*. See also Alan Ryan, *J.S. Mill* (London: Routledge, 1974), 53.
107. J.S. Mill, Letter to Cairnes (1871), in *The Later Letters of John Stuart Mill 1849–1873 Part IV*, vol. 17, *The Collected Works of John Stuart Mill*, ed. Francis E. Mineka and Dwight N. Lindley (Toronto: University of Toronto Press, 1972), 1829. He took a similar line on the issue of women's suffrage in 1872, writing that a "Conservative who will vote for women's suffrage should be, in general, preferred to a professed Liberal who will not." Mill, Letter to Robertson (1872), 17:1917.
108. J.S. Mill, Editor's Introduction, in *Essays on Equality, Law, and Education*, vol. 21, *The Collected Works of John Stuart Mill*, ed. John M. Robson (Toronto: University of Toronto Press, 1984), xxviii.
109. J.S. Mill, *On Liberty and Other Writings*, ed. Stefan Collini (Cambridge: Cambridge University Press, 1989), vii; Urbinati and Zakaras, *J.S. Mill's Political Thought*, 1–2.
110. Ryan, "Mill in a Liberal Landscape," 497.
111. Wall, *The Cambridge Companion to Liberalism*, 1.
112. "The Literature of Liberalism—Open Future."

# Chapter 3

1. Elements of the argument presented in this chapter first appeared in Menaka Philips, "Troubling Appropriations: JS Mill, Liberalism, and the Virtues of Uncertainty," *European Journal of Political Theory* 18, no. 1 (January 1, 2019): 68–88.
2. Terence Ball, "The Formation of Character: Mill's 'Ethology' Reconsidered," *Polity* 33, no. 1 (2000): 25–48; Shefali Misra, "Friend, nor Foe: Mill's Liberal Multiculturalism," *European Journal of Political Theory* 11, no. 3 (2012): 1–19; Wendy Brown, *Regulating Aversion: Tolerance in the Age of Identity and Empire* (Princeton: Princeton University Press, 2006); Uday Mehta, "Liberal Strategies of Exclusion," in *Tensions of Empire*, ed. Fredrick Cooper and Ann Laura Stoler (Berkeley: University of California Press, 1997), 59–86; Saba Mahmood, *Politics of Piety: The Islamic Revival and the Feminist Subject* (Princeton: Princeton University Press, 2005).

168 NOTES

3. J.T. Levy, *Rationalism, Pluralism, and Freedom* (Oxford University Press, 2015), 10.
4. Don Herzog, "Review: The Enlightenment, Republicanism, and Other Ghostly Afflictions," *Political Theory* 31, no. 2 (2003): 296.
5. John M. Robson, *The Improvement of Mankind: The Social and Political Thought of John Stuart Mill* (Toronto: University of Toronto Press, 1968), 85; Nicholas Capaldi, *John Stuart Mill: A Biography* (Cambridge: Cambridge University Press, 2004); John Skorupski, *Why Read Mill Today?* (London: Routledge, 2006).
6. John Gray, "Bibliographical Essay, John Stuart Mill: Traditional and Revisionist Interpretations," *Literature of Liberty: A Review of Contemporary Liberal Thought* 2, no. 2 (1979): 33.
7. J.S. Mill, *Autobiography*, in *Autobiography and Literary Essays*, vol. 1, *The Collected Works of John Stuart Mill* ed. John M. Robson and Jack Stillinger (Toronto: Toronto University Press, 1981), 5.
8. Elizabeth S. Anderson, "John Stuart Mill and Experiments in Living," *Ethics* 102, no. 1 (1991): 4–26; Martha Nussbaum, "Mill between Aristotle and Bentham," *Daedalus* 133, no. 2 (2004): 60–68; Samuel Clark, "Pleasure as Self-Discovery," *Ratio* 25, no. 3 (2012): 260–76; Ball, "The Formation of Character: Mill's 'Ethology' Reconsidered."
9. Mill, Editor's Introduction, in *Autobiography and Literary Essays*, 1:vii–xxx.
10. Mill, *Autobiography*, 1:5.
11. J.S. Mill, "Bentham," in *Essays on Ethics, Religion and Society*, vol. 10, *The Collected Works of John Stuart Mill*, ed. John M. Robson (Toronto: University of Toronto Press, 1969), 90; J.S. Mill, *On Liberty*, in *Essays on Politics and Society*, vol. 18, *The Collected Works of John Stuart Mill*, ed. John M. Robson (Toronto: University of Toronto Press, 1977).
12. Eldon J. Eisenach, "Mill's 'Autobiography' As Political Theory," *History of Political Thought* 8, no. 1 (1987): 111–29.
13. Nussbaum, "Mill between Aristotle and Bentham."
14. Isaiah Berlin, *Four Essays on Liberty* (London: Oxford University Press, 1969), 175.
15. Quoted in Capaldi, *John Stuart Mill: A Biography*, 20.
16. Mill, *Autobiography*, 1:27.
17. Mill, 1:25.
18. Mill, 1:25, 5.
19. Mill, 1:59, 61.
20. Mill, 1:37.
21. Mill, 1:63.
22. Mill, 1:129.
23. Mill, 1:27.
24. Mill, 1:87.
25. Lynn Zastoupil, "India, J.S. Mill, and 'Western' Culture," in *J.S. Mill's Encounter with India*, ed. Martin Moir, Douglas Peers, and Lynn Zastoupil (Toronto: University of Toronto Press, 1999), 137.
26. Mill, *Autobiography*, 1:87.
27. Mill, 1:69.
28. Mill, 1:139.

29. Stefan Collini, *Public Moralists: Political Thought and Intellectual Life in Britain* (Oxford: Clarendon Press, 1991), 122.
30. Mill, *Autobiography*, 1:139.
31. Mill, 1:5.
32. Mill, 1:149.
33. Mill, 1:149.
34. Mill, 1:52.
35. Mill, 1:175.
36. Mill, 1:163.
37. Mill, 1:175.
38. Mill, 1:613.
39. Mill, 1:613.
40. Mill, 1:113.
41. Robert Cumming, *Human Nature and History*, vol. 1 (Chicago: University of Chicago, 1969), 287.
42. Mill, *Autobiography*, 1:165. See also Thomas Macaulay, *Mill on Government*, in *The Miscellaneous Writings of Lord Macaulay* (London: Longman, Green, Longman, and Roberts, 1823), 285.
43. Gray, "Bibliographical Essay, John Stuart Mill: Traditional and Revisionist Interpretations," 29.
44. Mill, "Bentham," 10:91.
45. Mill, 10:91, 92.
46. Mill, 10:92.
47. Mill, *Autobiography*, 1:112–13.
48. Mill, 1:117.
49. Robson, *The Improvement of Mankind: The Social and Political Thought of John Stuart Mill*, 76.
50. Mill, *Autobiography*, 1:156.
51. Skorupski, *Why Read Mill Today?*, 4.
52. Mill, *Autobiography*, 1:173.
53. Mill, 1:175.
54. Capaldi, *John Stuart Mill: A Biography*, 92.
55. Robson, *The Improvement of Mankind: The Social and Political Thought of John Stuart Mill*, 78.
56. Mill, *Autobiography*, 1:219, 221.
57. Mill, "Coleridge," 10:122.
58. Mill, 10:122.
59. Mill, *Autobiography*, 1:171.
60. Mill, 1:253.
61. Mill, 1:169.
62. Ball, "The Formation of Character: Mill's 'Ethology' Reconsidered," 37.
63. Mill noted this in his dedication to Taylor in *On Liberty*. Mill, *Essays on Politics and Society*, 18:216.

64. Harriet Taylor Mill, *The Complete Works of Harriet Taylor Mill*, ed. Jo Ellen Jacobs and Paula Harms Payne (Bloomington: Indiana University Press, 1998), 31.
65. H.O. Pappe, *John Stuart Mill and the Harriet Taylor Myth*, Social Science Monographs (Melbourne: Melbourne University Press, 1960); Francis E. Mineka, "The Autobiography and the Lady," *University of Toronto Quarterly* 32, no. 3 (1963): 301–6; Susan Moller Okin, *Women in Western Political Thought* (Princeton: Princeton University Press, 1979).
66. Carole Pateman, *The Sexual Contract* (Stanford: Stanford University Press, 1988), 160.
67. Some readers might wonder how Taylor's editorial role in the composition of Mill's *Autobiography* should affect our reading of the text. Jack Stillinger's reconstruction of the evolution of the *Autobiography* offers some guidance here. Though one can detect something of the patriarchal bastion Pateman observes in his descriptions of Taylor's editorial role as, variously, that of the "wicked sister-and daughter-in-law," the "Victorian prude" or Mill's "mother-protector"—Stillinger later acknowledges a complex reality of intellectual production, namely, the wide-ranging fact of "the joint or multiple authorship of works presented (and generally thought of) as having been written by a single author." That fact should suggest that Mill's *Autobiography* is no different than many others in the nature of its production. And indeed, recognizing the collaborative labors that go into textual production might allow us to put to bed the tradition of making intellectual biography a narrative of "great men" thinking "great thoughts," as Terrell Carver argues. But in the case of Mill and Taylor, we should also not assume that Taylor's editorial hand simply substituted for Mill's autobiographical exploration. He did have the opportunity to review her notes, and even as many were accepted, some were altered or rejected. He continued to edit and revise the text until 1870—more than a decade following her death. In short, we can read the *Autobiography* as a collaborative effort on their part to preserve, and to present, Mill's account of his life. But that collaborative relationship was an essential part of the "great man" later generations have come to know. Jack Stillinger, "Who Wrote J.S. Mill's Autobiography," *Victorian Studies* 27 (1983): 21. See also: Terrell Carver, "'Mere Auxiliaries to the Movement:' How Intellectual Biography Obscures Marx's and Engels's Gendered Political Partnerships.," in *The Wives of Western Philosophy: Gender Politics in Intellectual Labor*, ed. Jennifer Forestal and Menaka Philips (New York: Routledge, 2020), 169; Cecilia Mazanec, "#ThanksForTyping Spotlights Unnamed Women In Literary Acknowledgments," NPR.org, March 30, 2017, https://www.npr.org/2017/03/30/521931310/-thanksfortyping-spotlights-unnamed-women-in-literary-acknowledgements.
68. Menaka Philips, "The 'Beloved and Deplored' Memory of Harriet Taylor Mill: Rethinking Gender and Intellectual Labor in the Canon," in *The Wives of Western Philosophy: Gender Politics in Intellectual Labor*, ed. Jennifer Forestal and Menaka Philips (New York: Routledge, 2020), 147–66.
69. Alice S. Rossi, ed., *Essays on Sex Equality* (Chicago: University of Chicago Press, 1970); Janet A. Seiz and Michèle A. Pujol, "Harriet Taylor Mill," *The American Economic Review* 90, no. 2 (2000): 476–79; Penelope Deutscher, "When Feminism Is 'High' and Ignorance Is 'Low': Harriet Taylor Mill on the Progress of the Species," *Hypatia* 21, no.

3 (2006): 136–50; Helen McCabe, "'Political ... Civil and Domestic Slavery': Harriet Taylor Mill and Anna Doyle Wheeler on Marriage, Servitude, and Socialism," *British Journal for the History of Philosophy* 29, no. 2 (March 4, 2021): 226–43.

70. Mill, *Autobiography*, 1:253.
71. John Dewey, *The Quest for Certainty* (Carbondale & Edwardsville: Southern Illinois University Press, 1988), 154. See also: James Farr, "John Dewey and American Political Science," *American Journal of Political Science* 43, no. 2 (1999): 520–41; Geoff Dancy, "Human Rights Pragmatism: Belief, Inquiry, and Action," *European Journal of International Relations* 22, no. 3 (September 1, 2016): 512–35.
72. J.S. Mill, *A System of Logic Ratiocinative and Inductive, Books IV–VI*, vol. 8, *The Collected Works of John Stuart Mill*, ed. John M. Robson (Toronto: University of Toronto Press, 1974), 840.
73. Ashcraft, "John Stuart Mill and the Theoretical Foundations of Democratic Socialism," 169.
74. Bhikhu Parekh, "Decolonizing Liberalism," in *The End of "Isms"? Reflections on the Fate of Ideological Politics after Communism's Collapse*, ed. Aleksandras Shtromas (Oxford: Blackwell Publishers, 1994), 11.
75. Eddy Souffrant, *Formal Transgressions: John Stuart Mill's Philosophy of International Affairs* (Oxford: Rowman & Littlefield, 2000), 57, 60.
76. John Gray, "Pluralism and Toleration in Contemporary Political Philosophy," *Political Studies* 48, no. 2 (2000): 323–33.
77. J.S. Mill, *Subjection of Women*, in *Essays on Equality, Law, and Education*, vol. 21, *The Collected Works of John Stuart Mill*, ed. John M. Robson (Toronto: University of Toronto Press, 1984), 313.
78. Mill, *On Liberty*, 18:262.
79. Mill, 18:262.
80. Souffrant, *Formal Transgressions: John Stuart Mill's Philosophy of International Affairs*, 54, 77.
81. Mill, *Autobiography*, 1:613.
82. Jonathan Riley, "Individuality, Custom and Progress," *Utilitas* 3, no. 2 (1991): 220. See also: Jennie C. Ikuta, *Contesting Conformity: Democracy and the Paradox of Political Belonging* (New York: Oxford University Press, 2020).
83. Mill, *On Liberty*, 18:262; Alan Ryan, *J.S. Mill* (London: Routledge, 1974).
84. Mill, *Subjection of Women*, 21:307–8, 324, 325.
85. Brown, *Regulating Aversion: Tolerance in the Age of Identity and Empire*; Catharine MacKinnon, *Toward a Feminist Theory of the State* (Cambridge: Harvard University Press, 1989).
86. Eisenach, "Mill's Autobiography as Political Theory," 114.
87. Mill, *On Liberty*, 18:232.
88. Nadia Urbinati, *Mill on Democracy: From the Athenian Polis to Representative Government* (Chicago: University of Chicago Press, 2002), 203.
89. Mill, *On Liberty*, 18:223.
90. David Dyzenhaus, "John Stuart Mill and the Harm of Pornography," in *Mill's On Liberty*, ed. Gerald Dworkin (Oxford: Rowman & Littlefield, 1997), 31–54;

Robert Skipper, "Mill and Pornography," in *Mill's On Liberty*, ed. Gerald Dworkin (Oxford: Rowman & Littlefield, 1997), 55–60; Lorna N. Bracewell, *Why We Lost the Sex Wars: Sexual Freedom in the #MeToo Era* (Minneapolis: University of Minnesota Press, 2021), 90–98.
91. Sarah Conly, *Against Autonomy: Justifying Coercive Paternalism* (Cambridge: Cambridge University Press, 2013); Donald Dripps, "The Liberal Critique of the Harm Principle," *Criminal Justice Ethics* 17, no. 2 (1998): 3–18.
92. John Gray, *Liberalisms: Essays in Political Philosophy* (London: Routledge, 1989), 222.
93. Leslie Green, "Internal Minorities and Their Rights," in *The Rights of Minority Cultures*, ed. Will Kymlicka (Oxford: Oxford University Press, 1995), 256–74.
94. Mill, *On Liberty*, 18:224.
95. Mill, 18:232.
96. Mill, 18:276.
97. This reading of the HP can extend Nadia Urbinati's argument that Mill's work on democratic institutions, voting practices, and citizenship privileges deliberation. Urbinati, *Mill on Democracy: From the Athenian Polis to Representative Government*.
98. Mill, *On Liberty*, 18:277.

# Chapter 4

1. His friend Alexander Bain remarked that Mill "postulates a degree of equality that does not chime in with the least biased observers." Alexander Bain, *John Stuart Mill: A Criticism with Personal Recollections* (London: Longmans, Green, and Co, 1882), 131; Maria Morales, ed., *Mill's Subjection of Women* (Oxford: Rowman & Littlefield Publishers, Inc., 2005), xiii.
2. John M. Robson, "Mill in Parliament: The View from the Comic Papers," *Utilitas* 2, no. 1 (May 1990): 102–43; Joan Wallach Scott, *Sex and Secularism* (Princeton: Princeton University Press, 2017), 106.
3. Ernest Jones, *The Life and Work of Sigmund Freud*, vol. 1 (New York: Basic Books, 1953), 176.
4. The Representation of the People Act of 1918 allowed British women over thirty who met property qualifications to vote in parliamentary elections. The franchise was fully extended in 1928. Richard Reeves, *John Stuart Mill: Victorian Firebrand* (London: Atlantic Books, 2007), 448; Bruce L. Kinzer, Anne P. Robson, and John M. Robson, *A Moralist in and out of Parliament: John Stuart Mill at Westminster, 1865–1868* (Toronto: University of Toronto Press, 1992).
5. Harriet Taylor Mill, *The Complete Works of Harriet Taylor Mill*, ed. Jo Ellen Jacobs and Paula Harms Payne (Bloomington: Indiana University Press, 1998).
6. J.S. Mill, "Women's Suffrage," in *Public and Parliamentary Speeches Part II*, vol. 29, *The Collected Works of John Stuart Mill*, ed. John M. Robson and Bruce L. Kinzer (Toronto: University of Toronto Press, 1988), 388.
7. J.S. Mill, *Autobiography*, in *Autobiography and Literary Essays*, vol. 1, *The Collected Works of John Stuart Mill*, ed. John M. Robson and Jack Stillinger (Toronto: Toronto University Press, 1981), 52.

8. Mill, *Autobiography*, 1:612.
9. Nicholas Capaldi, *John Stuart Mill: A Biography* (Cambridge: Cambridge University Press, 2004), 4.
10. J.S. Mill, *Subjection of Women*, in *Essays on Equality, Law, and Education*, vol. 21, *The Collected Works of John Stuart Mill* ed. John M. Robson (Toronto: University of Toronto Press, 1984), 261.
11. James Mill, *James Mill: Political Writings*, ed. Terence Ball (Cambridge: Cambridge University Press, 1992), 27.
12. Menaka Philips, "The 'Beloved and Deplored' Memory of Harriet Taylor Mill: Rethinking Gender and Intellectual Labor in the Canon," in *The Wives of Western Philosophy: Gender Politics in Intellectual Labor*, ed. Jennifer Forestal and Menaka Philips (New York: Routledge, 2020), 147–66.
13. Susan Moller Okin, *Justice, Gender, and The Family*, 2008 edition (New York: Basic Books, 1989), 14.
14. Maria Morales, "Rational Freedom in John Stuart Mill," in *J.S. Mill's Political Thought*, ed. Nadia Urbinati and Alex Zakaras (New York: Cambridge University Press, 2007), 46; Ruth Abbey, *The Return of Feminist Liberalism* (Montreal: McGill-Queen's University Press, 2011).
15. Wendy Donner, "John Stuart Mill's Liberal Feminism," in *Mill's Subjection of Women*, ed. Maria Morales (Oxford: Rowman & Littlefield Publishers, Inc., 2005), 1–12.
16. Donner, "John Stuart Mill's Liberal Feminism," 2.
17. Julia Annas, "Mill and the Subjection of Women," in *Mill's Subjection of Women*, ed. Maria Morales (Oxford: Rowman & Littlefield, 2005), 56–57, 69. Jennifer Ring, "Mill's *The Subjection of Women*: The Methodological Limits of Liberal Feminism," *Review of Politics* 47, no. 1 (1985): 27–44.
18. Janet Halley, *Split Decisions: How and Why to Take a Break from Feminism* (Princeton: Princeton University Press, 2006), 322–23.
19. Halley, *Split Decisions: How and Why to Take a Break from Feminism*, 333–34.
20. Keith Burgess-Jackson, "John Stuart Mill, Radical Feminist," in *Mill's Subjection of Women*, ed. Maria Morales (Oxford: Rowman & Littlefield Publishers, Inc., 2005), 71–97.
21. Burgess-Jackson, "John Stuart Mill, Radical Feminist," 88.
22. Saba Mahmood, *Politics of Piety: The Islamic Revival and the Feminist Subject* (Princeton: Princeton University Press, 2005), 10.
23. Menaka Philips, "Feminist Preoccupations: Liberalism as Method in Debates Concerning Gender and Culture," *Signs: Journal of Women in Culture and Society* 44, no. 4 (May 21, 2019): 955–77.
24. Mahmood, *Politics of Piety: The Islamic Revival and the Feminist Subject*, fn 15, 10.
25. Mahmood, 10.
26. Mill, *Subjection of Women*, 21:262. Emphasis added.
27. Mill, 21:263.
28. Mahmood, *Politics of Piety: The Islamic Revival and the Feminist Subject*, 15.
29. Catharine MacKinnon, *Toward a Feminist Theory of the State* (Cambridge: Harvard University Press, 1989), 7.
30. MacKinnon, *Toward a Feminist Theory of the State*, 45.

31. MacKinnon, 45–46.
32. Catharine A. MacKinnon, "'The Case' Responds," *American Political Science Review* 95, no. 3 (2001): 709.
33. Don Herzog, "'Is(n't) Catharine MacKinnon a Liberal?,'" *Newsletter on Philosophy and Law—The American Philosophical Association* 12, no. 2 (2013): 12, 15.
34. Mill, *Subjection of Women*, 21:277.
35. Mill, 21:313.
36. J.S. Mill, *On Liberty*, in *Essays on Politics and Society*, vol. 18, *The Collected Works of John Stuart Mill*, ed. John M. Robson (Toronto: University of Toronto Press, 1977), 231.
37. Mill, *On Liberty*, 18:232.
38. Mill, 18:267.
39. Bruce Baum, *Rereading Power and Freedom in J.S. Mill* (Toronto: University of Toronto Press, 2000), 2.
40. Herzog, "'Is(n't) Catharine MacKinnon a Liberal?,'" 15.
41. MacKinnon, "'The Case' Responds," 709.
42. Catharine MacKinnon, "Shakespeare's Sister in Philosophy and Reality: A Response," *Newsletter on Philosophy and Law—The American Philosophical Association* 12, no. 2 (2013): 18.
43. See for instance Brown's assessment of MacKinnon's take on issues like pornography. Wendy Brown, *States of Injury* (Princeton: Princeton University Press, 1995).
44. Wendy Brown, *Regulating Aversion: Tolerance in the Age of Identity and Empire* (Princeton: Princeton University Press, 2006), 5.
45. Brown, *Regulating Aversion: Tolerance in the Age of Identity and Empire*, 63.
46. Brown, 73.
47. Brown, 65.
48. Mill, *Subjection of Women*, 21:235.
49. Brown, *Regulating Aversion: Tolerance in the Age of Identity and Empire*, 152.
50. C. L. Ten, "Democracy, Socialism and the Working Classes," in *The Cambridge Companion to Mill*, ed. John Skorupski (Cambridge: Cambridge University Press, 1998), 372–95; Linda Zerilli, *Signifying Women: Culture and Chaos in Rousseau, Burke, and Mill* (Ithaca: Cornell University Press, 1994).
51. Uday Mehta, *Liberalism and Empire* (Chicago: University of Chicago Press, 1999); David Williams, "John Stuart Mill and the Practice of Colonial Rule in India," *Journal of International Political Theory* 17, no. 3 (2021): 412–28.
52. Mill, *Subjection of Women*, 21:276.
53. Mill, 21:271.
54. Mill, 21:272.
55. Mill, 21:301.
56. Mill, 21:284.
57. Mill, "Statement on Marriage," 21:97.
58. Mill, "On Marriage," 21:41.
59. Mill, *Subjection of Women*, 21:264.
60. Mill, 21:265.

## NOTES 175

61. Mill, "The Negro Question," 21:92.
62. Mill, "State of Society in America," 18:93.
63. Mill, *Subjection of Women*, 21:281.
64. Mill, 21:280.
65. Mill, 21:281.
66. Mill, 21:277.
67. Mill, 21:263.
68. Mill, 21:264.
69. Mill, 21:307.
70. Mill, 21:308.
71. Mill, 21:289.
72. Mill, 21:271.
73. Mill, 21:321-22.
74. Mill, 21:322.
75. Mill, 21:322.
76. Mill, 21:287, 324.
77. Mill, 21:284, 324.
78. Mill, 21:320-21.
79. Mill, 21:324.
80. Mill, 21:324-25.
81. Mill, 21:325.
82. Mill, 21:295.
83. Mill, 21:324.
84. Mill, 21:226.
85. Mill, 21:325.
86. Mill, *On Liberty*, 18:266.
87. Mill, *Autobiography*, 1:265.
88. J.S. Mill, "Claims of Labour," in *Essays on Economics and Society I*, vol. 4, *The Collected Works of John Stuart Mill*, ed. John M. Robson (Toronto: Toronto University Press, 1967), 370.
89. Alan Ryan, *J.S. Mill* (London: Routledge, 1974), 157.
90. J.S. Mill, Letter to Bain (1869), in *The Later Letters of John Stuart Mill 1849-1873 Part IV*, vol. 17, *The Collected Works of John Stuart Mill*, ed. Francis E. Mineka and Dwight N. Lindley (Toronto: University of Toronto Press, 1972), 1623-24.
91. Taylor Mill, *The Complete Works of Harriet Taylor Mill*, 332.
92. Taylor Mill, 23.
93. Mill, "Contagious Diseases Acts," 21:355.
94. J.S. Mill, "St. Simonism in London, Feb. 2 1834," in *Newspaper Writings August 1831— October 1834 Part II*, ed. Anne P. Robson and John M. Robson, vol. 23, *The Collected Works of John Stuart Mill* (Toronto: University of Toronto Press, 1986), 679.
95. John Morely, *Essay 3: Mr. Mill's Autobiography*, vol. 3, *Critical Miscellanies* (London: MacMillan and Co., 1904), 77, http://www.gutenberg.org.
96. Mill, "On Marriage," 21:42 Emphasis added.
97. Mill, *Subjection of Women*, 21:306.

98. Annas, "Mill and the Subjection of Women," 63.
99. Mill, *Subjection of Women*, 21:298.
100. Carole Pateman, *The Sexual Contract* (Stanford: Stanford University Press, 1988), 163.
101. Mill, *Subjection of Women*, 21:298.
102. In a 1998 Egyptian translation of *Subjection*, the translator, Dr. Imam 'Abd al-Fattah Imam, appropriates Mill to characterize the Muslim family: "and since the family's role was raising children and implanting values, this demands that all threads be gathered in a single hand that has a higher degree (*daraja*) to decide matters having to do with the reproduction of the family, especially moral questions. And these are usually in the hand of the husband in his capacity as source of the family income. So, men are in charge of (*qawwa-mun 'ala*) women in what they [men] expend of their monies—and this is what Mill calls for, precisely." Marilyn Booth, "Islamic Politics, Street Literature, and John Stuart Mill: Composing Gendered Ideals in 1990s Egypt," *Feminist Studies* 39, no. 3 (2013): 616.
103. Mill, *Subjection of Women*, 21:297–98.
104. Mill, 21:298.
105. Mill, "On Marriage," 21:43.
106. Annas, "Mill and the Subjection of Women," 60; Burgess-Jackson, "John Stuart Mill, Radical Feminist," 86.
107. Taylor Mill, *The Complete Works of Harriet Taylor Mill*, 59.
108. Taylor Mill, 60.
109. Mill, "St. Simonism in London, Feb. 2 1834, 23:680.

# Chapter 5

1. Incidentally, Elliot was a contemporary and avid reader of Mill. Avrom Fleishman, *George Eliot's Intellectual Life* (Cambridge: Cambridge University Press, 2010).
2. J.S. Mill, "Spirit of the Age (I)," in *Newspaper Writings December 1822–July 1831 Part I*, ed. Anne P. Robson and John M. Robson, vol. 22, *The Collected Works of John Stuart Mill* (Toronto: University of Toronto Press, 1986), 228–29.
3. Mill, "Spirit of the Age (1)," 22:233.
4. Maria Morales, ed., *Mill's Subjection of Women* (Oxford: Rowman & Littlefield Publishers, Inc., 2005); Catharine A. MacKinnon, "Sexuality, Pornography, and Method: Pleasure under Patriarchy," *Ethics* 99, no. 2 (1989): 314–46; Wendy Brown, *Regulating Aversion: Tolerance in the Age of Identity and Empire* (Princeton: Princeton University Press, 2006).
5. Inder S. Marwah, *Liberalism, Diversity and Domination: Kant, Mill and the Government of Difference* (Cambridge: Cambridge University Press, 2019), 128.
6. C. L. Ten, "Democracy, Socialism and the Working Classes," in *The Cambridge Companion to Mill*, ed. John Skorupski (Cambridge: Cambridge University Press, 1998), 384.

7. Jennifer Pitts, *A Turn to Empire* (Princeton: Princeton University Press, 2005), 160; Uday Mehta, "Liberal Strategies of Exclusion," in *Tensions of Empire*, ed. Fredrick Cooper and Ann Laura Stoler (Berkeley: University of California Press, 1997), 77.
8. Linda Zerilli, *Signifying Women: Culture and Chaos in Rousseau, Burke, and Mill* (Ithaca: Cornell University Press, 1994), 97.
9. J.S. Mill, "On Marriage," in *Essays on Equality, Law, and Education*, vol. 21, *The Collected Works of John Stuart Mill*, ed. John M. Robson (Toronto: University of Toronto Press, 1984), 42.
10. J.S. Mill, "Thoughts on Parliamentary Reform," in *Essays on Politics and Society II*, vol. 19, *The Collected Works of John Stuart Mill*, ed. John M. Robson (Toronto: University of Toronto Press, 1977), 315.
11. J.S. Mill, *Autobiography*, in *Autobiography and Literary Essays*, vol. 1, *The Collected Works of John Stuart Mill*, ed. John M. Robson and Jack Stillinger (Toronto: Toronto University Press, 1981), 239.
12. Helen McCabe, "Harriet Taylor and John Stuart Mill's Socialism," *Nineteenth-Century Prose* 47, no. 1 (2020): 197.
13. Taylor's contributions to Mill's political thought and development are discussed in Chapter 3. I address the gendered dynamics of scholarship on the Mill-Taylor collaboration in other work: Menaka Philips, "The 'Beloved and Deplored' Memory of Harriet Taylor Mill: Rethinking Gender and Intellectual Labor in the Canon," in *The Wives of Western Philosophy: Gender Politics in Intellectual Labor*, ed. Jennifer Forestal and Menaka Philips (New York: Routledge, 2020), 147–66.
14. Robert B. Ekelund and Robert D. Tollison, "The New Political Economy of J. S. Mill: The Means to Social Justice," *The Canadian Journal of Economics / Revue Canadienne d'Economique* 9, no. 2 (1976): 214.
15. Quentin Taylor, "John Stuart Mill, Political Economist: A Reassessment," *The Independent Review* 21, no. 1 (2016): 92.
16. Samuel Hollander, *The Economics of John Stuart Mill* (Toronto: University of Toronto Press, 1985), 793.
17. Pedro Schwartz, "John Stuart Mill and Socialism," *The Mill News Letter* 4, no. 1 (1968): 13, 14.
18. Scotty Hendricks, "Why John Stuart Mill Was a Capitalist—Big Think," *Big Think* (blog), June 6, 2018, https://bigthink.com/scotty-hendricks/why-john-stuart-mill-was-a-capitalist. For incisive critiques of this view see: Bruce Baum, "J.S. Mill and Liberal Socialism," in *J.S. Mill's Political Thought*, ed. Nadia Urbinati and Alex Zakaras (New York: Cambridge University Press, 2007), 98–123; Jonathan Riley, "Mill's Political Economy: Ricardian Science and Liberal Utilitarian Art," in *The Cambridge Companion to Mill*, ed. John Skorupski, 1st edition (Cambridge University Press, 1998), 293–337.
19. J. E. Broadbent, "The Importance of Class in the Political Theory of John Stuart Mill," *Canadian Journal of Political Science / Revue Canadienne de Science Politique* 1, no. 3 (1968): 286.
20. Broadbent, "The Importance of Class in the Political Theory of John Stuart Mill," 270.

21. Richard Ashcraft, "Class Conflict and Constitutionalism in JS Mill's Political Thought," in *Liberalism and the Moral Life*, ed. Nancy Rosenblum (Cambridge: Cambridge University Press, 1989), 122–23. On Mill's skepticism regarding socialism's relation to liberty see Richard J. Arneson, "Mill's Doubts about Freedom under Socialism," *Canadian Journal of Philosophy; Supplementary Volume; Calgary, Alta.* 5 (January 1, 1979): 231–49.
22. Baum, "J.S. Mill and Liberal Socialism," 100; Chris Barker, *Educating Liberty: Democracy and Aristocracy in J.S. Mill's Political Thought* (Rochester, NY: University of Rochester Press, 2018), 57.
23. Baum, "J.S. Mill and Liberal Socialism," 718, 724.
24. Helen McCabe, *John Stuart Mill, Socialist* (Montreal: McGill-Queen's University Press, 2021), 15.
25. J.S. Mill, Letter to Potter (1865), in *The Later Letters of John Stuart Mill 1849–1873 Part III*, vol. 16, *The Collected Works of John Stuart Mill* (Toronto: University of Toronto Press, 1972), 1014–15.
26. Ashcraft, "Class Conflict and Constitutionalism in JS Mill's Political Thought," 122–23.
27. Ashcraft, 126; Barker, *Educating Liberty*, 82.
28. Mill, "Contest in America," 21:136.
29. The Slavery Abolition Act of 1833 outlawed slavery in the British Empire, with the exception of some territories administered by the East India Company; slavery was outlawed in British India in 1843. Mill, 21:125–42.
30. Mill, *Subjection of Women*, 21:274.
31. J.S. Mill, "Chapters on Socialism," in *Essays on Economics and Society II*, vol. 5, *The Collected Works of John Stuart Mill* (Toronto: University of Toronto Press, 1967), 710.
32. J.S. Mill, "Claims of Labour," in *Essays on Economics and Society I*, vol. 4, *The Collected Works of John Stuart Mill*, ed. John M. Robson (Toronto: University of Toronto Press, 1967), 367.
33. Mill, "Chapters on Socialism," 5:710.
34. Mill, 5:629. Emphasis added.
35. Mill, 5:710.
36. Mill, 5:715.
37. J.S. Mill, *Principles of Political Economy Books III–IV*, vol. 3, *The Collected Works of John Stuart Mill*, ed. John M. Robson (Toronto: Toronto University Press, 1965), 759.
38. Mill, *Principles of Political Economy Books III–IV*, 3:760.
39. Mill, "Claims of Labour," 4:371.
40. Marwah, *Liberalism, Diversity and Domination*, 146.
41. Mill, "Chapters on Socialism," 5:711. Emphasis added.
42. Mill, V.W. Bladen's introduction, *Principles of Political Economy Books I–II*, vol. 2, *The Collected Works of John Stuart Mill*, ed. John M. Robson (Toronto: Toronto University Press, 1965), xxxvii.
43. McCabe offers a nuanced account of how liberty and equality, but also fraternity, form Mill's socialism. Helen McCabe, "Mill and Socialism: A Reply to Capaldi," *The Tocqueville Review / La Revue Tocqueville* 33, no. 1 (March 24, 2012): 145–64.

44. Baum, "J.S. Mill and Liberal Socialism," 100.
45. Mill, "Newman's Political Economy," 5:443.
46. Mill, *Autobiography*, 1:175.
47. Mill, "Chapters on Socialism," 5:753.
48. Mill, *Principles of Political Economy Books I–II*, 2:209; "Newman's Political Economy," 5:443.
49. "Chapters on Socialism," 5:710.
50. Mill, *Autobiography*, 1:238.
51. Mill, *Principles of Political Economy Books I–II*, 2:209.
52. Mill, Bladen's introduction, 2:xxxvii.
53. Ekelund and Tollison, "The New Political Economy of J. S. Mill," 214.
54. Mill, *Principles of Political Economy Books III–V*, 3:794.
55. Mill, 3:795.
56. Mill, 3:769.
57. Mill, 3:762.
58. Mill, *Autobiography*, 1:238.
59. Mill, "de Tocqueville on Democracy in America (II)," in *Essays on Politics and Society*, vol. 18, *The Collected Works of John Stuart Mill*, ed. John M. Robson (Toronto: Toronto University Press, 1977), 198.
60. Mill, "de Tocqueville (II)," 18:191.
61. Gregory Claeys, "Justice, Independence, and Industrial Democracy: The Development of John Stuart Mill's Views on Socialism," *The Journal of Politics* 49, no. 1 (1987): 128. See also: Philippe Gillig and Philippe Légé, "J. S. Mill on Cooperatives: From Mistrust to Praise—the Constitution of a Liberal Thought in the First Half of the 19th Century," *Cahiers d'économie Politique / Papers in Political Economy* 73, no. 2 (December 28, 2017): 197–221.
62. Mill, *Principles of Political Economy Books III–IV*, 3:793.
63. Claeys, "Justice, Independence, and Industrial Democracy," 134.
64. Barker, *Educating Liberty*, 51.
65. Mill, "de Tocqueville (II)," 18:198.
66. Mill, *Principles of Political Economy Books III–IV*, 3:944.
67. Mill, 3:763.
68. Mill, "French News, Jan. 9, 1831," 22:235.
69. Mill, "Thoughts on Parliamentary Reform," 19:324.
70. Mill, "Parliamentary Reform Bill Mar. 6, 1831," 22:277.
71. J.S. Mill, "Representation of the People (1866)," in *Public and Parliamentary Speeches Part I November 1850–November 1868*, ed. Bruce L Kinzer and John M Robson, vol. 28, *The Collected Works of John Stuart Mill* (Toronto: University of Toronto Press, 1988), 64.
72. Mill, "Representation of the People (1866)," 28:65.
73. Mill, 28:65.
74. Mill, 28:61.
75. Mill, "Electoral Franchise for Women (1866)," 28:91–93.
76. Mill, "Admission of Women to the Electoral Franchise (1867)," 28:158.
77. Mill, *Autobiography*, 1:285.

78. Mill, "Admission of Women," 28:157.
79. Mill, *Considerations*, 19:469.
80. Mill, 19:469.
81. Mill, "Thoughts on Parliamentary Reform," 19:322.
82. Pitts, *A Turn to Empire*; Mehta, "Liberal Strategies of Exclusion"; Alan Ryan, *J.S. Mill* (London: Routledge, 1974); Bruce Baum, *Rereading Power and Freedom in J.S. Mill* (Toronto: University of Toronto Press, 2000).
83. Mill, "Attack on Literature, June 12, 1831," 22:326–27.
84. Mill, *Considerations*, 19:470.
85. Mill, "Contagious Diseases Acts," 21:368–69.
86. Mill, *Considerations*, 19:471.
87. Mill, "On Marriage," 21:42.
88. Zerilli, *Signifying Women: Culture and Chaos in Rousseau, Burke, and Mill*, 121.
89. Nadia Urbinati, *Mill on Democracy: From the Athenian Polis to Representative Government* (Chicago: University of Chicago Press, 2002), 121, 100.
90. Bruce Baum, "Governing 'Democratic' Equality: Mill, Tawney, and Liberal Democratic Governmentality," *Political Research Quarterly* 65, no. 4 (December 1, 2012): 717.
91. Bruce L. Kinzer, "J.S. Mill and the Secret Ballot," *Historical Reflections / Réflexions Historiques* 5, no. 1 (1978): 19–39; Joseph Hamburger, *Intellectuals in Politics: John Stuart Mill and the Philosophic Radicals* (New Haven: Yale University Press, 1965).
92. Mill, "Use and Abuse of the Ballot, Nov. 28, 1830," 22:194.
93. Mill, 22:194.
94. J.S. Mill, Letter to de Tocqueville (1837), in *The Earlier Letters 1812–1848 Part I*, ed. Francis E. Mineka, vol. 12, *The Collected Works of John Stuart Mill* (Toronto: University of Toronto Press, 1963), 317.
95. Mill, "Thoughts on Parliamentary Reform," 19:331.
96. Mill, "Use and Abuse of the Ballot, Nov. 28, 1830," 22:195.
97. Mill, "Thoughts on Parliamentary Reform," 19:332.
98. J.S. Mill, "Reorganization of the Reform Party," in *Essays on England, Ireland, and the Empire*, vol. 6, *The Collected Works of John Stuart Mill*, ed. John M. Robson (Toronto: University of Toronto Press, 1982), 482.
99. Mill, "Thoughts on Parliamentary Reform," 19:333.
100. Mill, *Considerations*, 19:488.
101. Mill, "Reorganization of the Reform Party," 6:482.
102. Mill, 6:482.
103. Mill, 6:483.
104. Mill, *Principles of Political Economy Books III–IV*, 3:760.
105. Mill, "Reorganization of the Reform Party," 6:489.
106. Mill, *Considerations*, 19:493.
107. Mill, 19:490; "Thoughts on Parliamentary Reform," 19:334.
108. Urbinati, *Mill on Democracy: From the Athenian Polis to Representative Government*, 122.
109. Kinzer, "J.S. Mill and the Secret Ballot," 27.

110. Mill, "Thoughts on Parliamentary Reform," 19:336.
111. "John Stuart Mill on Parliamentary Reform," *The New York Times*, May 7, 1865, sec. Archives, https://www.nytimes.com/1865/05/07/archives/john-stuart-mill-on-parliamentary-reform.html.
112. Mill, *Considerations*, 19:477.
113. Mill, 19:447.
114. Mill, 19:508. See also: Jonathan Riley, "Mill's Neo-Athenian Model of Liberal Democracy," in *J.S. Mill's Political Thought*, ed. Nadia Urbinati and Alex Zakaras (New York: Cambridge University Press, 2007), 221–49.
115. Mill, "Claims of Labour," 4:376.
116. Mill, "Chapters on Socialism," 5:710.
117. Mill, "Claims of Labour," 4:376.
118. John Rawls, *A Theory of Justice* (Cambridge: Harvard University Press, 2003), 205.
119. J. Joseph Miller, "J.S. Mill on Plural Voting, Competence and Participation," *History of Political Thought* 24, no. 4 (2003): 664.
120. Zerilli, *Signifying Women: Culture and Chaos in Rousseau, Burke, and Mill*, 121.
121. Zerilli, 135.
122. Zerilli, 121–22.
123. Mill, *Autobiography*, 1:219.
124. Barker, *Educating Liberty*, 115.
125. Wendy Donner and Richard Fumerton, *Mill*, 1st edition (Malden, MA: Wiley-Blackwell, 2009); Baum, *Rereading Power and Freedom in J.S. Mill*; Maria Morales, *Perfect Equality: John Stuart Mill on Well-Constituted Communities* (Boulder & New York: Rowman & Littlefield Publishers, Inc., 1996).
126. Dale E. Miller, "The Place of Plural Voting in Mill's Conception of Representative Government," *The Review of Politics* 77, no. 3 (ed 2015): 414.
127. Urbinati for instance suggests that Mill began to have doubts about plural voting when he considered that it might be used to benefit propertied interests, but that his doubts reflected the "effectiveness of plural voting, not its logic." Urbinati, *Mill on Democracy: From the Athenian Polis to Representative Government*, 94–95; Mill, *Essays on Politics and Society II*, 19:354.
128. Mill, "de Tocqueville (II)," 18:167.
129. Mill, "Claims of Labour," 4:376.
130. Mill, *Considerations*, 19:442.
131. Mill, *Subjection of Women*, 21:301.
132. Mill, 21:301 This might place Mill in conversation with 20th century feminist literature on class and the development of a feminist standpoint.
133. Katherine Smits, "John Stuart Mill and the Social Construction of Identity," *History of Political Thought* 25, no. 2 (2004): 311.
134. Wendy Brown, *States of Injury* (Princeton: Princeton University Press, 1995), 61.
135. Judith Butler, *Gender Trouble: Feminism and the Subversion of Identity* (New York: Routledge, 1999), 189–90.
136. Mill, *Considerations*, 19:445.
137. Mill, 19:446.

## Chapter 6

1. Duncan Bell, *Reordering the World: Essays on Liberalism and Empire* (Princeton: Princeton University Press, 2016), 211.
2. Jennifer Pitts, "Political Theory of Empire and Imperialism," *Annual Review of Political Science* 13 (2010): 212.
3. Pitts, "Political Theory of Empire and Imperialism," 223.
4. Sheldon Pollack, "Empire and Imitation," in *Lessons of Empire: Imperial Histories and American Power*, ed. Craig Calhoun, Fredrick Cooper, and Kevin W Moore (New York: New Press, 2006), 176.
5. Mary G. Dietz, "Between Polis and Empire: Aristotle's Politics," *American Political Science Review* 106, no. 2 (May 2012): 275.
6. Pitts, "Political Theory of Empire and Imperialism," 219.
7. Uday Mehta, *Liberalism and Empire* (Chicago: University of Chicago Press, 1999), 1; Thomas McCarthy, *Race, Empire and the Idea of Human Development* (Cambridge: Cambridge University Press, 2009), 166; Shiraz Dossa, "Liberal Imperialism?: Natives, Muslims, and Others," *Political Theory* 30, no. 5 (October 1, 2002): 739; Karuna Mantena, "The Crisis of Liberal Imperialism," *Histoire@Politique* 11, no. 2 (June 3, 2010), https://doi.org/10.3917/hp.011.0002; A. Sartori, *Liberalism in Empire: An Alternative History* (University of California Press, 2014); Bell, *Reordering the World*; Jeanne Morefield, *Covenants without Swords: Idealist Liberalism and the Spirit of Empire* (Princeton: Princeton University Press, 2009).
8. Margaret Kohn and Kavita Reddy, "Colonialism," in *The Stanford Encyclopedia of Philosophy*, Fall 2017, ed. Edward N. Zalta, https://plato.stanford.edu/archives/fall2017/entries/colonialism/.
9. McCarthy, *Race, Empire and the Idea of Human Development*, 169.
10. Daniel I. O'Neill, *Edmund Burke and the Conservative Logic of Empire* (California: University of California Press, 2016), 3.
11. O'Neill, *Edmund Burke and the Conservative Logic of Empire*, 2.
12. Eileen P. Sullivan, "Liberalism and Imperialism: J. S. Mill's Defense of the British Empire," *Journal of the History of Ideas* 44, no. 4 (1983): 599.
13. Sullivan, "Liberalism and Imperialism"; Jennifer Pitts, "Legislator of the World? A Rereading of Bentham on Colonies," *Political Theory* 31, no. 2 (April 1, 2003): 200–34. For a more critical view see: O'Neill, *Edmund Burke and the Conservative Logic of Empire*; Inder S. Marwah, *Liberalism, Diversity and Domination: Kant, Mill and the Government of Difference* (Cambridge: Cambridge University Press, 2019).
14. Uday Mehta, "Liberal Strategies of Exclusion," in *Tensions of Empire*, ed. Fredrick Cooper and Ann Laura Stoler (Berkeley: University of California Press, 1997), 75.
15. J.S. Mill, *On Liberty*, in *Essays on Politics and Society*, vol. 18, *The Collected Works of John Stuart Mill*, ed. John M. Robson (Toronto: University of Toronto Press, 1977), 224; Mehta, "Liberal Strategies of Exclusion," 75.
16. Mehta, *Liberalism and Empire*, 194.

17. Mehta, 103; Jennifer Pitts, *A Turn to Empire* (Princeton: Princeton University Press, 2005), 20.
18. Pitts, *A Turn to Empire*, 5.
19. Pitts, 4.
20. I discuss these practices in Chapter 2. See also: Duncan Bell, "What Is Liberalism?," *Political Theory* 42, no. 6 (2014): 682–715.
21. Pitts, *A Turn to Empire*, 3.
22. Pitts, 4.
23. Jennifer Pitts, "Republicanism, Liberalism, and Empire in Postrevolutionary France," in *Empire and Modern Political Thought*, ed. Sankar Muthu (New York: Cambridge University Press, 2012), 286; Pitts, *A Turn to Empire*, 238.
24. Pitts, *A Turn to Empire*, 238.
25. Karuna Mantena, *Alibis of Empire* (Princeton: Princeton University Press, 2010), 44.
26. Mantena, *Alibis of Empire*, 31, 35.
27. Mantena, 43.
28. Karuna Mantena, "Mill and the Imperial Predicament," in *J.S. Mill's Political Thought*, ed. Nadia Urbinati and Alex Zakaras (New York: Cambridge University Press, 2007), 301.
29. Marwah, *Liberalism, Diversity and Domination*, 177.
30. Marwah, 198.
31. Barbara Arneil, *Domestic Colonies: The Turn Inward to Colony* (Oxford; New York: Oxford University Press, 2017), 14.
32. Barbara Arneil, "Liberal Colonialism, Domestic Colonies and Citizenship," *History of Political Thought* 33, no. 3 (2012): 491–523.
33. Mark Tunick, "Tolerant Imperialism: John Stuart Mill's Defense of British Rule in India," *The Review of Politics* 68, no. 4 (2006): 589.
34. Nadia Urbinati, "The Many Heads of the Hydra: J.S. Mill on Despotism," in *J.S. Mill's Political Thought*, ed. Nadia Urbinati and Alex Zakaras (New York: Cambridge University Press, 2007), 95.
35. Urbinati, "The Many Heads of the Hydra," 76.
36. Urbinati, 69.
37. Mantena, *Alibis of Empire*; Jonathan Riley, "Individuality, Custom and Progress," *Utilitas* 3, no. 2 (1991): 217–44.
38. See Chapter 5.
39. Wendy Donner, "John Stuart Mill's Liberal Feminism," in *Mill's Subjection of Women*, ed. Maria Morales (Oxford: Rowman & Littlefield Publishers, Inc., 2005), 1–12; John Howes, "Mill on Women and Human Development," in *Mill's Subjection of Women*, ed. Maria Morales (Oxford: Rowman & Littlefield Publishers, Inc., 2005), 13–23; Susan Moller Okin, "John Stuart Mill's Feminism," in *Mill's Subjection of Women*, ed. Maria Morales (Oxford: Rowman & Littlefield Publishers, Inc., 2005), 24–51.
40. C. L. Ten, *Mill on Liberty* (New York: Oxford University Press, 1980), 109–23.

41. Terence Ball, "The Formation of Character: Mill's 'Ethology' Reconsidered," *Polity* 33, no. 1 (2000): 47; Chris Barker, *Educating Liberty: Democracy and Aristocracy in J.S. Mill's Political Thought* (Rochester, NY: University of Rochester Press, 2018), 239.
42. Pitts, *A Turn to Empire*, 160; Mehta, "Liberal Strategies of Exclusion," 77.
43. Alan Ryan, *J.S. Mill* (London: Routledge, 1974), 147.
44. Bruce Baum, *Rereading Power and Freedom in J.S. Mill* (Toronto: University of Toronto Press, 2000), 90, 149–50.
45. J.S. Mill, "The East India Company's Charter," in *Writings on India*, vol. 30, *The Collected Works of John Stuart Mill*, ed. John M. Robson, Martin Moir, and Zawahir Moir (Toronto: University of Toronto Press, 1990), 51.
46. Catherine Hall, "The Economy of Intellectual Prestige: Thomas Carlyle, John Stuart Mill, and the Case of Governor Eyre," *Cultural Critique*, no. 12 (1989): 188.
47. Mill, "East India Company's Charter," 30:51.
48. Mill, 30:65.
49. Mill, Editor's Introduction, 30:xliv.
50. J.S. Mill, "On Marriage," in *Essays on Equality, Law, and Education*, vol. 21, *The Collected Works of John Stuart Mill*, ed. John M. Robson (Toronto: University of Toronto Press, 1984), 42.
51. Urbinati, "The Many Heads of the Hydra," 95.
52. Urbinati, 97; Pitts, *A Turn to Empire*, 161; Tunick, "Tolerant Imperialism," 599.
53. J. Joseph Miller, "J.S. Mill on Plural Voting, Competence and Participation," *History of Political Thought* 24, no. 4 (2003): 647–67.
54. A key figure involved in establishing British colonies in New Zealand and South Australia, and in the crafting of the Durham Report on Canada, Wakefield argued in favor of exporting English laborers to Australia and New Zealand as a means of alleviating what he, and Mill, considered to be the overpopulation problem in the metropole. Edward R. Kittrell, "Wakefield's Scheme of Systematic Colonization and Classical Economics," *The American Journal of Economics and Sociology* 32, no. 1 (1973): 87–111.
55. J.S. Mill, *Principles of Political Economy Books III–IV*, vol. 3, *The Collected Works of John Stuart Mill*, ed. John M. Robson (Toronto: Toronto University Press, 1965), 963.
56. Mill, *Principles of Political Economy Books III–IV*, 3:963.
57. Mill, "On Marriage," 21:43. See also Chapter 4.
58. Ewa Atanassow, "Colonization and Democracy: Tocqueville Reconsidered," *American Political Science Review* 111, no. 1 (February 2017): 83–96; Cheryl B. Welch, "Out of Africa: Tocqueville's Imperial Voyages," *Review of Middle East Studies* 45, no. 1 (2011): 53–61; August Nimtz, "The Eurocentric Marx and Engels and Other Related Myths," in *Marxism, Modernity and Postcolonial Studies*, ed. Crystal Bartolovich and Neil Lazarus (Cambridge: Cambridge University Press, 2002), 65–80; Shlomo Avineri, "Marx and Modernization," *The Review of Politics* 31, no. 2 (1969): 172–88.
59. Pitts, *A Turn to Empire*, 238.
60. Homi Bhabha and Bhikhu Parekh, "Identities on Parade: A Conversation," *Marxism Today*, June 1989, 27.
61. Mill, "Address to the University of St. Andrews," 21:226.

NOTES 185

62. J.S. Mill, "England and Ireland," in *Essays on England, Ireland, and the Empire*, vol. 6, *The Collected Works of John Stuart Mill*, ed. John M. Robson (Toronto: University of Toronto Press, 1982), 508, 11.
63. Mill, *Subjection of Women*, 21:277.
64. Mill, "The Negro Question," 21:93.
65. Mill, *Subjection of Women*, 21:277.
66. Mill, "England and Ireland," 6:508–9.
67. Sullivan, "Liberalism and Imperialism," 615.
68. Mill, "Maine on Village Communities," 30:223.
69. Abram L. Harris, "John Stuart Mill: Servant of the East India Company," *The Canadian Journal of Economics and Political Science / Revue Canadienne d'Economique et de Science Politique* 30, no. 2 (1964): 190.
70. Mill, "Memorandom of Improvements," 30:125.
71. J.S. Mill, *Considerations*, in *Essays on Politics and Society II*, vol. 19, *The Collected Works of John Stuart Mill*, ed. John M. Robson (Toronto: University of Toronto Press, 1977), 570, 569.
72. Lynn Zastoupil, "India, J.S. Mill, and 'Western' Culture," in *J.S. Mill's Encounter with India*, ed. Martin Moir, Douglas Peers, and Lynn Zastoupil (Toronto: University of Toronto Press, 1999), 127. In his enlightening article, Ambirajan argues that Mill's seminal writings (more than his work with the Company) had the "greatest and most abiding impact on the modern history of the Indian subcontinent." S. Ambirajan, "John Stuart Mill and India," in *J.S. Mill's Encounter with India*, ed. Martin Moir, Douglas Peers, and Lynn Zastoupil (Toronto: University of Toronto Press, 1999), 257.
73. Lynn Zastoupil, *John Stuart Mill and India* (Stanford: Stanford University Press, 1994), 39–41.
74. Shefali Misra, "Friend, nor Foe: Mill's Liberal Multiculturalism," *European Journal of Political Theory* 11, no. 3 (2012): 14.
75. Mill, "On Liberty," 18:262.
76. Mill, Editor's Introduction, 30:xlviii; J.S. Mill, Letter to Taylor (1837), *The Later Letters of John Stuart Mill 1849–1873 Part IV*, vol. 17, *The Collected Works of John Stuart Mill*, ed. Francis E. Mineka and Dwight N. Lindley (Toronto: University of Toronto Press, 1972), 1969–70.
77. Thomas Macaulay, *Speeches by Lord Macaulay: With His Minute on Indian Education* (London: Oxford University Press, 1935), 349.
78. Mill, Letter to Taylor (1837), 17:1970 fn. 3.
79. Mill, *Considerations*, 19:574.
80. Mill, 19:575.
81. J.S. Mill, *Autobiography*, in *Autobiography and Literary Essays*, vol. 1, *The Collected Works of John Stuart Mill*, ed. John M. Robson and Jack Stillinger (Toronto: Toronto University Press, 1981), 87.
82. Mill, *Considerations*, 19:577, 573.
83. Mill testified before the House of Lords against the dissolution of the EIC's charter, arguing that direct rule would turn "Indian questions [into] party questions" and

India would become "a subject for discussions, of which the real object would be to effect a change in the administration of the Government of England." Mill, "East India Company's Charter," 30:50.
84. Mill, "England and Ireland," 6:519.
85. Mill, 6:519.
86. Mill, 6:519.
87. Jimmy Casas Klausen, "Violence and Epistemology: J. S. Mill's Indians after the 'Mutiny,'" *Political Research Quarterly* 69, no. 1 (March 1, 2016): 105.
88. Klausen, "Violence and Epistemology," 99; Tocqueville is arguably a better representative of the uncomplicated view of Indian subjects which Klausen attributes to Mill. In a letter to an English friend following the India uprising, Tocqueville suggests that "the horrible events in India are not in any way an uprising against oppression. It is the revolt of barbarism against pride." Alexis de Tocqueville, *Selected Letters on Politics and Society*, ed. Roger Boesche, trans. James Toupin (California: University of California Press, 1986), 364.
89. Mill, "Minute on the Black Act," 30:13.
90. Mill, *Considerations*, 19:411.
91. Gayatri Chakravorty Spivak, "Can the Subaltern Speak?," in *Marxism and the Interpretation of Culture*, ed. C. Nelson and L. Grossberg (Chicago: University of Illinois Press, 1988), 271–313; Uma Narayan, *Dislocating Cultures: Identities, Traditions, and Third World Feminism* (New York: Routledge, 1997).
92. Harriet Taylor Mill, *The Complete Works of Harriet Taylor Mill*, ed. Jo Ellen Jacobs and Paula Harms Payne (Bloomington: Indiana University Press, 1998), 87.
93. Mill, "Minute on the Black Act," 30:14.
94. Mill, 30:15.
95. See footnote: Mill, *On Liberty*, 18:240–41.
96. Mill, *On Liberty*, 18:240.
97. Mill, *Considerations*, 19:571.
98. J.S. Mill, Letter to Chapman (1866), in *The Later Letters of John Stuart Mill 1849–1873 Part III*, vol. 16, *The Collected Works of John Stuart Mill*, ed. Francis E. Mineka and Dwight N. Lindley (Toronto: University of Toronto Press, 1972), 1136.
99. David Williams, "John Stuart Mill and the Practice of Colonial Rule in India," *Journal of International Political Theory* 17, no. 3 (2021): 423, 421. See also: David Williams, *Progress, Pluralism, and Politics: Liberalism and Colonialism, Past and Present* (Montreal; Kingston; London; Chicago: McGill-Queen's University Press, 2021).
100. Mill, *Principles of Political Economy Books III–IV*, 3:963.
101. Pitts, *A Turn to Empire*, 154. See also: Pratap Bhanu Mehta, "Liberalism, Nation, and Empire: The Case of John Stuart Mill," in *Empire and Modern Political Thought*, ed. Sankar Muthu (New York: Cambridge University Press, 2012), 232–60.
102. Gad Heuman, *The Killing Time: The Morant Bay Rebellion Jamaica*, 1st edition (Knoxville: University of Tennessee Press, 1994); Mill detailed some of the treatment of victims in his questioning of the Chancellor of the Exchequer. J.S. Mill, "Disturbances in Jamaica," in *Public and Parliamentary Speeches Part I November 1850–November 1868*, ed. Bruce L Kinzer and John M Robson, vol. 28, *The Collected Works of John Stuart Mill* (Toronto: University of Toronto Press, 1988), 95.

103. Klausen, "Violence and Epistemology," 102.
104. Pitts, *A Turn to Empire*, 151. See also Mantena, "The Crisis of Liberal Imperialism."
105. Klausen, "Violence and Epistemology," 97.
106. Pitts, *A Turn to Empire*, 162.
107. Mantena, "The Crisis of Liberal Imperialism," 11.
108. Mill, Letter to Urquhart (1866), in *The Later Letters of John Stuart Mill 1849–1873 Part III*, 16:1206.
109. Mill, *Considerations*, 19:571.
110. Mill, "Statement of the Jamaica Committee (1866)," 21:424.
111. Mill, 21:423.
112. Pitts, *A Turn to Empire*, 153.
113. Mill, *Autobiography*, 1:281.
114. Pitts, *A Turn to Empire*, 151; Klausen, "Violence and Epistemology," 97.
115. Mill, Letter to Hazard (1865), 16:1117–18.
116. Mill, , "East India Company's Charter," 30:65. Emphasis added.
117. Notably, Mill maintained the same educative qualification for extending the vote to freedman and poor whites in the south that he advocated for in England. See Mill, Letter to Dickson (1865), 16:1102.
118. J.S. Mill, Letter to Arnold (1866), in *Additional Letters of John Stuart Mill*, vol. 32, *The Collected Works of John Stuart Mill*, ed. Marion Filipiuk, Michael Laine and John M. Robson (Toronto: University of Toronto Press, 1991), 161.
119. Mill, *Subjection of Women*, 21:324.
120. Mill, *Considerations*, 19:571.
121. Mill, 19:571.
122. Mill, Letter to Aspland (1868), 16:1365. Emphasis added.
123. Mill, 16:1365.
124. Mill, *Autobiography*, 1:281.
125. Mill, Letter to Fawcett (1866), 16:1131.
126. Mill, Letter to Pratten (1868), 16:1410.
127. Mill, 16:1411.
128. Mill, Letter to Rae (1865), 16:1126.
129. Bell, *Reordering the World*, 214.
130. J.S. Mill, "Claims of Labour," *Essays on Economics and Society I*, vol. 4, *The Collected Works of John Stuart Mill*, ed. John M. Robson (Toronto: Toronto University Press, 1967), 367.
131. Mill, *Autobiography*, 1:613.

# Chapter 7

1. Lionel Barber, Alex Barker, and Henry Foy, "Vladimir Putin Says Liberalism Has 'Become Obsolete,'" *Financial Times*, June 27, 2019, https://www.ft.com/content/670039ec-98f3-11e9-9573-ee5cbb98ed36; Edward Luce, *The Retreat of Western Liberalism* (New York: Atlantic Monthly Press, 2017).

2. Paolo Gerbaudo, "Liberal Democracy Is in Trouble—and Liberals Won't Save It," *Jacobin*, May 2, 2020, https://www.jacobinmag.com/2020/05/post-democracy-after-crises-colin-crouch-review-liberalism.

3. Patrick J. Deneen, *Why Liberalism Failed* (New Haven: Yale University Press, 2018), 20, 187.

4. Deneen, *Why Liberalism Failed*; Catharine A. MacKinnon, "'The Case' Responds," *The American Political Science Review* 95, no. 3 (2001): 709–11; Wendy Brown, "Neo-Liberalism and the End of Liberal Democracy," *Theory & Event* 7, no. 1 (2003) doi:10.1353/tae.2003.0020..

5. Saba Mahmood, *Politics of Piety: The Islamic Revival and the Feminist Subject* (Princeton: Princeton University Press, 2005), 50.

6. Mahmood, *Politics of Piety*, 44.

7. Mahmood, 149.

8. Mahmood, 8.

9. Mahmood, 10.

10. J.S. Mill, *A System of Logic Ratiocinative and Inductive, Books IV-VI*, vol. 8, *The Collected Works of John Stuart Mill*, ed. John M. Robson (Toronto: University of Toronto Press, 1973), 681.

11. Speaking of Hajja Faiza's lessons, Mahmood observes that though she sees herself as the disseminator of "correct information," based on her reading of religious doctrines, and of existing juristic debates about them, Hajja Faiza still insists "that each individual remained responsible for the choices she made and the actions she took." Mahmood, *Politics of Piety*, 86; Menaka Philips, "Troubling Appropriations: JS Mill, Liberalism, and the Virtues of Uncertainty," *European Journal of Political Theory* 18, no. 1 (January 1, 2019): 68–88.

12. Menaka Philips, "Feminist Preoccupations: Liberalism as Method in Debates Concerning Gender and Culture," *Signs: Journal of Women in Culture and Society* 44, no. 4 (May 21, 2019): 955–77.

13. Linda Zerilli, "Towards a Feminist Theory of Judgment," *Signs* 34, no. 2 (2009): 303.

14. Jennifer Pitts, "Political Theory of Empire and Imperialism," *Annual Review of Political Science* 13 (2010): 216.

15. Thomas McCarthy, *Race, Empire and the Idea of Human Development* (Cambridge: Cambridge University Press, 2009), 169.

16. Henry Farrell and Abraham L. Newman, "Weaponized Interdependence: How Global Economic Networks Shape State Coercion," *International Security* 44, no. 1 (August 5, 2019): 42–79.

17. Alexander Cooley and Daniel H. Nexon, "'The Empire Will Compensate You': The Structural Dynamics of the U.S. Overseas Basing Network," *Perspectives on Politics* 11, no. 4 (2013): 1034–50; Daniel H. Nexon and Thomas Wright, "What's at Stake in the American Empire Debate," *American Political Science Review* 101, no. 2 (2007): 253–71; Sumantra Maitra, "How China Is Slowly Becoming The World's Largest Imperialist Power," *The Federalist*, November 22, 2019, https://thefederalist.

com/2019/11/22/how-china-is-slowly-becoming-the-worlds-largest-imperialist-power/; Sarah A. Topol, "What Does Putin Really Want?," *The New York Times*, June 25, 2019, sec. Magazine, https://www.nytimes.com/2019/06/25/magazine/russia-united-states-world-politics.html.
18. Judith Butler, "Contingent Foundations," in *Feminist Contentions*, ed. Judith Butler, Drucilla Cornell, Nancy Fraser, and Seyla Benhabib (New York: Routledge, 1995), 39.
19. Butler, "Contingent Foundations," 41.
20. Butler, 41.
21. Richard Reeves, *John Stuart Mill: Victorian Firebrand* (London: Atlantic Books, 2007), 8.
22. Karl Marx and Frederick Engels, *Marx and Engels 1843–1844*, vol. 3, *Collected Works* (New York: International Publishers, 1975), 142.
23. John Morely, *Essay 3: Mr. Mill's Autobiography*, vol. 3, *Critical Miscellanies* (London: MacMillan and Co., 1904), http://www.gutenberg.org.
24. Marx and Engels, *Marx and Engels 1843–1844*, 3:149.
25. "But since we cannot divest ourselves of preconceived notions, there is no known means of eliminating their influence but by frequently using the differently coloured glasses of other people: and those of other nations, as the most different, are the best." J.S. Mill, "Address to the Students of St. Andrews," *Essays on Equality, Law, and Education*, vol. 21, *The Collected Works of John Stuart Mill*, ed. John M. Robson (Toronto: University of Toronto Press, 1984), 226.

# Bibliography

Abbey, Ruth. *The Return of Feminist Liberalism*. Montreal: McGill-Queen's University Press, 2011.
Abu-Lughod, Lila. *Do Muslim Women Need Saving?* Cambridge: Harvard University Press, 2013.
Adcock, R. *Liberalism and the Emergence of American Political Science: A Transatlantic Tale*. New York: Oxford University Press, 2014.
Adcock, Robert, Mark Bevir, and Shannon C. Stimson. *Modern Political Science: Anglo-American Exchanges since 1880*. Princeton Paperbacks. Princeton: University Press, 2007.
Alter, Adam. "The Power of Names." *The New Yorker*, May 29, 2013.
Ambirajan, S. "John Stuart Mill and India." In *J.S. Mill's Encounter with India*, edited by Martin Moir, Douglas Peers, and Lynn Zastoupil, 221–64. Toronto: University of Toronto Press, 1999.
Amine, Loubna El. "Beyond East and West: Reorienting Political Theory through the Prism of Modernity." *Perspectives on Politics* 14, no. 1 (2016): 102–29.
Anderson, Elizabeth S. "John Stuart Mill and Experiments in Living." *Ethics* 102, no. 1 (1991): 4–26.
Annas, Julia. "Mill and the Subjection of Women." In *Mill's Subjection of Women*, edited by Maria Morales, 52–70. Oxford: Rowman & Littlefield, 2005.
Armitage, David. "John Locke: Theorist of Empire?" In *Empire and Modern Political Thought*, edited by Sankar Muthu, 85–111. New York: Cambridge University Press, 2012.
Arneil, Barbara. *Domestic Colonies: The Turn Inward to Colony*. Oxford; New York: Oxford University Press, 2017.
Arneil, Barbara. "Liberal Colonialism, Domestic Colonies and Citizenship." *History of Political Thought* 33, no. 3 (2012): 491–523.
Arneson, Richard J. "Mill's Doubts about Freedom under Socialism." *Canadian Journal of Philosophy; Supplementary Volume; Calgary, Alta.* 5 (January 1, 1979): 231–49.
Asad, Talal. *On Suicide Bombing*. New York: Columbia University Press, 2007.
Ashcraft, Richard. "Class Conflict and Constitutionalism in JS Mill's Political Thought." In *Liberalism and the Moral Life*, edited by Nancy Rosenblum, 105–26. Cambridge: Cambridge University Press, 1989.
Ashcraft, Richard. "John Stuart Mill and the Theoretical Foundations of Democratic Socialism." In *Mill and the Moral Character of Liberalism*, edited by Eldon J Eisenach, 169–90. Pennsylvania: Pennsylvania State University Press, 1998.
Atanassow, Ewa. "Colonization and Democracy: Tocqueville Reconsidered." *American Political Science Review* 111, no. 1 (February 2017): 83–96.
Avineri, Shlomo. "Marx and Modernization." *The Review of Politics* 31, no. 2 (1969): 172–88.

# BIBLIOGRAPHY

Bain, Alexander. *John Stuart Mill: A Criticism with Personal Recollections*. London: Longmans, Green, and Co, 1882.

Ball, Terence. "From Paradigms to Research Programs: Towards a Post-Kuhnian Political Science." *American Journal of Political Science* 20, no. 1 (February 1976): 151–77.

Ball, Terence. "The Formation of Character: Mill's 'Ethology' Reconsidered." *Polity* 33, no. 1 (2000): 25–48.

Ball, Terence, and Richard Dagger, eds. *Political Ideologies and the Democratic Ideal*. 8th edition. New York: Pearson/Longman, 2011.

Ball, Terence, and Richard Dagger. "The 'L-Word': A Short History of Liberalism." *Political Science Teacher* 3, no. 1 (1990): 1–6.

Barber, Lionel, Alex Barker, and Henry Foy. "Vladimir Putin Says Liberalism Has 'Become Obsolete.'" *Financial Times*, June 27, 2019. https://www.ft.com/content/67003 9ec-98f3-11e9-9573-ee5cbb98ed36.

Barker, Chris. *Educating Liberty: Democracy and Aristocracy in J.S. Mill's Political Thought*. Rochester, NY: University of Rochester Press, 2018.

Barnes, Henry. "Cannes Faces Backlash after Women Reportedly Barred from Film Screening for Not Wearing High Heels." *The Guardian*, May 19, 2015, sec. Film.

Baum, Bruce. "Governing 'Democratic' Equality: Mill, Tawney, and Liberal Democratic Governmentality." *Political Research Quarterly* 65, no. 4 (December 1, 2012): 714–31.

Baum, Bruce. "J.S. Mill and Liberal Socialism." In *J.S. Mill's Political Thought*, edited by Nadia Urbinati and Alex Zakaras, 98–123. New York: Cambridge University Press, 2007.

Baum, Bruce. *Rereading Power and Freedom in J.S. Mill*. Toronto: University of Toronto Press, 2000.

Bell, Duncan. *Reordering the World: Essays on Liberalism and Empire*. Princeton: Princeton University Press, 2016.

Bell, Duncan. "What Is Liberalism?" *Political Theory* 42, no. 6 (2014): 682–715.

Benhabib, Seyla. "Jürgen Habermas's 90th Birthday." *Medium*, July 2, 2019. https://medium.com/@arendt_center/j%C3%BCrgen-habermass-90th-birthday-2c2a720a4f5b.

Benhabib, Seyla. *Situating the Self*. New York: Routledge, 1992.

Benhabib, Seyla. "The Liberal Imagination and the Four Dogmas of Multiculturalism." *Yale Journal of Criticism* 12, no. 2 (1999): 401–13.

Berkenpas, Josh. "'The Behavioural Revolution'? A Genealogy of a Concept." *European Political Science* 15, no. 2 (June 2016): 233–50.

Berlin, Isaiah. *Four Essays on Liberty*. London: Oxford University Press, 1969.

Berndston, Erkki. "The Development of Political Science: Methodological Problems of Comparative Research." In *The Development of Political Science: A Comparative Survey*, edited by David Easton, John G. Gunnell, and Luigi Graziano, 34–58. New York: Routledge, 1991.

Berns, Lawrence. "Thomas Hobbes." In *History of Political Philosophy*, edited by Leo Strauss and Joseph Cropsey, 396–420. Chicago: University of Chicago Press, 2012.

Bhabha, Homi, and Parekh, Bikhu. "Identities on Parade: A Conversation." *Marxism Today*, June 1989, 24–29.

Blondel, Jean. *The Discipline of Politics*. Boston: Butterworth-Heinemann, 1981.

Bloom, Allan. *The Closing of the American Mind*. New York: Simon and Schuster, 1987.

Booth, Marilyn. "Islamic Politics, Street Literature, and John Stuart Mill: Composing Gendered Ideals in 1990s Egypt." *Feminist Studies* 39, no. 3 (2013): 596–627.

Bracewell, Lorna N. *Why We Lost the Sex Wars: Sexual Freedom in the #MeToo Era.* Minneapolis: University of Minnesota Press, 2021.
Broadbent, J.E. "The Importance of Class in the Political Theory of John Stuart Mill." *Canadian Journal of Political Science / Revue Canadienne de Science Politique* 1, no. 3 (1968): 270–87.
Brown, W. *Undoing the Demos: Neoliberalism's Stealth Revolution.* New York: Zone Books, 2015.
Brown, Wendy. *Edgework: Critical Essays on Knowledge and Politics.* Princeton: Princeton University Press, 2005.
Brown, Wendy. "Neo-Liberalism and the End of Liberal Democracy." *Theory & Event* 7, no. 1 (2003). https://doi:10.1353/tae.2003.0020.
Brown, Wendy. *Regulating Aversion: Tolerance in the Age of Identity and Empire.* Princeton: Princeton University Press, 2006.
Brown, Wendy. *States of Injury.* Princeton: Princeton University Press, 1995.
Burgess-Jackson, Keith. "John Stuart Mill, Radical Feminist." In *Mill's Subjection of Women*, edited by Maria Morales, 71–97. Oxford: Rowman & Littlefield, 2005.
Butler, Judith. "Contingent Foundations." In *Feminist Contentions*, edited by Judith Butler, Drucilla Cornell, Nancy Fraser, and Seyla Benhabib, 35–67. New York: Routledge, 1995.
Butler, Judith. *Gender Trouble: Feminism and the Subversion of Identity.* New York: Routledge, 1999.
Capaldi, Nicholas. *John Stuart Mill: A Biography.* Cambridge: Cambridge University Press, 2004.
Carver, Terrell. "'Mere Auxiliaries to the Movement:' How Intellectual Biography Obscures Marx's and Engels's Gendered Political Partnerships." In *The Wives of Western Philosophy: Gender Politics in Intellectual Labor*, edited by Jennifer Forestal and Menaka Philips, 1st edition, 167–84. New York: Routledge, 2020.
Cassidy, John. "Liberalism Will Survive Obamacare." *The New Yorker*, November 27, 2013.
Chait, Jonathan. "Trump Thinks Putin's Attack on 'Western-Style Liberalism' Was about California." *New York Magazine*, June 29, 2019. http://nymag.com/intelligencer/2019/06/trump-thinks-western-style-liberalism-is-about-california.html.
Cheung, Helier. "Is Putin Right? Is Liberalism Really Dead?," June 28, 2019, sec. Europe. https://www.bbc.com/news/world-europe-48798875.
Churchill, Winston. *Liberalism and the Social Problem.* London: Hodder & Stoughton, 1909.
Claeys, Gregory. "Justice, Independence, and Industrial Democracy: The Development of John Stuart Mill's Views on Socialism." *The Journal of Politics* 49, no. 1 (1987): 122–47.
Clark, Samuel. "Pleasure as Self-Discovery." *Ratio* 25, no. 3 (2012): 260–76.
Cohen, Joshua, Matthew Howard, and Martha Nussbaum, eds. *Is Multiculturalism Bad for Women.* Princeton: Princeton University Press, 1999.
Cohen, Roger. "Opinion | The Death of Liberalism." *The New York Times*, April 14, 2016, sec. Opinion. https://www.nytimes.com/2016/04/14/opinion/the-death-of-liberalism.html.
Collini, Stefan. "Liberalism and the Legacy of Mill." *The Historical Journal* 20, no. 1 (1977): 237–54.
Collini, Stefan. *Public Moralists: Political Thought and Intellectual Life in Britain.* Oxford: Clarendon Press, 1991.
Conly, Sarah. *Against Autonomy: Justifying Coercive Paternalism.* Cambridge: Cambridge University Press, 2013.

Cooley, Alexander, and Daniel H. Nexon. "'The Empire Will Compensate You': The Structural Dynamics of the U.S. Overseas Basing Network." *Perspectives on Politics* 11, no. 4 (2013): 1034–50.

Coulthard, Glen Sean. *Red Skin, White Masks: Rejecting the Colonial Politics of Recognition*. Minneapolis: University of Minnesota Press, 2014.

Cowling, Maurice. *Mill and Liberalism*. Cambridge: Cambridge University Press, 1963.

Crick, Bernard. *The American Science of Politics: Its Origins and Conditions*. Berkeley: University of California Press, 1959.

Cumming, Robert. *Human Nature and History*. Vol. 1. Chicago: University of Chicago, 1969.

Dallmayr, Fred. *Post-Liberalism: Recovering a Shared World*. Oxford; New York: Oxford University Press, 2019.

Dancy, Geoff. "Human Rights Pragmatism: Belief, Inquiry, and Action." *European Journal of International Relations* 22, no. 3 (September 1, 2016): 512–35.

Deneen, Patrick J. *Why Liberalism Failed*. New Haven: Yale University Press, 2018.

Deutscher, Penelope. "When Feminism Is 'High' and Ignorance Is 'Low': Harriet Taylor Mill on the Progress of the Species." *Hypatia* 21, no. 3 (2006): 136–50.

Dewey, John. *Liberalism and Social Action*. Great Books in Philosophy. Amherst, NY: Prometheus Books, 1999.

Dewey, John. *The Quest for Certainty*. Carbondale; Edwardsville: Southern Illinois University Press, 1988.

Dietz, Mary G. "Between Polis and Empire: Aristotle's Politics." *American Political Science Review* 106, no. 2 (May 2012): 275–93.

Donner, Wendy. "John Stuart Mill's Liberal Feminism." In *Mill's Subjection of Women*, edited by Maria Morales, 1–12. Oxford: Rowman & Littlefield, 2005.

Donner, Wendy, and Richard Fumerton. *Mill*. 1st edition. Malden, MA: Wiley-Blackwell, 2009.

Dossa, Shiraz. "Liberal Imperialism?: Natives, Muslims, and Others." *Political Theory* 30, no. 5 (October 1, 2002): 738–45.

Douthat, Ross. "Is There Life After Liberalism?" *The New York Times*, January 13, 2018, sec. Opinion. https://www.nytimes.com/2018/01/13/opinion/sunday/life-after-liberalism.html.

Dripps, Donald. "The Liberal Critique of the Harm Principle." *Criminal Justice Ethics* 17, no. 2 (1998): 3–18.

Dryzek, John S. "Revolutions without Enemies: Key Transformations in Political Science." *American Political Science Review* 100, no. 4 (2006): 487–92.

Dyzenhaus, David. "John Stuart Mill and the Harm of Pornography." In *Mill's On Liberty*, edited by Gerald Dworkin, 31–54. Oxford: Rowman & Littlefield, 1997.

Easton, David, John G. Gunnell, and Luigi Graziano. *The Development of Political Science: A Comparative Survey*. London; New York: Routledge, 1991.

"Against the Tyranny of the Majority." *The Economist*, August 4, 2018. https://www.economist.com/schools-brief/2018/08/04/against-the-tyranny-of-the-majority.

Editorial Board. "No, Mr. Putin, Western Liberalism Is Not Obsolete." *Financial Times*, June 28, 2019, sec. Opinion. https://www.ft.com/content/34f3edc0-9990-11e9-9573-ee5cbb98ed36.

Eisenach, Eldon J. "Mill's 'Autobiography' as Political Theory." *History of Political Thought* 8, no. 1 (1987): 111–29.

Ekelund, Robert B., and Robert D. Tollison. "The New Political Economy of J. S. Mill: The Means to Social Justice." *The Canadian Journal of Economics / Revue Canadienne d'Economique* 9, no. 2 (1976): 213-31.

Eliot, George. *Middlemarch*. Ware: Wordsworth Editions Ltd, 1994.

Euben, Roxanne L. *Enemy in the Mirror: Islamic Fundamentalism and the Limits of Modern Rationalism: A Work of Comparative Political Theory*. Princeton: Princeton University Press, 1999.

Farr, James. "John Dewey and American Political Science." *American Journal of Political Science* 43, no. 2 (1999): 520-41.

Farr, James. "Remembering the Revolution: Behavioralism in American Political Science." In *Political Science in History*, edited by James Farr, John S Dryzek, and Stephen T Leonard, 198-224. Cambridge: Cambridge University Press, 1995.

Farrell, Henry, and Abraham L. Newman. "Weaponized Interdependence: How Global Economic Networks Shape State Coercion." *International Security* 44, no. 1 (August 5, 2019): 42-79.

Fawcett, E. *Liberalism: The Life of an Idea*. Princeton: Princeton University Press, 2018.

Fawcett, Millicent Garrett. *What I Remember*. New York: G.P. Putnam's Sons, 1925.

Fleishman, Avrom. *George Eliot's Intellectual Life*. Cambridge: Cambridge University Press, 2010.

Forestal, Jennifer, and Menaka Philips, eds. *The Wives of Western Philosophy: Gender Politics in Intellectual Labor*. 1st edition. New York, NY: Routledge, 2020.

Forrester, Katrina. *In the Shadow of Justice: Postwar Liberalism and the Remaking of Political Philosophy*. Princeton: Princeton University Press, 2019.

Forrester, Katrina. "The Crisis of Liberalism: Why Centrist Politics Can No Longer Explain the World." *The Guardian*, November 18, 2019, sec. Books. https://www.theguardian.com/books/2019/nov/18/crisis-in-liberalism-katrina-forrester.

Freeden, Michael. *Liberalism: A Very Short Introduction*. Vol. 434. Very Short Introductions. Oxford: Oxford University Press, 2015.

Fukuyama, Francis. "Against Identity Politics: The New Tribalism and the Crisis of Democracy." *Foreign Affairs* 97, no. 5 (October 9, 2018): 90-112.

Fukuyama, Francis. Francis Fukuyama On Why Liberal Democracy Is in Trouble. NPR, April 4, 2017. https://www.npr.org/2017/04/04/522554630/francis-fukuyama-on-why-liberal-democracy-is-in-trouble.

Fukuyama, Francis. "Francis Fukuyama: Putin's War on the Liberal Order." *Financial Times*, March 3, 2022. https://www.ft.com/content/d0331b51-5d0e-4132-9f97-c3f41c7d75b3.

Fukuyama, Francis. *Liberalism and Its Discontents*. New York: Farrar, Straus and Giroux, 2022.

Fukuyama, Francis. "The End of History?" *The National Interest*, no. 16 (Summer 1989): 3-18.

Galston, William. "Defending Liberalism." *American Political Science Review* 76, no. 3 (1982): 621-29.

Gardels, Nathan. "Opinion | Francis Fukuyama: Identity Politics Is Undermining Democracy." *Washington Post*, September 18, 2018. https://www.washingtonpost.com/news/theworldpost/wp/2018/09/18/identity-politics/.

Gerbaudo, Paolo. "Liberal Democracy Is in Trouble—and Liberals Won't Save It." *Jacobin*, May 2, 2020. https://www.jacobinmag.com/2020/05/post-democracy-after-crises-colin-crouch-review-liberalism.

Geuss, Raymond. "A Republic of Discussion: Habermas at Ninety." *The Point Magazine*, June 18, 2019. https://thepointmag.com/2019/politics/republic-of-discussion-habermas-at-ninety.

Geuss, Raymond. *Not Thinking Like a Liberal*: Cambridge: Belknap Press of Harvard University Press, 2022.

Gillig, Philippe, and Philippe Légé. "J. S. Mill on Cooperatives: From Mistrust to Praise—the Constitution of a Liberal Thought in the First Half of the 19th Century." *Cahiers d'economie Politique / Papers in Political Economy* 73, no. 2 (December 28, 2017): 197–221.

Glickman, Lawrence B. "Forgotten Men." *Boston Review*, December 12, 2017. http://bostonreview.net/politics/lawrence-b-glickman-forgotten-men-the-long-road-from-fdr-to-trump.

Gray, John. "Bibliographical Essay, John Stuart Mill: Traditional and Revisionist Interpretations." *Literature of Liberty: A Review of Contemporary Liberal Thought* 2, no. 2 (1979): 1–129.

Gray, John. *Liberalism*. Minneapolis: University of Minnesota Press, 1995.

Gray, John. *Liberalisms: Essays in Political Philosophy*. London: Routledge, 1989.

Gray, John. "Pluralism and Toleration in Contemporary Political Philosophy." *Political Studies* 48, no. 2 (2000): 323–33.

Gray, John. "Why Liberalism Is in Crisis." *New Statesman* (blog), January 26, 2022. https://www.newstatesman.com/ideas/2022/01/the-light-that-failed-why-liberalism-is-in-crisis.

Green, Leslie. "Internal Minorities and Their Rights." In *The Rights of Minority Cultures*, edited by Will Kymlicka, 256–74. Oxford: Oxford University Press, 1995.

Greenstone, David. "Political Culture and American Political Development: Liberty, Union and the Liberal Bipolarity." *Studies in American Political Development* 1 (1986): 1–49.

Gross, Jonathan David. *Byron: The Erotic Liberal*. Lanham, MD: Rowman & Littlefield Publishers, 2000.

Gunnell, John G. "American Political Science, Liberalism, and the Invention of Political Theory." *American Political Science Review* 82, no. 1 (1988): 71–87.

Gunnell, John G. "Behavioralism." In *The Encyclopedia of Political Thought*, edited by Michael Gibbons, Diana Coole, Elisabeth Ellis, and Kennan Ferguson, 272–77. Wiley-Blackwell, 2014.

Gunnell, John G. "Louis Hartz and the Liberal Metaphor: A Half-Century Later." *Studies in American Political Development* 19, no. 2 (October 2005): 196–205.

Gunnell, John G. "Pluralism and the Fate of Perestroika: A Historical Reflection." *Perspectives on Politics* 13, no. 02 (2015): 408–15.

Gunnell, John G. "Political Science, History of." In *The Encyclopedia of Political Science*, edited by George Thomas Kurian, 1276–89. Washington: CQ Press, 2013.

Gunnell, John G. "The Founding of the American Political Science Association: Discipline, Profession, Political Theory, and Politics." *American Political Science Review* 100, no. 4 (November 2006): 479–86.

Habermas, Jurgen. "Reconciliation through the Public Use of Reason: Remarks on John Rawls's Political Liberalism." *The Journal of Philosophy* 92, no. 3 (1995): 109–31.

Hall, Catherine. "The Economy of Intellectual Prestige: Thomas Carlyle, John Stuart Mill, and the Case of Governor Eyre." *Cultural Critique*, no. 12 (1989): 167–96.

Halley, Janet. *Split Decisions: How and Why to Take a Break from Feminism*. Princeton: Princeton University Press, 2006.

Hamburger, Joseph. *Intellectuals in Politics: John Stuart Mill and the Philosophic Radicals.* New Haven: Yale University Press, 1965.

Hanchard, Michael. "Contours of Black Political Thought: An Introduction and Perspective." *Political Theory* 38, no. 4 (August 1, 2010): 510-36.

Harris, Abram L. "John Stuart Mill: Servant of the East India Company." *The Canadian Journal of Economics and Political Science / Revue Canadienne d'Economique et de Science Politique* 30, no. 2 (1964): 185-202.

Hartz, Louis. *The Liberal Tradition in America.* New York: Harcourt Brace Jovanovich Publishers, 1955.

Hassanzadeh, Navid. "The Canon and Comparative Political Thought." *Journal of International Political Theory* 11, no. 2 (June 1, 2015): 184-202.

Hawkesworth, Mary. "From Constitutive Outside to the Politics of Extinction: Critical Race Theory, Feminist Theory, and Political Theory." *Political Research Quarterly* 63, no. 3 (2010): 686-96.

Hendricks, Scotty. "Why John Stuart Mill Was a Capitalist - Big Think." *Big Think* (blog), June 6, 2018. https://bigthink.com/scotty-hendricks/why-john-stuart-mill-was-a-capitalist.

Herzog, Don. "'Is(n't) Catharine MacKinnon a Liberal?'" *Newsletter on Philosophy and Law—The American Philosophical Association* 12, no. 2 (2013): 11-16.

Herzog, Don. "Review: The Enlightenment, Republicanism, and Other Ghostly Afflictions." *Political Theory* 31, no. 2 (2003): 295-301.

Heuman, Gad. *The Killing Time: The Morant Bay Rebellion Jamaica.* 1st edition. Knoxville: University of Tennessee Press, 1994.

Heywood, Andrew. *Political Ideologies: An Introduction.* New York: St. Martin's Press, 1992.

Hill, John Lawrence. *The Prophet of Modern Constitutional Liberalism: John Stuart Mill and the Supreme Court.* Cambridge: Cambridge University Press, 2020.

Himmelfarb, Gertrude. *On Liberty and Liberalism: The Case of John Stuart Mill.* New York: Alfred A. Knopf, 1974.

Hollander, Samuel. *The Economics of John Stuart Mill.* Toronto: University of Toronto Press, 1985.

hooks, bell. "Theory as Liberatory Practice." *Yale Journal of Law & Feminism* 4, no. 1 (1991): 1-12.

Hoover, Herbert. *The Challenge to Liberty.* New York: Scribner's and Sons, 1934.

Hopgood, S. *The Endtimes of Human Rights.* Ithaca: Cornell University Press, 2013.

Hörnqvist, Michael. "Machiavelli's Three Desires." In *Empire and Modern Political Thought*, edited by Sankar Muthu, 7-29. New York: Cambridge University Press, 2012.

Horowitz, Irving Louis. "Louis Hartz and the Liberal Tradition: From Consensus to Crack-Up." *Modern Age* 47, no. 3 (2005): 201-9.

Howes, John. "Mill on Women and Human Development." In *Mill's Subjection of Women*, edited by Maria Morales, 13-23. Oxford: Rowman & Littlefield, 2005.

Hueglin, Thomas. *Classical Debates for the 21st Century: Rethinking Political Thought.* Toronto: Broadview Press, 2008.

Hulliung, Mark. *The American Liberal Tradition Reconsidered: The Contested Legacy of Louis Hartz.* American Political Thought. Lawrence: University Press of Kansas, 2010.

Ikuta, Jennie C. *Contesting Conformity: Democracy and the Paradox of Political Belonging.* New York: Oxford University Press, 2020.

Jaggar, Alison M. "'Saving Amina': Global Justice for Women and Intercultural Dialogue." *Ethics & International Affairs* 19, no. 03 (2005): 55-75.

Jay, Martin. "'The Liberal Idea Has Become Obsolete': Putin, Geuss and Habermas." *The Point Magazine*, July 5, 2019. https://thepointmag.com/2019/criticism/the-liberal-idea-has-become-obsolete-putin-geuss-and-habermas.

Jenco, Leigh K. "Histories of Thought and Comparative Political Theory: The Curious Thesis of 'Chinese Origins for Western Knowledge,' 1860–1895." *Political Theory* 42, no. 6 (December 1, 2014): 658–81.

"John Stuart Mill on Parliamentary Reform." *The New York Times*, May 7, 1865, sec. Archives. https://www.nytimes.com/1865/05/07/archives/john-stuart-mill-on-parliamentary-reform.html.

Jones, Ernest. *The Life and Work of Sigmund Freud*. New York: Basic Books, 1953.

Katznelson, Ira. "APSA Presidential Address: At the Court of Chaos: Political Science in an Age of Perpetual Fear." *Perspectives on Politics* 5, no. 1 (2007): 3–15.

Kelly, Paul. *Liberalism*. Cambridge: Polity, 2004.

Kinzer, Bruce L. "J.S. Mill and the Secret Ballot." *Historical Reflections / Réflexions Historiques* 5, no. 1 (1978): 19–39.

Kinzer, Bruce L, Anne P. Robson, and John M. Robson. *A Moralist in and out of Parliament: John Stuart Mill at Westminster, 1865–1868*. Toronto: University of Toronto Press, 1992.

Kirchner, Emil. *Liberal Parties in Western Europe*. Cambridge: Cambridge University Press, 1988.

Kittrell, Edward R. "Wakefield's Scheme of Systematic Colonization and Classical Economics." *The American Journal of Economics and Sociology* 32, no. 1 (1973): 87–111.

Klausen, Jimmy Casas. "Violence and Epistemology: J. S. Mill's Indians after the 'Mutiny.'" *Political Research Quarterly* 69, no. 1 (March 1, 2016): 96–107.

Klein, Daniel B. "The Origin of 'Liberalism.'" *The Atlantic*, February 13, 2014. https://www.theatlantic.com/politics/archive/2014/02/the-origin-of-liberalism/283780/.

Kohn, Margaret, and Kavita Reddy. "Colonialism." In *The Stanford Encyclopedia of Philosophy*, Fall 2017, edited by Edward N. Zalta. https://plato.stanford.edu/archives/fall2017/entries/colonialism/.

Kurtenbach, Elaine, and Klug Foster. "G-20 Leaders Clash over Values, Face Calls to Protect Growth." AP News, June 28, 2019. https://www.apnews.com/6d4457a0692e44b29e3793e7cc7e0ecb.

Kymlicka, Will. "Liberal Multiculturalism as a Political Theory of State–Minority Relations." *Political Theory* 46, no. 1 (February 1, 2018): 81–91.

Kymlicka, Will. *Liberalism, Community, and Culture*. Oxford: Clarendon Press, 1989.

Kymlicka, Will, ed. *The Rights of Minority Cultures*. Oxford: Oxford University Press, 1995.

Laski, Harold. *The Rise of European Liberalism: An Essay in Interpretation*. London: George Allen & Unwin, 1947.

Laslett, Peter. *Philosophy Politics and Society*. 1st edition. Oxford: Blackwell Publishers, 1956.

Levy, J.T. *Rationalism, Pluralism, and Freedom*. Oxford: Oxford University Press, 2015.

Linker, Damon. "An Ominous Prophecy for Liberalism." *The Week*, January 22, 2018. https://theweek.com/articles/749378/ominous-prophecy-liberalism.

Lloyd, John. "The New Illiberal International." *New Statesman*, July 18, 2018. https://www.newstatesman.com/world/2018/07/new-illiberal-international.

Lowi, Theodore. *The End of Liberalism: The Second Republic of the United States*. New York: W.W. Norton & Company, 1969.

Luce, Edward. *The Retreat of Western Liberalism*. New York: Atlantic Monthly Press, 2017.

## BIBLIOGRAPHY 199

Luke, Timothy W., and Patrick J. McGovern. "The Rebels' Yell: Mr. Perestroika and the Causes of This Rebellion in Context." *PS: Political Science & Politics* 43, no. 04 (October 2010): 729–31.

Macaulay, Thomas. *Mill on Government. The Miscellaneous Writings of Lord Macaulay.* Vol. 1. London: Longman, Green, Longman, and Roberts, 1823.

Macaulay, Thomas. *Speeches by Lord Macaulay: With His Minute on Indian Education.* London: Oxford University Press, 1935.

MacKinnon, Catharine. "Shakespeare's Sister in Philosophy and Reality: A Response." *Newsletter on Philosophy and Law—The American Philosophical Association* 12, no. 2 (2013): 16–21.

MacKinnon, Catharine. *Toward a Feminist Theory of the State.* Cambridge: Harvard University Press, 1989.

MacKinnon, Catharine A. "Sexuality, Pornography, and Method: Pleasure under Patriarchy." *Ethics* 99, no. 2 (1989): 314–46.

MacKinnon, Catharine A. "'The Case' Responds." *American Political Science Review* 95, no. 3 (2001): 709–11.

Mahmood, Saba. *Politics of Piety: The Islamic Revival and the Feminist Subject.* Princeton: Princeton University Press, 2005.

Maitra, Sumantra. "How China Is Slowly Becoming the World's Largest Imperialist Power." *The Federalist*, November 22, 2019. https://thefederalist.com/2019/11/22/how-china-is-slowly-becoming-the-worlds-largest-imperialist-power/.

Mantena, Karuna. *Alibis of Empire.* Princeton: Princeton University Press, 2010.

Mantena, Karuna. "Mill and the Imperial Predicament." In *J.S. Mill's Political Thought*, edited by Nadia Urbinati and Alex Zakaras, 298–318. New York: Cambridge University Press, 2007.

Mantena, Karuna. "The Crisis of Liberal Imperialism." *Histoire@Politique* 11, no. 2 (June 3, 2010). https://doi.org/10.3917/hp.011.0002.

Marwah, Inder S. *Liberalism, Diversity and Domination: Kant, Mill and the Government of Difference.* Cambridge: Cambridge University Press, 2019.

Marx, Karl, and Frederick Engels. *Marx and Engels 1843–1844.* Vol. 3. 50 vols. *Collected Works.* New York: International Publishers, 1975.

Massad, Joseph. *Islam in Liberalism.* Chicago: University of Chicago Press, 2015.

Mazanec, Cecilia. "#ThanksForTyping Spotlights Unnamed Women in Literary Acknowledgments." NPR.org, March 30, 2017. https://www.npr.org/2017/03/30/521931310/-thanksfortyping-spotlights-unnamed-women-in-literary-acknowledgements.

McCabe, Helen. "Harriet Taylor and John Stuart Mill's Socialism." *Nineteenth-Century Prose* 47, no. 1 (2020): 197–234.

McCabe, Helen. *John Stuart Mill, Socialist.* Montreal: McGill-Queen's University Press, 2021.

McCabe, Helen. "Mill and Socialism: A Reply to Capaldi." *The Tocqueville Review / La Revue Tocqueville* 33, no. 1 (March 24, 2012): 145–64.

McCabe, Helen. "'Political . . . Civil and Domestic Slavery': Harriet Taylor Mill and Anna Doyle Wheeler on Marriage, Servitude, and Socialism." *British Journal for the History of Philosophy* 29, no. 2 (March 4, 2021): 226–43.

McCarthy, Thomas. *Race, Empire and the Idea of Human Development.* Cambridge: Cambridge University Press, 2009.

McDonough, Kevin, and Walter Feinberg, eds. *Citizenship and Education in Liberal-Democratic Societies: Teaching for Cosmopolitan Values and Collective Identities.* Oxford: Oxford University Press, 2003. https://doi.org/10.1093/0199253668.001.0001.

Mehta, Pratap Bhanu. "Liberalism, Nation, and Empire: The Case of John Stuart Mill." In *Empire and Modern Political Thought*, edited by Sankar Muthu, 232–60. New York: Cambridge University Press, 2012.

Mehta, Uday. "Liberal Strategies of Exclusion." In *Tensions of Empire*, edited by Fredrick Cooper and Ann Laura Stoler, 59–86. Berkeley: University of California Press, 1997.

Mehta, Uday. *Liberalism and Empire*. Chicago: University of Chicago Press, 1999.

Menand, Louis. "Francis Fukuyama Postpones the End of History." *The New Yorker*, August 27, 2018. https://www.newyorker.com/magazine/2018/09/03/francis-fukuyama-postpones-the-end-of-history.

Mill, James. *James Mill: Political Writings*. Edited by Terence Ball. Cambridge: Cambridge University Press, 1992.

Mill, J.S. *A System of Logic Ratiocinative and Inductive, Books IV–VI*. Vol. 8. 33 vols. *The Collected Works of John Stuart Mill*. Edited by John M. Robson. Toronto: University of Toronto Press, 1974.

Mill, J.S. *Additional Letters of John Stuart Mill*. Vol. 32. 33 vols. *The Collected Works of John Stuart Mill*. Edited by Marion Filipiuk, Michael Laine, and John M. Robson. Toronto: University of Toronto Press, 1991.

Mill, J.S. *Autobiography and Literary Essays*. Vol. 1. 33 vols. *The Collected Works of John Stuart Mill*. Edited by John M. Robson and Jack Stillinger. Toronto: University of Toronto Press, 1981.

Mill, J.S. *Essays on Economics and Society I*. Vol. 4. 33 vols. *The Collected Works of John Stuart Mill*. Edited by John M. Robson. Toronto: Toronto University Press, 1967.

Mill, J.S. *Essays on Economics and Society II*. Vol. 5. 33 vols. *The Collected Works of John Stuart Mill*. Edited by John M. Robson. Toronto: University of Toronto Press, 1967.

Mill, J.S. *Essays on England, Ireland, and the Empire*. Vol. 6. 33 vols. *The Collected Works of John Stuart Mill*. Edited by John M. Robson. Toronto: University of Toronto Press, 1982.

Mill, J.S. *Essays on Equality, Law, and Education*. Vol. 21. 33 vols. *The Collected Works of John Stuart Mill*. Edited by John M. Robson. Toronto: University of Toronto Press, 1984.

Mill, J.S. *Essays on Ethics, Religion and Society*. Vol. 10. 33 vols. *The Collected Works of John Stuart Mill*. Edited by John M. Robson. Toronto: University of Toronto Press, 1969.

Mill, J.S. *Essays on Politics and Society*. Vol. 18. 33 vols. *The Collected Works of John Stuart Mill*. Edited by John M. Robson. Toronto: University of Toronto Press, 1977.

Mill, J.S. *Essays on Politics and Society II*. Vol. 19. 33 vols. *The Collected Works of John Stuart Mill*. Edited by John M. Robson. Toronto: University of Toronto Press, 1977.

Mill, J.S. *Newspaper Writings August 1831–October 1834 Part II*. Vol. 23. 33 vols. *The Collected Works of John Stuart Mill*. Edited by Anne P. Robson and John M. Robson. Toronto: University of Toronto Press, 1986.

Mill, J.S. *Newspaper Writings December 1822–July 1831 Part I*. Vol. 22. 33 vols. *The Collected Works of John Stuart Mill*. Edited by Anne P Robson and John M Robson. Toronto: University of Toronto Press, 1986.

Mill, J.S. *On Liberty and Other Writings*. Edited by Stefan Collini. Cambridge: Cambridge University Press, 1989.

Mill, J.S. *Principles of Political Economy Books I–II*. Vol. 2. 33 vols. *The Collected Works of John Stuart Mill*. Edited by John M. Robson. Toronto: University of Toronto Press, 1965.

Mill, J.S. *Principles of Political Economy Books III–V*. Vol. 3. 33 vols. *The Collected Works of John Stuart Mill*. Edited by John M. Robson. Toronto: University of Toronto Press, 1965.

Mill, J.S. *Public and Parliamentary Speeches Part I November 1850–November 1868.* Vol. 28. 33 vols. *The Collected Works of John Stuart Mill.* Edited by John M. Robson and Bruce L. Kinzer. Toronto: University of Toronto Press, 1988.

Mill, J.S. *Public and Parliamentary Speeches Part II July 1869—March 1873.* Vol. 29. 33 vols. *The Collected Works of John Stuart Mill.* Edited by John M. Robson and Bruce L. Kinzer. Toronto: University of Toronto Press, 1988.

Mill, J.S. *The Earlier Letters 1812–1848 Part I.* Vol. 12. 33 vols. *The Collected Works of John Stuart Mill.* Edited by Francis E. Mineka. Toronto: University of Toronto Press, 1963.

Mill, J.S. *The Later Letters of John Stuart Mill 1849–1873 Part III.* Vol. 16. 33 vols. *The Collected Works of John Stuart Mill.* Edited by Francis E. Mineka and Dwight N. Lindley. Toronto: University of Toronto Press, 1972.

Mill, J.S. *The Later Letters of John Stuart Mill 1849–1873 Part IV.* Vol. 17. 33 vols. *The Collected Works of John Stuart Mill.* Edited by Francis E. Mineka and Dwight N. Lindley.Toronto: University of Toronto Press, 1972.

Mill, J.S. *Writings on India.* Vol. 30. 33 vols. *The Collected Works of John Stuart Mill.* Edited by John M. Robson, Martin Moir, and Zawahir Moir. Toronto: University of Toronto Press, 1990.

Miller, Dale E. "The Place of Plural Voting in Mill's Conception of Representative Government." *The Review of Politics* 77, no. 3 (ed 2015): 399–423.

Miller, J. Joseph. "J.S. Mill on Plural Voting, Competence and Participation." *History of Political Thought* 24, no. 4 (2003): 647–67.

Mineka, Francis E. "The Autobiography and the Lady." *University of Toronto Quarterly* 32, no. 3 (1963): 301–6.

Mises, Ludwig von. *Liberalism in the Classical Tradition.* 3rd edition. New York: Cobden Press, 1985.

Misra, Shefali. "Friend, nor Foe: Mill's Liberal Multiculturalism." *European Journal of Political Theory* 11, no. 3 (2012): 1–19.

Morales, Maria, ed. *Mill's Subjection of Women.* Oxford: Rowman & Littlefield, 2005.

Morales, Maria. *Perfect Equality: John Stuart Mill on Well-Constituted Communities.* Boulder; New York: Rowman & Littlefield, 1996.

Morales, Maria. "Rational Freedom in John Stuart Mill." In *J.S. Mill's Political Thought*, edited by Nadia Urbinati and Alex Zakaras, 43–65. New York: Cambridge University Press, 2007.

Morefield, Jeanne. *Covenants without Swords: Idealist Liberalism and the Spirit of Empire.* Princeton: Princeton University Press, 2009.

Morely, John. *Essay 3: Mr. Mill's Autobiography.* Vol. 3. 3 vols. *Critical Miscellanies.* London: MacMillan and Co., 1904. http://www.gutenberg.org.

Nagel, Thomas. "Rawls and Liberalism." In *The Cambridge Companion to Rawls*, edited by Samuel Freeman, 62–85. Cambridge: Cambridge University Press, 2002.

Narayan, Uma. *Dislocating Cultures: Identities, Traditions, and Third World Feminism.* New York: Routledge, 1997.

New York Times. "OBITUARY, John Stuart Mill." May 10, 1873. https://www.nytimes.com/1873/05/10/archives/obituary-john-stuart-mill.html.

Nexon, Daniel H., and Thomas Wright. "What's at Stake in the American Empire Debate." *American Political Science Review* 101, no. 2 (2007): 253–71.

Nimtz, August. "The Eurocentric Marx and Engels and Other Related Myths." In *Marxism, Modernity and Postcolonial Studies*, edited by Crystal Bartolovich and Neil Lazarus, 65–80. Cambridge: Cambridge University Press, 2002.

Nozick, Robert. "Distributive Justice." In *Communitarianism and Individualism*, edited by Shlomo Avineri and Avner de-Shalit, 137–50. Oxford: Oxford University Press, 1992.

Nussbaum, Martha. "Mill between Aristotle and Bentham." *Daedalus* 133, no. 2 (2004): 60–68.

Nussbaum, Martha. *Women and Human Development: The Capabilities Approach*. Cambridge: Cambridge University Press, 2000.

Okin, Susan Moller. "Feminism and Multiculturalism: Some Tensions." *Ethics* 108, no. 4 (1998): 661–84.

Okin, Susan Moller. "John Stuart Mill's Feminism." In *Mill's Subjection of Women*, edited by Maria Morales, 24–51. Oxford: Rowman & Littlefield, 2005.

Okin, Susan Moller. *Justice, Gender, and The Family*. 2008 edition. New York: Basic Books, 1989.

Okin, Susan Moller. *Women in Western Political Thought*. Princeton: Princeton University Press, 1979.

O'Neill, Daniel I. *Edmund Burke and the Conservative Logic of Empire*. California: University of California Press, 2016.

Pappe, H.O. *John Stuart Mill and the Harriet Taylor Myth*. Social Science Monographs. Melbourne: Melbourne University Press, 1960.

Parekh, Bhikhu. "A Varied Moral World." In *Is Multiculturalism Bad for Women?*, edited by Joshua Cohen, Matthew Howard, and Martha Nussbaum, 69–75. Princeton: Princeton University Press, 1999.

Parekh, Bhikhu. "Decolonizing Liberalism." In *The End of "Isms"? Reflections on the Fate of Ideological Politics after Communism's Collapse*, edited by Aleksandras Shtromas, 85–103. Oxford: Blackwell Publishers, 1994.

Pateman, Carole. *The Sexual Contract*. Stanford: Stanford University Press, 1988.

Philips, Anne. *Multiculturalism without Culture*. Princeton: Princeton University Press, 2009.

Philips, Menaka. "Feminist Preoccupations: Liberalism as Method in Debates Concerning Gender and Culture." *Signs: Journal of Women in Culture and Society* 44, no. 4 (May 21, 2019): 955–77.

Philips, Menaka. "The 'Beloved and Deplored' Memory of Harriet Taylor Mill: Rethinking Gender and Intellectual Labor in the Canon." In *The Wives of Western Philosophy: Gender Politics in Intellectual Labor*, edited by Jennifer Forestal and Menaka Philips, 147–66. New York: Routledge, 2020.

Philips, Menaka. "Troubling Appropriations: JS Mill, Liberalism, and the Virtues of Uncertainty." *European Journal of Political Theory* 18, no. 1 (January 1, 2019): 68–88.

Pitts, Jennifer. *A Turn to Empire*. Princeton: Princeton University Press, 2005.

Pitts, Jennifer. "Legislator of the World? A Rereading of Bentham on Colonies." *Political Theory* 31, no. 2 (April 1, 2003): 200–34.

Pitts, Jennifer. "Political Theory of Empire and Imperialism." *Annual Review of Political Science* 13 (2010): 211–35.

Pitts, Jennifer. "Republicanism, Liberalism, and Empire in Postrevolutionary France." In *Empire and Modern Political Thought*, edited by Sankar Muthu, 261–91. New York: Cambridge University Press, 2012.

Pollack, Sheldon. "Empire and Imitation." In *Lessons of Empire: Imperial Histories and American Power*, edited by Craig Calhoun, Fredrick Cooper, and Kevin W Moore, 175–88. New York: New Press, 2006.

"Putin Derides Liberalism as 'Obsolete' before G20 Summit." *Al Jazeera*, June 28, 2019. https://www.aljazeera.com/news/2019/06/putin-derides-liberalism-obsolete-g20-summit-190628052108100.html.

Rawls, John. *A Theory of Justice*. Cambridge: Harvard University Press, 2003.

Rawls, John. *Justice as Fairness*. Cambridge: Belknap Press of Harvard University Press, 2003.

Reeves, Richard. "John Stuart Mill and What's Lacking in American Liberalism." *The Wall Street Journal* (blog), May 20, 2014. http://blogs.wsj.com/washwire/2014/05/20/john-stuart-mill-and-whats-lacking-in-american-liberalism/.

Reeves, Richard. *John Stuart Mill: Victorian Firebrand*. London: Atlantic Books, 2007.

Ricci, David M. "Contradictions of a Political Discipline." In *Discipline and History: Political Science in the United States*, edited by James Farr and Raymond Seidelman, 165–78. Ann Arbor: The University of Michigan Press, 1993.

Riley, Jonathan. "Individuality, Custom and Progress." *Utilitas* 3, no. 2 (1991): 217–44.

Riley, Jonathan. "Mill's Neo-Athenian Model of Liberal Democracy." In *J.S. Mill's Political Thought*, edited by Nadia Urbinati and Alex Zakaras, 221–49. New York: Cambridge University Press, 2007.

Riley, Jonathan. "Mill's Political Economy: Ricardian Science and Liberal Utilitarian Art." In *The Cambridge Companion to Mill*, edited by John Skorupski, 1st ed., 293–337. Cambridge University Press, 1998.

Ring, Jennifer. "Mill's *The Subjection of Women*: The Methodological Limits of Liberal Feminism." *Review of Politics* 47, no. 1 (1985): 27–44.

Roache, Madeline. "Russian President Putin Calls Liberalism 'Obsolete' Amid G20." *Time*, June 28, 2019. https://time.com/5616982/putin-liberalism-g20/.

Robson, John M. "Mill in Parliament: The View from the Comic Papers." *Utilitas* 2, no. 1 (May 1990): 102–43.

Robson, John M. *The Improvement of Mankind: The Social and Political Thought of John Stuart Mill*. Toronto: University of Toronto Press, 1968.

Rosenblatt, Helena. *The Lost History of Liberalism: From Ancient Rome to the Twenty-First Century*. Princeton: Princeton University Press, 2018.

Ross, Dorothy. "Against Canons: Liberating the Social Sciences." *Society* 29, no. 1 (1991): 10–13.

Ross, Dorothy. "Robert Adcock. Liberalism and the Emergence of American Political Science: A Transatlantic Tale. Oxford: Oxford University Press, 2014." *American Political Thought* 4, no. 4 (September 2015): 669–72.

Ross, Dorothy. *The Origins of American Social Science*. Cambridge: Cambridge University Press, 1991.

Rossi, Alice S., ed. *Essays on Sex Equality*. Chicago: University of Chicago Press, 1970.

Rothbard, Murray N. *An Austrian Perspective on the History of Economic Thought*. Vol. 2. Ludwig von Mises Institute. Alabama: Edward Elgar Publishing Ltd., 1995.

Ryan, Alan. *J.S. Mill*. London: Routledge, 1974.

Ryan, Alan. "Mill in a Liberal Landscape." In *The Cambridge Companion to Mill*, edited by John Skorupski, 497–540. Cambridge: Cambridge University Press, 1998.

Samuelson, Robert J. "Opinion | Does Vladimir Putin Have a Point?" *Washington Post*, July 8, 2019, sec. Opinions. https://www.washingtonpost.com/opinions/putin-declared-that-liberalism-is-obsolete-is-he-right/2019/07/08/a6f13070-a1a3-11e9-b732-41a79c2551bf_story.html.

Sandel, Michael. *Liberalism and the Limits of Justice*. Cambridge: Cambridge University Press, 1998.
Sandel, Michael. "The Procedural Republic and the Unencumbered Self." *Political Theory* 12, no. 1 (1984): 81–96.
Sartori, A. *Liberalism in Empire: An Alternative History*. California: University of California Press, 2014.
Schaeffer, Denise. "Feminism and Liberalism Reconsidered: The Case of Catharine MacKinnon." *American Political Science Review* 95, no. 3 (September 2001): 699–708.
Schwartz, Pedro. "John Stuart Mill and Socialism." *The Mill News Letter* 4, no. 1 (1968): 11–15.
Scott, Joan Wallach. *Sex and Secularism*. Princeton: Princeton University Press, 2017.
Seidelman, Raymond. "Political Scientists, Disenchanted Realists, and Disappearing Democrats." In *Discipline and History: Political Science in the United States*, edited by James Farr and Raymond Seidelman, 311–25. Ann Arbor: The University of Michigan Press, 1993.
Seiz, Janet A., and Michèle A. Pujol. "Harriet Taylor Mill." *The American Economic Review* 90, no. 2 (2000): 476–79.
Shklar, Judith N. *Political Thought and Political Thinkers*. Chicago: University of Chicago Press, 1998.
Shklar, Judith N. "Redeeming American Political Theory." *American Political Science Review* 85, no. 1 (March 1991): 3–15.
Siedentop, Larry. *Inventing the Individual: The Origins of Western Liberalism*. Cambridge: Belknap Press, 2014.
Skinner, Quentin. "Meaning and Understanding in the History of Ideas." In *Meaning and Context: Quentin Skinner and His Critics*, edited by James Tully, 29–67. Princeton: Princeton University Press, 1998.
Skipper, Robert. "Mill and Pornography." In *Mill's On Liberty*, edited by Gerald Dworkin, 55–60. Oxford: Rowman & Littlefield, 1997.
Skorupski, John. *Why Read Mill Today?* London: Routledge, 2006.
Skowronek, Stephen. "The Reassociation of Ideas and Purposes: Racism, Liberalism, and the American Political Tradition." *American Political Science Review* 100, no. 3 (2006): 384–401.
Smith, Rogers. "Beyond Tocqueville, Myrdal and Hartz: The Multiple Traditions in America." *American Political Science Review* 87, no. 3 (1993): 549–66.
Smits, Katherine. "John Stuart Mill and the Social Construction of Identity." *History of Political Thought* 25, no. 2 (2004): 298–324.
Souffrant, Eddy. *Formal Transgressions: John Stuart Mill's Philosophy of International Affairs*. Oxford: Rowman & Littlefield, 2000.
Spivak, Gayatri Chakravorty. "Can the Subaltern Speak?" In *Marxism and the Interpretation of Culture*, edited by C. Nelson and L. Grossberg, 271–313. Chicago: University of Illinois Press, 1988.
Stanley, Timothy, and Lee Alexander. "It's Still Not the End of History." *The Atlantic*, September 1, 2014. https://www.theatlantic.com/politics/archive/2014/09/its-still-not-the-end-of-history-francis-fukuyama/379394/.
Stephen, Leslie. *The English Utilitarians: John Stuart Mill*. Vol. 3. London: Duckworth & Co., 1900.
Stillinger, Jack. "Who Wrote J.S. Mill's Autobiography." *Victorian Studies* 27 (1983): 7–23.

Storing, Herbert J., ed. *Essays on the Scientific Study of Politics*. New York: Holt, Rinehart, & Winston, 1962.

Strauss, Leo. *Liberalism Ancient and Modern*. 1st edition. Chicago: University of Chicago Press, 1968.

Sullivan, Eileen P. "Liberalism and Imperialism: J. S. Mill's Defense of the British Empire." *Journal of the History of Ideas* 44, no. 4 (1983): 599–617.

Sunstein, Cass. "It's For Your Own Good!" *The New York Review of Books*, March 7, 2013.

Sylvester, Rachel. "Jeremy Browne: 'Many Lib Dems Support the Opposite of True Liberalism.'" *The Times*, 2014. https://www.thetimes.co.uk/article/jeremy-browne-many-lib-dems-support-the-opposite-of-true-liberalism-86zckcvnl20.

Taylor Mill, Harriet. *The Complete Works of Harriet Taylor Mill*. Edited by Jo Ellen Jacobs and Paula Harms Payne. Bloomington: Indiana University Press, 1998.

Taylor, Quentin. "John Stuart Mill, Political Economist: A Reassessment." *The Independent Review* 21, no. 1 (2016): 73–94.

Ten, C.L. "Democracy, Socialism and the Working Classes." In *The Cambridge Companion to Mill*, edited by John Skorupski, 372–95. Cambridge: Cambridge University Press, 1998.

Ten, C.L. *Mill on Liberty*. New York: Oxford University Press, 1980.

"The Literature of Liberalism—Open Future." *The Economist*, August 29, 2018. https://www.economist.com/open-future/2018/08/29/the-literature-of-liberalism.

Thompson, Dennis. "Mill in Parliament." In *J.S. Mill's Political Thought*, edited by Nadia Urbinati and Alex Zakaras, 166–99. New York: Cambridge University Press, 2007.

Tocqueville, Alexis de. *Selected Letters on Politics and Society*. Edited by Roger Boesche. Translated by James Toupin. California: University of California Press, 1986.

Topol, Sarah A. "What Does Putin Really Want?" *The New York Times*, June 25, 2019, sec. Magazine. https://www.nytimes.com/2019/06/25/magazine/russia-united-states-world-politics.html.

Traub, James. "Liberalism Isn't Dead—but It's Very Sick." *Foreign Policy*, May 10, 2022. https://foreignpolicy.com/2022/05/10/liberalism-democracy-decline-autocracy-mounk-fukuyama-books/.

Tunick, Mark. "Tolerant Imperialism: John Stuart Mill's Defense of British Rule in India." *The Review of Politics* 68, no. 4 (2006): 586–611.

Urbinati, Nadia. *Mill on Democracy: From the Athenian Polis to Representative Government*. Chicago: University of Chicago Press, 2002.

Urbinati, Nadia. "The Many Heads of the Hydra: J.S. Mill on Despotism." In *J.S. Mill's Political Thought*, edited by Nadia Urbinati and Alex Zakaras, 66–97. New York: Cambridge University Press, 2007.

Urbinati, Nadia, and Alex Zakaras, eds. *J.S. Mill's Political Thought*. New York: Cambridge University Press, 2007.

Waldron, Jeremy. "Mill on Liberty and on the Contagious Diseases Acts." In *J.S. Mill's Political Thought*, edited by Nadia Urbinati and Alex Zakaras, 11–42. New York: Cambridge University Press, 2007.

Wall, Steven. *The Cambridge Companion to Liberalism*. Cambridge: Cambridge University Press, 2015.

Weiss, Penny A. *Canon Fodder: Historical Women Political Thinkers*. Pennsylvania: The Pennsylvania State University Press, 2009.

Welch, Cheryl B. "Out of Africa: Tocqueville's Imperial Voyages." *Review of Middle East Studies* 45, no. 1 (2011): 53–61.

Whewell, W. "Comte and Positivism, MacMillan's Magazine," 1866. Mill-Taylor Collection/45, London School of Economics.

Williams, David. "John Stuart Mill and the Practice of Colonial Rule in India." *Journal of International Political Theory* 17, no. 3 (2021): 412–28.

Williams, David. *Progress, Pluralism, and Politics: Liberalism and Colonialism, Past and Present*. Montreal; Kingston; London; Chicago: McGill-Queen's University Press, 2021.

Williams, Melissa S. "Deparochializing Democratic Theory." In *Deparochializing Political Theory*, edited by Melissa S. Williams, 201–29. Cambridge: Cambridge University Press, 2020. https://doi.org/10.1017/9781108635042.009.

Wolf, Martin. "Liberalism Will Endure but Must Be Renewed." *Financial Times*, July 2, 2019. https://www.ft.com/content/52dc93d2-9c1f-11e9-9c06-a4640c9feebb.

Wolin, Sheldon S. "Political Theory as a Vocation." *American Political Science Review* 63, no. 4 (1969): 1062–82.

Wright, Bryan. "I'm a Democrat but There's Something Great about Trump's Travel Ban." *Fox News*, January 31, 2017.

Young, Iris Marion. *Inclusion and Democracy*. New York: Oxford University Press, 2000.

Zastoupil, Lynn. "India, J.S. Mill, and 'Western' Culture." In *J.S. Mill's Encounter with India*, edited by Martin Moir, Douglas Peers, and Lynn Zastoupil, 111–48. Toronto: University of Toronto Press, 1999.

Zastoupil, Lynn *John Stuart Mill and India*. Stanford: Stanford University Press, 1994.

Zelizer, Julian. "Opinion: Obamacare and the Failure of Half-Baked Liberalism." CNN—Opinion, November 11, 2013.

Zerilli, Linda. *Signifying Women: Culture and Chaos in Rousseau, Burke, and Mill*. Ithaca: Cornell University Press, 1994.

Zerilli, Linda. "Towards a Feminist Theory of Judgment." *Signs* 34, no. 2 (2009): 295–317.

# Index

*For the benefit of digital users, indexed terms that span two pages (e.g., 52–53) may, on occasion, appear on only one of those pages.*

Adorno, Theodor, 3–4
Alter, Adam, 1
Ambirajan, S., 185n.72
American militarism, 116–17
Annas, Julia, 63
Arendt, Hannah, 3–4
Arneil, Barbara, 122
Ashcraft, Richard, 37, 51
authoritarianism, ix, 18–19
*Autobiography* (Mill)
　discussion of mental crisis in, 44–49
　and dogmas, 148
　drafting of, 40–41, 45–46, 56–58, 60, 170n.67
　emphasis on social conditions, 54
　and gender equality, 50
　and imperialism, 138
　"many-sided" thought in, 11, 25–26, 38, 47–48, 52–53, 55–56
　reception of, 7, 91–92, 151–52

Bain, Alexander, 81, 172n.1
Ball, Terence, 24–25, 26, 49
Barker, Chris, 99, 111
Baum, Bruce, 30–31, 32–33, 92–93, 105, 124
Bell, Duncan, 4–5, 16, 21, 141
benevolent despotism, 128–41
Benhabib, Seyla, x
Bentham, Jeremy, 11, 24–25, 34, 41, 43–44, 45–47, 116–17, 120–21
Bentham, Sir Samuel, 42
"Bentham" (Mill), 46–47, 75
Bentinck, William, 131
Berlin, Isaiah, 26, 30–31, 41
Berndston, Erkki, 17–18
Black Act of 1836, 133–34, 137–38

Bloom, Allan, 30
Bogle, Paul, 136–37
Bolsonaro, Jair, ix
British Empire, 12–13, 43, 58, 74, 90, 114–15, 120, 124, 126, 133, 136, 138, 141–42. *See also* East India Company; imperialism; India
Broadbent, J.E., 92
Brown, Wendy, 2–3, 53–54, 65, 71–73, 113–14, 145–46, 174n.43
Burgess-Jackson, Keith, 64
Burke, Edmund, 22–23, 116–17, 118, 120–21
Butler, Judith, 113–14, 150

canonization, xii–xiii, 7, 8–10, 16–17, 21, 25, 149
Capaldi, Nicholas, 28, 38
capitalism, 91–92, 98, 111
Carlyle, Thomas, 76
Catholicism, 48, 145–46
Caucus for a New Political Science, 20
censorship, 55
"Chapters on Socialism" (Mill), 94
China, 149–50
citizenship
　benefits of, 100
　duties of, 94–95, 107–8, 110, 112, 124–25
　and empire, 122
　practices of, 32–33, 72–73, 102, 104–5
　qualifications for, 90–91, 124–25
civilizational progress, 121, 127
"Claims of Labor, The" (Mill), 94
class
　conditions of, 54, 89–90
　and identity, 57–58, 113, 114

class (cont.)
 and political representation, 88, 93, 100–1, 102, 107–8, 112–13, 124–25
 structural exclusion of, 94–95 (see also gender; poverty)
class inequality, 93, 95, 102–3. See also inequality
Clifford, Dr., 59
"Coleridge" (Mill), 34, 48–49
Collini, Stefan, 34, 165n.82
communism, 96–97
Comte, Auguste, 48, 49–50, 111, 126
conformity, 52, 148
conscription, 16, 20–25. See also retrojection
*Considerations on Representative Government* (Mill), 102, 133–34
Contagious Diseases Acts, 33, 59–60
cottiers, 129–30
Cowling, Maurice, 30
critical thinking, 41–42, 43, 45, 47
critique, task of, 150–51
cultural diversity, 129

Dagger, Richard, 24–25, 26
*Daily Telegraph*, 139–40
Davies, Emily, 101–2
democracy, xi, 8, 20, 57–58, 89–90, 98, 113. See also liberalism
*Democracy in America* (Tocqueville), 98
Deneen, Patrick, 145–46
despotism, 57–58, 120, 122–23, 128–41, 143. See also imperialism
Dewey, John, 2, 51
Dietz, Mary, 116–17
 "Memorandum of the Improvements in the Administration of India" (Mill), 130
divorce, 49–50, 81–82, 83–84, 86. See also marriage
dogmas, 11, 41–43, 52, 148–49. See also local customs
domestic abuse, 59–60, 134
domestic labor, 49–50, 72–73, 83–84, 85–86, 90
Donner, Wendy, 63, 74
Dossa, Shiraz, 117

Dumont, Étienne, 43–44

East India Company, 32, 41, 43, 116, 128, 130–31, 137–38. See also British Empire
east/west dichotomy, 149–50
*Economist*, x–xi, 26
education
 and gender norms, 75, 78–79, 86
 of John Stuart Mill, 41–47
 and producing social change, 83–84
 as requirement for suffrage, 104–5, 108–9, 112–13, 124–25, 127, 187n.117
Elliot, George, 88, 176n.1
*Enfranchisement of Women* (Taylor), 85
English principles, 61, 94–95, 138–39
ethnocentrism, 32
*Examiner*, 82, 100
Eyre, Edward, 136–37, 138, 139–41

Farr, James, 19
Fawcett, Edmund, 24
Fawcett, Henry, 140–41
Fawcett, Millicent, 59
feminism, 9, 21, 31, 59–60, 62–63, 65–66. See also liberal feminism
*Financial Times, The*, ix
France, 110, 112–13, 128
Freeden, Michael, 24
free press, 15–16
Freud, Sigmund, 59
Fukuyama, Francis, x

G20 summit, ix, 15
Garrett, Elizabeth, 101–2
gender
 and citizenship, 71
 and inequality, 11–12, 39, 68–69, 78–79, 85–87, 90
 perceived natural hierarchies, 75–76
 social norms of, 53, 54, 60–61, 75, 77 (see also class)
gender equity, xii–xiii, 13, 31, 50, 57–58, 62, 74, 125–26. See also inequality; women's suffrage
Geuss, Raymond, x, 158n.13

globalization, x, 9, 116–17, 149–50
Google Ngram, 1
gradualist strategy, 12, 57–58, 61, 74, 81, 82, 86, 103, 104, 108, 110–11, 113–14, 124–25, 127, 143–44. *See also* paternalist strategy; radical strategy
Gray, John, 30, 38–39, 52
Gunnell, John, 4, 19

Halley, Janet, 63, 64
harm principle, 33, 54–56, 63–64, 172n.97. *See also* Mill, John Stuart
Harris, Abram, 130
Hartz, Louis, 4, 19–20, 34–35
Hazard, Rowland, 138–39
Herodotus, 41
Herzog, Don, 23, 68, 69
Himmelfarb, Gertrude, 29–30, 165n.82
Hobbes, Thomas, 6, 22–23, 24–25
Hoover, Herbert, x
Horkheimer, Max, 3–4
hothouse characters, 78, 102
human nature, 7, 46, 48, 49–50, 51, 68–69, 75, 76–77, 120
hysteria, 77

ideology
  genealogies of, 146, 150
  and identity, 23–24
  labels of, 6, 33, 35, 49, 99–100
  rigidity of, 61–62
  *See also* liberalism
imperialism
  critiques of, 126–27, 128
  economic interests of, 126–27, 136, 184n.54
  perceptions of, 12–13, 57–58, 116–17, 123, 140–41
  violence of, 135–36, 137–38, 141
  *See also* British Empire; despotism; liberal imperialism
India
  indirect rule in, 132
  local customs of, 43, 130–32
  perceptions of, 124–26, 185n.72
  political subjectivity in, 133–34, 142, 186n.88

self-governance of, 125–26, 133–34, 139
*See also* British Empire
individual agency, 2, 45–46, 61, 147–48
individuality, 7, 30, 48, 52, 54–55, 57–58, 68, 69, 93–94
individual liberty, 15–16, 24–25, 26, 30–31, 63. *See also* liberty
inequality, x, 11–12, 39. *See also* class inequality; gender equity
International Political Science Association, 18
international relations, 116–17
Ireland, 129–30, 132
Islam, 147–48, 176n.102

Jamaica, 34, 136–37, 138, 139–40, 186n.102
Jamaica Committee, 116, 136–37, 138, 139–41
Jay, Martin, x, 158n.13
Judaism, 71

Kinzer, Bruce, 108
Klausen, Jimmy Casas, 133
Kymlicka, Will, 30–31

labor supply, 126–27, 184n.54
laissez-faire markets, 24–25
Laski, Harold, 2
Le Pen, Marie, ix
LGBTQ rights, ix
liberal, as label, 1, 16, 21, 22, 64–65, 120–21, 165n.69
liberal feminism, 11–12, 31, 63, 64–66, 86, 148–49. *See also* feminism
liberal imperialism, 32, 117, 118–19, 120, 127–28, 142, 149–50. *See also* imperialism
liberalism
  critiques of, ix–x, 29, 53–54
  discursive resilience of, xi–xii, 3, 21, 23–24
  elasticity of, 2–4, 15–16, 21–22, 24, 34–35
  and empire, 12–13, 117–18, 120–21, 142
  features of, 15–16, 18–19, 63, 68, 120–21
  framings of, 10, 19

liberalism (*cont.*)
  and the harm principle, 54–55
  history and lineage of, 1–2, 5, 21–22, 24–25, 26–27, 29, 30–31, 32, 34, 37, 39–40, 61–62, 68, 92–93, 155n.3
  ideological functions of, 23–25, 26–27, 96–97, 117
  narratives of, 19–21, 32–33, 145
  scholarly receptions of, x, 10–11, 13–14, 27–28, 51–52, 145
  *See also* democracy; ideology; liberalism trap; liberty; Mill, John Stuart
*Liberalism and Empire* (Mehta), 117
liberalism trap
  and feminism, 71–74
  limitations of, xi–xii, 8–9, 10–11, 70, 141–42
  persistence of, 20–21
  refusal of, 38, 119
  rigidity of, 5, 146, 152–53
  *See also* liberalism
Liberal Party, 33, 165n.69
liberal pedagogies, 20–25, 35
*Liberal Tradition in America, The* (Hartz), 4
libertarianism, 55
liberty, 26, 27, 32–33, 35, 39, 43, 48, 97–98, 99–100, 152. *See also* liberalism; individual liberty
Lieber, Francis, 18
local customs, 130, 131–32, 148. *See also* dogmas
Locke, John, 6, 21, 22–23, 24–25, 92, 118, 149
*Logic* (Mill), 75
*longue durée* perspective, 125–26
Lowi, Theodore, 19–20

Macaulay, Thomas, 46, 131
MacKinnon, Catharine, 31, 53–54, 65, 67–70, 72–73, 80, 145–46, 174n.43
Mahmood, Saba, 31, 65–67, 73, 147–48, 188n.11
Mantena, Karuna, 121–22
"Many Heads of the Hyrda, The" (Urbinati), 122–23
marriage, 49–50, 56, 59–61, 63–64, 75, 78–80, 83–85, 104–5, 125–26. *See also* divorce

Marwah, Inder, 122
Marx, Karl, 128, 152
Marxism, 113–14
Massey, William, 134–35
McCabe, Helen, 31, 92–93
McCarthy, Thomas, 117–18
Mehta, Uday, 117, 120, 142
melancholic colonialism, 141
*Middlemarch* (Elliot), 88
Mill, Harriet, 60
Mill, James, 7–8, 11, 41, 42, 43–44, 45–46, 60, 116–17, 120–21, 122. *See also* Mill, John Stuart
Mill, John Stuart
  alternate readings of, 29–30, 32–33, 37–38, 49, 119, 122–23
  canonization of, 16–17, 39–40
  critiques of liberalism, 29
  education of, 11, 40–44, 56–58
  and empire, 12–13, 32, 57–58, 74, 116–17, 118–19, 120, 121–23, 126–41, 149–50
  feminist politics of, 11–12, 61–62, 64, 65–70, 72, 80, 83–84, 85–87, 89–90, 118–19, 123–24, 148–49
  gender politics of, 31, 50, 59, 75–76
  iconic status of, xii, 6–9, 14, 25, 28, 29, 36, 61–63, 68–70, 73–74, 91–92, 116–18, 146–47
  legacy of, 15, 25–26, 59
  mental crisis of, 41, 44–49
  political career of, 32, 33, 34, 43, 59–60, 81, 101, 105–6, 108–9, 110–11, 129–31, 136–37, 165n.69
  and political economy, 31–32, 89, 91–92, 96–97, 99, 102–3
  reception of, 16, 18, 27, 28, 30–31, 32–33, 53–54, 92–93, 176n.102
  rhetorical strategies of, 93–95
  role as critic, 150–53
  and socialism, 97–98
  *See also* harm principle; liberalism; Mill, James; Taylor, Harriet; uncertainty; *specific works*
*Mill and the Moral Character of Liberalism* (Ashcraft), 37
Mises, Ludwig von, 29–30
Misra, Shefali, 130–31
modernity, failures of, 145–46
Moir, Martin, 125

morality, 68, 95–96, 111, 130, 137–38, 141, 143–44
Morant Bay massacre, 136–37, 140–41
Morely, John, 82, 151–52
multiculturalism, ix

Nagel, Thomas, 2
"Nature" (Mill), 75
"Negro Question, The" (Mill), 76
neoliberalism, 118, 149
*New Yorker, The*, 1
*New York Times*, 15, 25–26, 109
New Zealand, 135–36, 184n.54
Nozick, Robert, 30–31

*Oberon*, 45
Okin, Susan Moller, 31, 62–63
oligarchs, ix
O'Neill, Daniel, 118
*On Liberty* (Mill), 6–7, 26, 28–30, 34–35, 41–42, 53, 55–56, 75, 93, 120, 130–31, 148
"On Marriage" (Mill), 83, 104–5
open ballots, 104–5, 108, 111–12, 125. *See also* secret ballots
Orbán, Viktor, ix
overpopulation, 126
Owenism, 48, 97–98

Parekh, Bhikhu, 52, 129
Pateman, Carole, 31, 50, 62–63
paternalism, 57–58, 84–85, 122–24
paternalist strategy, 12, 61, 74, 86, 103, 113–14, 123–24, 143–44. *See also* gradualist strategy; radical strategy
personality cults, ix
philosophy, 48
Pitts, Jennifer, 22, 120–21
Plato, 41, 42
plural votes, 103–4, 109–10, 111–12, 114, 125–26
political correctness, 63
political economy, 31–32
political science
  academic traditions of, 3–4, 9–10, 17–18, 19–20
  dominance of liberalism in, xi–xii, 10–11, 16
  and empire studies, 116–17
  pedagogical strategies of, 23–25, 35

political spectrum, 27, 48–49, 91–92, 145–46
*Politics of Piety* (Mahmood), 65–67
Pollack, Sheldon, 116–17
positivist methodologies, 19
postcolonialism, xii–xiii, 21
poststructuralism, 65
poverty, 54, 90–91, 94–95. *See also* class
power, 32–33, 64–65, 71, 78–79, 139–41
*Principles of Political Economy* (Mill), 97
private property, 98, 100
public opinion, x, 107–8
public sphere, 4, 15, 18, 72–73
Putin, Vladimir, ix–x, xi, 158n.13

race, 9, 76–77, 122–23, 135–36
radical strategy, 11–13, 33, 61–62, 63, 74, 80, 88–89, 91, 93, 104–5, 108–9, 113, 114, 118–19, 123, 127–28, 143, 146–47, 152. *See also* gradualist strategy; paternalist strategy
Rawls, John, 20–21, 30–31, 110–11
Reeves, Richard, 8, 27
Reform Acts, 81, 88, 100, 101–2, 104, 105–6, 140–41
refusal, 38
*Regulating Aversion* (Brown), 71–73
religious tolerance, 15–16, 26–27
Representation of the People Act of 1918, 172n.2
retrojection, 16, 21–23, 25. *See also* conscription
Ricci, David, 18
Robson, John, 38, 48
Roosevelt, Franklin Delano, 18
Ross, Dorothy, 17–18
Rothbard, Murray, 29–30
Russia, xi, 149–50
Ryan, Alan, 34–35, 81, 124

Salvini, Matteo, ix
Sandel, Michael, 30–31
scholarly debates, x, 4, 15, 27–28
Scott, Joan, 62–63
secret ballots, 104–6, 108. *See also* open ballots
Seidelman, Raymond, 18, 21
self-determination, 125–26, 142–43
Sepoy uprising of 1857, 133, 135, 137–38
sexism, 59–60, 91–92

sexual agency, 63, 71
Shklar, Judith, 2
Skinner, Quentin, 13–14
Skorupski, John, 38
slavery, 54, 75–76, 80–81, 93–96
Smith, Adam, 24–25, 120–21
Smits, Katherine, 113
social contract, 24–25
socialism, 8, 29, 31, 48, 91–92, 93–94, 96–98, 99–100, 112–13
social relations, 26–27, 52–53, 68–70, 80–81, 83, 95
sociology, 68, 86–87
Socratic dialogues, 42
Souffrant, Eddy, 52–53
"Spirit of the Age, The" (Mill), 145
Stillinger, Jack, 170n.67
Strauss, Leo, 3–4, 19–20
St. Simonian thought, 48, 96–97
*Subjection of Women, The* (Mill), 50, 53, 63, 68, 72–73, 75, 81–82, 83–85, 88–89, 90, 93–94, 101–2, 108–9, 125–26, 176n.102
suffrage. *See* universal suffrage; women's suffrage
Sullivan, Eileen, 120
Sumner, William Graham, 18

Taylor, Harriet, 41, 49–50, 59–61, 69–70, 75, 81–82, 85, 91–92, 98, 134, 170n.67, 176n.3, *See also* Mill, John Stuart
Taylor, John, 81–82
Taylor, Quentin, 91–92
Ten, C.L., 28, 29, 89–90, 104–5, 123–24
*Theory of Justice* (Rawls), 20–21
Thompson, Dennis, 33
Tocqueville, Alexis de, 18, 98, 105–6, 116–17, 120–21, 128, 186n.88
Tory party, 34
totalitarianism, 30
*Toward a Feminist Theory of the State* (MacKinnon), 67–70
Trump, Donald, ix, 145–46

Tunick, Mark, 122–23
*Turn to Empire, A* (Pitt), 120–21
Tusk, Donald, ix
tyranny, 26–27

uncertainty
  development of, 44, 52–53, 60–61, 68–69, 90–91
  and dual positionality, 142–43
  and the harm principle, 55–56
  political potentials of, 11, 38–39, 48–49, 51, 56–58, 86, 97–98, 123, 128–29, 146–47
  recovery of, xii, 25–26, 74, 116–17, 139, 150–51
  *See also* Mill, John Stuart
United States, x, 2, 4, 17–18, 20, 34–35, 93–94, 116–17, 138–39, 149–50
universal suffrage, 107, 114–15, 124–25
Urbinati, Nadia, 8, 32–33, 105, 122–23, 125–26, 172n.97
"Use and Abuse of the Ballot" (Mill), 105–6
utilitarianism, 8, 24–25, 46, 47–48
Utilitarian Society, 43

Wakefield, Edward Gibbon, 126, 184n.54
Waldron, Jeremy, 33
Weiss, Penny, 9
*What I Remember* (Fawcett), 59
*Why Liberalism Failed* (Deneen), 145–46
Williams, David, 136
Wollstonecraft, Mary, 71
women's suffrage, 12, 59, 61, 75, 78–80, 81, 83, 89–91, 101–2, 104–5, 114–15, 172n.4, *See also* gender equity
World Wars, 4, 18–20

Xenophon, 41

Zakaras, Alex, 8
Zastoupil, Lynn, 43, 130–31
Zerilli, Linda, 111